**DO NOT REMOVE
CARDS FROM POCKET**

PSYCHIC

PSYCHIC

AWAKENING THE POWER WITHIN YOU

CAROLE KENNEDY

CB
CONTEMPORARY
BOOKS
CHICAGO · NEW YORK

Library of Congress Cataloging-in-Publication Data

Kennedy, Carole.
    Psychic : awakening the power within you.

    Bibliography: p. 373
    1. Extrasensory perception.   2. Fortune-telling.
I. Title.
BF1321.K46   1988   133.8   88-18140
ISBN 0-8092-4703-8

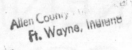
All illustrations by Meg Winston.

Published by Contemporary Books, Inc.
180 North Michigan Avenue, Chicago, Illinois 60601
Manufactured in the United States of America
Library of Congress Catalog Card Number: 88-18140
International Standard Book Number: 0-8092-4703-8

Published simultaneously in Canada by Beaverbooks, Ltd.
195 Allstate Parkway, Valleywood Business Park
Markham, Ontario L3R 4T8 Canada

Dedicated to the ones I love
I'd like to express heartfelt appreciation to the following:
Kay
Sheila
Joy and Meg
Debbie L.
Shir/Lyn
Stacy P.
But most of all—God!
Love and kisses to all patient families (especially Margie and Stanley)
and supportive husbands—Jim, Geoffrey, Joe/George

CONTENTS

INTRODUCTION

IN RECENT YEARS, the public's interest in New Age activities and skills, such as ESP, parapsychology, and the unexplained, has increased dramatically. People are not only curious about these topics, they are open about their curiosity. Numerous ESP books, some of which are bestsellers, are finding their way to library and bookstore shelves everywhere. Although much information is currently available, there is a growing hunger for more.

I find this new interest in ESP sort of amusing. First, as I'll demonstrate in Chapter 2, ESP *isn't* new. It's been around longer than written language. Second, while each person's individual discovery of his or her psychic abilities is new, history has shown that ESP comes and goes in popularity. Most psychics think all this hoopla is ridiculous, because they're just doing what they've always done. But now *everyone* wants psychic knowledge, and psychics are swamped with questions: How does it work? Can I do it? Tell me about me. Right now psychics are a hot commodity; only a few years ago we were considered weird! Of course, there are reasons why people are becoming interested in psychic phenomena. Astrologers and metaphysicians have been forecasting this resurgence for the past twenty years.

Although ESP is all the rage now, it is not new in our world. It has been in existence for centuries—even before the beginning of recorded history. But many superstitions and prejudices existed concerning ESP abilities. Years of intensive research have slowly but surely validated occurrences of psychic phenomena and given credibility to the field of parapsychology. As the research data accumulate, many earlier prejudices are being overcome.

The high interest in ESP books and classes is evidence that the acceptance level is growing fast. People not only want to have ESP used on them (as in a card or palm reading), but they also want to use ESP themselves. It is not coincidental that classes in positive thinking, body language, meditation, goal seeking, and the like are currently at the top of seminar lists. These self-improvement topics teach the use of natural abilities to further understanding and success. Many people do not realize that the methods used to reach these goals are ESP-related and can be considered introductory to the development of ESP skills.

People attend self-help seminars and New Age classes for very normal reasons. They want success. They want to understand the way other people think and act. They want good relationships and marriages. They want to understand how to better achieve their goals. They want to be happy.

People have begun to seek psychic help for many of the same reasons. They are beginning to realize that psychic phenomena are not mystical. To a psychic, having ESP is like having the ability to learn to read: you can ignore your ability and remain illiterate, or you can make use of the basic tools you've been given and learn to use your ability to its fullest.

WHAT'S THE BIG SECRET?

I feel that my psychic ability is a natural talent, just like an artist's or a musician's talent, and I am comfortable with my abilities. I see no reason to hide behind the traditional garb and costume of a fortune teller (the robe, the earrings, the crystal ball). I love the shocked expressions on clients' faces when I greet them in my office wearing jeans, T-shirt, and house shoes, wielding a cup of coffee instead of a crystal ball. Some psychics (usually those who want to impart an air of mystical superiority) make ESP *seem* mystical by purposely setting themselves apart from their clients. However, I want to let you in on the secret that ESP is something everyone can use—and without wearing weird clothes and dimming the lights.

Many people ask me how I got into ESP. This really gives me the giggles, because I did not get into ESP—it got into me. As with

most children, I was born with natural psychic ability. The difference came in how that ability was accepted by my family. Children
are known to be imaginative, and parents often ignore or squelch
budding psychic abilities. My grandmother, however, accepted my
experiences without question. When I blurted out information, I
was never chastised, though my grandmother was careful to teach
me how and when to use this information.

For example, when I was four years old, I saw a man with dark
shadows all around him. He was entirely surrounded by a gray-
black mist, and I was fascinated! I turned to my grandmother and
immediately blurted out what I had seen. I remember her shushing
me, saying, "Don't tell anyone else about these things you see—
just me." When the same man died two days later, my grandmother explained what she felt had happened. She said that I had
seen an illness or death aura and explained why it would not
exactly have made this man's day to have me run up and tell him, "I
think you're going to die" (lesson number one in tact for me). She
told me to inform no one but her when I saw or felt something,
and we would discuss why it would be right or wrong to enlighten
others with what I knew. She never made fun of me or of anything
I told her, but she knew that other people might not be as accepting of my talents as she was, and she did not want them to punish
me for my insights. In other words, she protected my ability to
grow. My abilities were not suppressed.

I believe that my grandmother was psychic herself. ESP tends to
run in families, because families who experience a high level of
psychic ability do not stifle it in their children or grandchildren. If
they're smart, they will put certain conditions on the usage;
psychically gifted children thus learn to be careful not to hurt the
feelings of others, and to watch what they say in public.

Being a kid, I could be baited into using my psychic abilities in
an inappropriate setting, despite my grandmother's best efforts.
In middle school one day, while in the classroom, I was minding
my own business (being a good kid for a change), combing my
hair and pulling my blouse down through the placket of my skirt.
My teacher calmly looked at me, called my name, and told me that
the activities I was engaged in should only be performed in a
boudoir. I'd never heard that word before, but as soon as she said it,
I had a vivid "flash" picture of *her* boudoir. At this point I stood
up in front of her (and the class) and said, "Well, I don't do in *my*

boudoir what you do in *your* boudoir!" I was promptly sent to the principal's office, and my family was called in to discuss my outburst. It was my grandmother, of course, who got me out of the mess. Later, after I satisfied her curiosity about what I had seen, she gave me another lesson in tact—and also a lesson on the birds and the bees.

When I pulled stunts like these and didn't watch what I said in public, I got plenty of strange looks. It took me forever to understand why people looked askance at me. I wasn't a slow learner, but I was a child, and I thought everyone saw and heard the same kind of things I did. I had no reason to think they didn't; I thought what I was experiencing was normal. I still do. After all, I was a normal kid. I played the same kinds of games you did, had the same kinds of dolls, pulled the same kinds of silly stunts, and made the same kinds of grades in school. Fortunately for me, my grandmother made me feel that I was, in truth, a normal child. She accepted me and my ESP, and thus provided a secure and stable environment for me.

In fact, my grandmother was one of the only sources of stability in my somewhat unique family life. I grew to depend on her for love and protection. She was my "touchstone." I could always count on her to be there. When I was twelve, my grandmother died. Because I had dreamed about her death before it happened, I was somewhat prepared when it did occur. I was inconsolable, but not as scared as I would have been with no foreknowledge. With her death, my source of protection and security was gone, yet my ESP began to fill in the gaps; it protected me from all the instability in my life. I began to rely more on my abilities, and they began to develop at an accelerated pace.

So, even as an adolescent I felt a sense of caring, protection, and understanding; no matter what I did, I knew I'd be OK. I find in my adult life that most people don't feel this sense of security. I believe that this protection comes from God, or a higher power if you will. My strong spiritual base, which for me encompasses the Christian doctrine, is the core of my ESP ability. I feel that ESP is God's way of communicating with me. The information I receive is His way of guiding me and helping me with decision making. There is no doubt in my mind that I am being protected, because I trust God and I trust the messages He sends through ESP. I am secure in the knowledge that whatever course my life might take, my ESP will help me to make the right moves and decisions. Not everyone has to share my belief in the Divine Spirit. However, most people, including nonbelievers, acknowledge the existence of something greater than themselves.

MEANWHILE, BACK AT THE RANCH

People are always asking me, "What's it like to be a psychic?" It is hard for people to comprehend that I am a wife, a mother, and a friend. Well, I have been happily married for twenty-seven years—to the same man—and have raised three sons. I live in an average American town, "Cookie Cutter City" I call it. I run an average American office, with an assistant, a secretary, two computers, two telephone lines, and a Mount Everest of bills. I owe on my Sears bill, too, but then I *told* you I was normal. I have friends who have withstood twenty years or more of my company. I am a normal, average person in all aspects save one: I have a very developed ESP ability.

My friends and family and I work well together in a give-and-take, democratic style. Sometimes, however, I'm so involved with my clients and friends that I'm literally oblivious to my surroundings. I am like the plumber whose pipes leak, or the seamstress who scotch tapes a loose hem. I'm always the last to know what is going on in my own home. Having ESP does not make you perfect.

Yet my close friends have all gotten used to my answering their questions before they ask them. They don't mind my finishing their sentences. In fact, they say they don't even notice it anymore! I once called a friend at 10:30 P.M. to interrupt a fuss between her and her husband. As soon as my friend answered the phone, I started right in with my lecture. I told her, "You and Geoff stop fussing right now. The project you are working on will work out just fine. The money you're griping about is not the issue, and you both know it. It is just frustrating to wait . . . I know that. But everything will work out in a matter of weeks. So, hush, and go to bed." My friend didn't even bother asking me how I knew they were fussing!

I told another friend, Debbie, that she would be making a job-related move to Florida within six months. Debbie laughingly said, "No way, I don't even know anyone in Florida." Four months later, she was on her way to a new job in Florida.

One thing that probably helps me keep my friendships is that I am careful not to be intrusive when I interact with my friends. I rarely offer information unless they request it because I respect their privacy. I follow this rule especially carefully with acquaintances, since they might find my information unwelcome. For instance, I entered an office recently for a business meeting and as the receptionist was showing us to the conference room, I picked up on the fact that she had a breathing problem and that it was treatable with medication. I kept all this information to myself. Only later when she approached me with questions did I take the opportunity to tell her the information I'd already received. She was relieved to hear that her problems weren't imaginary. I could never have given her this reassurance if she had not been ready to receive it.

I do find, however, that people invade *my* privacy—without really intending to, of course. They just don't realize how many people approach me in public. Once word gets out that I'm a psychic, I'm done for. People almost always ask me to answer "just one question." I've had people interrupt meals, follow me to the bathroom, and mob me at parties. At one point, I was so surrounded by people that I couldn't get into a waiting cab. Now it's fun, but enough's enough!

Occasionally, one of these "just one question" people will become a friend. One of my favorites is Charlie Chase, host of the talk show "Crook and Chase," whom I first met when I was a guest on his show. On the set one day, he said, "While I've got you . . . ," and proceeded to tell me that he and his wife were considering buying a house. I told him that the house was very large and was a bit unusual because it had three stories. I said it was in a bad state of disrepair and that there were many "unseen" repairs that might cost more than they wanted to spend. I then gave him the dollar amount it would take to buy the house. Later, Charlie and his wife had an appraisal made. From this, they found that the unseen repairs were going to be so costly that they decided against the purchase. The house later sold for almost the exact dollar amount I had given him. Because Charlie is a friend and colleague, and because he always tells such good dirty jokes, I don't mind helping him out from time to time.

Paradoxically, I find that family members, who have free access to all sorts of good information, don't ask as many questions. They prefer to see me as a mother or a wife, as the case may be. My husband, Jim, deals with my abilities with his usual quiet, "sneak up on your blind side" sense of humor. When his friends ask him what it's like to be married to a psychic, he tells them, "I just scramble my brains before I go into the house!" When there's a problem, however, I'm the first person he comes to. Jim is always a man of few words, and when something happens to puzzle or upset him, he will say one word—what?—and I'm supposed to solve his puzzle. He does listen to me (sometimes).

Being psychic has been an enormous help to me in raising my sons. They aren't always crazy about my knowing where they are going before they go, or my telling them they'd better have on clean underwear and wear their seat belts tonight, because I sense they are going to have a mishap in the car (not a big one, you understand—I would sit on them rather than allow them to go out that night). On the whole, though, I feel that my sons deal with my abilities pretty well. They feel protected and safe because they realize that sometimes mother does know best.

My ESP abilities have saved my sons from many unpleasant or potentially harmful occurrences. Like all kids, however, they don't always listen the way they should. The best example of this is one involving my youngest son. He was seventeen at the time and seldom drove the car fully dressed. Driving barefoot is against the law in Tennessee, but he thought he was cool and wouldn't get caught. I dreamed that he was driving with just jeans on—nothing else. I saw him going off the road and down an embankment. At the bottom, he hit something with the car and then came to a stop. I woke up, grabbed my son, and informed him of my dream. I cautioned him to wear shoes and underwear, and also to keep a shirt in the car, just in case. Because the road in the dream had a large, dangerous curve, I also told him to slow down and watch out. Two weeks later the door opened, and a boy wearing nothing but jeans limped in. His feet were sore from the walk home— *barefoot*. He told me that he had lost control of the car on a curve and needed $35 for a tow truck. I asked him where his shoes were, and he said he'd left them at a friend's. He was really mad at me because I was right, and I was mad at him because I was right! And if he'd listened to me, I'd have saved the $35 towing fee.

Over the years, in spite of the normal adolescent tendency to disregard parental direction, my sons have listened to and followed my directions for the most part. Besides, they sort of like having a mom that all their girlfriends want to meet!

A PSYCHIC'S WORK IS NEVER DONE, BECAUSE YOU NEVER RUN OUT OF QUESTIONS

People make several assumptions about psychics. One is that we know all. Another is that we are "on" twenty-four hours a day. Yet another is that we don't conduct our business as professionals.

People who think I know everything are in for a rude awakening. As I tell all my clients at their first reading, I *don't* walk on water (sometimes I have trouble on dry land). All I can do is set up the environment most conducive to *my* psychic flow. I don't see all and know all; I know what I know, and the rest is up for grabs.

As for being "on" all the time, no one wants to work twenty-four hours a day. Though I receive information all the time (and have no control over it), I often choose to deal with it later or not at all. If the information is getting in the way of something else I want to do (make love, clean the toilet, talk to a friend), I'll take care of it. Receiving psychic information is passive—I don't try to do it, and *no kind of effort on my part can get me information I wasn't meant to have*. The *work* comes in articulating and applying what I've received. When I'm working, I don't receive any *more* information; it just increases in intensity, because I'm ready for it. It's like a radio turned on all the time. When you want to hear the music, you turn up the volume and listen. When you aren't particularly interested in listening, you turn the volume down and go about your business.

Being a professional is important to me for several reasons. First, it is crucial to my psychic flow that I have a good environment in which to work. Second, I keep regular office hours as much for my own benefit as for that of the clients. I do, after all, have a family! Third, being a professional helps put an "unusual" service in a familiar setting. My office, just like a doctor's, has a secretary (who makes and confirms appointments), a waiting area, and a private office. Clients expect and receive confidentiality. You wouldn't catch an accountant dashing out of his office shouting, "Wow! You wouldn't believe the shambles this guy has made of his finances!" The same is true of me. What goes on within the four walls of my office remains there.

Because I feel good about myself, my main goal and purpose as a parapsychology counselor is to get people to feel good about themselves. By using my ESP abilities, I answer their questions and try to let them see their options in any given situation. Whether or not a client realizes it, coming in for a reading is really entering a classroom, the school of "you." One of my goals is to make people more aware psychically—to help them pay attention to the signals they get.

A good psychic will not allow a client to become dependent. Psychics are supposed to be guides, teachers, arbitrators. I take this as my personal creed. My clients make all the decisions affecting their own lives. And I try to teach them to listen to ESP signals themselves.

My classes are an extension of my role as a teacher. Clients have requested that I teach them more about how ESP works, how to develop it, and how to use it in everyday life. Everyone has the capacity to use this ESP ability, and I teach students the basic knowledge with which to do so.

In addition to my work as a counselor and teacher, I also help the police, insurance companies, and rescue squads find lost people or items upon request. These types of cases are interesting and add variety to my work.

A few years ago, Wink Brown of the Williamson County, Tennessee, Rescue Squad heard me on the radio and called to ask my help in locating the body of a man who'd drowned in the Harpeth River. The squad had searched unsuccessfully for two days. I received a mental picture of a man lying face down, wearing red gym shorts and a gold watch. He was snagged under a rock outcropping between two bridges. Wink listened carefully but insisted that the victim had last been seen skinny-dipping and therefore would not have been wearing shorts. Once Wink and his rescue squad located the two bridges, they did indeed find the man, submerged under a rock outcropping. He was, of course, wearing red gym shorts and a watch.

I do this kind of work regularly and never quite know what to expect when I pick up the phone. One day a friend, who also happens to be an arson investigator, gave me a call from North

Carolina to say he was stumped on a particular case. I immediately picked up a road of churk (reddish clay) and asked him if he was on a red clay road or close to it. He said yes. I told him to go ten miles down that road in the same direction and he should see another churk road off to his left. I told him that he'd find what he needed at the end of that road—either physical evidence or the arsonist—but he'd know it when he saw it. Later on, my friend called to say he had indeed found what he needed at the end of that road—gas containers with fingerprints, enough physical evidence to prosecute and win the case.

When I work with the police, they often show me photos of crime scenes, which I scan psychically. I just tell the police everything I pick up—names, dates, descriptions of locations, people, buildings, and events. Then I'm done. I provide them with the answers, and they just have to fit the puzzle pieces together. I have a documented accuracy rate of 85 to 95 percent. I *know* that most of what I pick up is valid (give me 10 percent for normal human error in interpretation), but documentation makes them feel better.

However, once a local newspaper reporter tracked me on a case. She was just waiting to say, "Aha! A charlatan." I did my thing and then left. A year and a half later, I got a call from the reporter, who told me that the case had been closed—successfully, thanks to my information. She said she was amazed that it had taken the police that long to get together the evidence to *prove* what I'd known eighteen months earlier! Information received psychically can save both time and money if used properly, and I'm glad to report that more and more police are using this unorthodox method of investigation (albeit after hours).

I BELIEVE IN MAGIC

I decided to write this book for several reasons. First, I want to take some of the mystery out of ESP, and show that it is a life tool that more of us should use. I want to give people concrete help for their daily lives, and psychic information can make it easier to do everything from washing clothes to making business decisions. Second, I'm hoping to help people to have as much fun with ESP as I do. It's wonderful to get information "out of nowhere." Last, but most important, I would like to share the joy of ESP. ESP-aware people experience comfort and security in an insecure world. They're happy with themselves. They have more friends, deeper loves, and fuller lives.

It's hard to believe that something as seemingly intangible as ESP can make that big a difference in your life. Wrong! Even though ESP may seem abstract, it has concrete applications. If you don't believe me, just give it a try. I've lived all my life as an ESP-sensitive person, and I love it. I never want to lose the feeling that all things are possible. I find being psychic a great comfort. I also find it to be great fun.

1
YOU ALREADY HAVE ESP ... YOU JUST DON'T KNOW IT

DO YOU AND a friend or sibling seem to know what's on each other's minds? Do you have wonderful beginner's luck at card games? Take this quiz and find out if you have a natural ability for ESP. The results will surprise you!

The following short quiz will help you identify your own personal ESP quotient. Answer yes or no to each question. At the end of the quiz is a scoring sheet.

SECTION I

1. Have you ever decided to do something when all the evidence told you to go in another direction?
2. Have you ever met someone and felt you'd known him or her before?
3. Have you ever experienced love (not lust!) at first sight?
4. Have you ever taken a different route home and had something interesting or unusual happen to you?
5. Have you ever just *known* something without knowing how you know it?
6. Have you ever felt the need to contact someone without knowing why?
7. Have you ever known instinctively that someone was lying to you over the phone?
8. Have you ever played a hunch (or the stock market) and had it pay off?

13

SECTION II

9. Do you often find yourself finishing other people's sentences?
10. Have you ever known a woman was pregnant before you were told?
11. Have you noticed that in times of personal crisis, helpful persons or resources were made available to you?
12. Have you ever known that the phone was going to ring or who was calling once it rang?
13. Do you know when your child, twin or other close sibling, or parent is unhappy, in danger, or sick? Especially when that person is out of your sight—maybe even far away?

SECTION III

14. Have you ever known the sex of a baby before its birth?
15. Are you particularly aware of lucky days in your life?
16. Are your particularly aware of lucky numbers in your life?
17. Have your ever gotten especially dressed up for no apparent reason, and were glad you did?
18. Do you have beginner's luck at cards, bingo, or gambling?

SECTION IV

19. Are your first impressions usually correct?
20. Have you experienced a recurring dream—over a period of time—and then had that dream come true?
21. Have you ever picked up on someone's health problems before the person told you about them?
22. Have you ever realized that an event that you had no control over was about to occur, that you "saw" it happening? This would include auto accidents (knowing that a driver is going to pull out in front of you), earthquakes, airplane crashes, and so on.

SECTION V

23. Have you ever felt positive or negative vibes (or feelings) upon entering a room?
24. Have you ever picked up a personal object and felt vibes from it? (This includes wallets, watches, rings, bracelets, or any favored object.)
25. Have you ever seen a photograph and immediately realized or felt you knew the story behind the photograph?

26. Have you ever, when observing a famous personality on TV, picked up clips of information concerning that person?

SECTION VI

27. Have you ever found yourself in a new situation but felt that you had been there before?
28. Has someone ever asked you to help recover a lost object, and by closing your eyes, you were able to visually locate the object?
29. Have you ever set out to "dream up" a solution to a problem and then gone to sleep . . . awaking with the solution?
30. Have you ever been in a situation where, on the surface, all appeared to be normal, but in an instant you *knew* (correctly) that something was out of sync? Did you also know what it was?

SECTION VII

31. Have you ever heard your name called but found no one there?
32. Have you ever heard a sound that no one else seemed to hear?
33. Have you ever heard a conversation being carried on by two people known to you (you were not present at the time), and you recognized the voices and knew what was said?

BONUS QUESTION

Have you ever doubted your sanity when one or more of the preceding events occurred?

HOW TO SCORE

Give yourself one point for each *yes* answer. Total the points, and read on to find how you rate.

31–33 points: You probably don't really need this book, but have fun reading it anyway!

26–30 points: In all probability, you're already using ESP in your life; you just may not have called it that. You should breeze through the exercises in the book!

21–25 points: Say, "I'm great!" and pat yourself on the back. You have a high degree of ESP ability—as you or your friends have probably already noticed.

16–20 points: Wonderful score! You have a good ability, and it can only get better. Go for it!

11–15 points: Not bad! You have a perfectly solid base from which to operate. Most of my students don't start out this well.

6–10 points: You have good working potential! When you see what you'll be able to do, you are in for a pleasant surprise!

1–5 points: Don't worry. By answering yes to even one question, you are ahead of the game. You *do* have the knack for ESP development—with a little effort, you will go far.

Zero points: Don't despair! Even if you answered no to all the questions, it could be that the questions just did not cover any of the events you have personally experienced. It could also be that you have been too inhibited and have been subconsciously blocking ESP experiences. You might want to read the chapter on meditation so that you can begin to release these inhibitions. Don't push yourself: when the student is ready, the teacher will be sent.

Bonus point: If you answered yes to this question, congratulations! You're part of the human race. Most people have felt this way, and I just wanted you to know it's OK. Once you have more psychic occurrences, you'll find this feeling easier to handle.

CATEGORIES

Section I: If you answered yes to questions in Section I, you have what is called "psychic flow." This is a mixture of several ESP activities joining together to process information. You may have the feeling of "knowing something" without knowing *how* you know. You're just sure your feeling is correct.

Section II: If you answered yes to questions in Section II, you have telepathic skills. Telepathy is the communication of one mind with another mind. It occurs frequently among good friends or close family members.

Section III: If you answered yes to questions in Section III, you have overall ESP ability, blending precognitive flashes with other skills, such as telepathy.

Section IV: If you answered yes to questions in Section IV, you have precognition, or foreknowledge.

Section V: If you answered yes to questions in Section V, you have an affinity for psychometry. Psychometry is the ability to obtain information about an object or its owner by coming into physical contact with the object. It is also the ability to pick up vibes from persons or objects or atmospheres.

Section VI: If you answered yes to questions in Section VI, you have experienced an occurrence of visual clairvoyance, the ability to visually perceive events or people, places, or things in your mind's eye. This is called "second sight."

Section VII: If you answered yes to questions in Section VII, then you have experienced an occurrence of audio clairvoyance. These occurrences can include a voice, knock, ringing noise, or any other sound that seems to bring a message.

I hope this quiz helped you to realize *you do* have ESP. You just might not have been conscious of it. But to be *more* aware of ESP, and to use it positively in your life, you must be prepared to change your mind set.

Over and over, people tell me, "I wish I could do what you do." *You can!* Do you remember when you first took swimming lessons and your teacher told you to do the impossible—get into the water? Well, guess what? That is exactly what I'm telling you to do. Jump in! We'll worry later about how great your technique is. This probably sounds simplistic, but that is the point. ESP is easy. You can do it.

I want to make you comfortable with ESP, to develop your trust in ESP, and to teach you to use ESP to your best advantage. I want you to become ESP-sensitive.

AS EASY AS 1-2-3

Most of your life, you have had to use books to learn how to do things—bake a cake, build a bookshelf, earn a degree. To do most things in life, all you need is to get equipment and instructions. You already have the equipment, as you will see in Chapter 2. This book will provide the instructions. The only other thing you need is an interest in having an ESP occurrence or in having more ESP occurrences.

To simplify the learning process, this book uses a "cookbook" formula of instruction: step-by-step, detailed instructions, or "recipes," for using ESP. The steps are simple, but you must not forget any or leave them out. After seven years of teaching, I find that my students respond best to this cookbook method.

Learning ESP is a bit like learning to make biscuits. Though you must take the time to follow a recipe, without forgetting a single step, biscuits are really quite easy to make. After some time has passed and you become familiar with the biscuit recipe, making biscuits becomes automatic. Before long you are very good at making biscuits. Likewise, if you take the time to follow my ESP recipes step by step, you can perfect your psychic repertoire. You may not be a raging success the first time out, but practice makes perfect.

Before you can get started, you must learn and understand certain basic concepts and procedures. I may use some clinical terminology in this book, but I promise to explain it in plain English. Eventually, you will *understand* the procedures and will begin to carry them out automatically. You'll find yourself remembering what to do without thinking about it; you may even feel comfortable enough with the rules to start bending them a bit.

Within the rest of this cookbook you will find several recipes for using your ESP. These include recipes for telepathy, precognition, audio and visual clairvoyance, psychometry, cards, palms, numerology, and psychic dreams, all of which will be discussed a bit later. I call them your ESP vehicles. By following the guidelines in this book, you will learn what your personal ESP vehicle is, how and why it works, and how to make the best use of it (or them).

Basically, you will move through three levels in developing your psychic ability:

Level 1: The first level involves memorization of the procedures and particulars of your chosen vehicle. Each vehicle has certain rules to follow and certain traditional meanings that must be learned before you can expect to feel comfortable with it. These meanings (found in the lines in a palm, in card progressions, or in dream symbols) are rooted in tradition and have evolved from truths accepted by psychics over generations. You must accept these "truths" as facts. To psychics they *are* facts, because they've been used for centuries, and they work. Soon, as you progress into the other levels, you will begin to have your own flashes or insights, which will merge with the "truths" you've been using—and they will become facts to you, too. In the meantime, try to think of this memorization as a starting point or building block. Don't become too hung up on this memorization, however. As you'll see when you start the palmistry or card chapter, there is a lot to memorize. Just do the best you can; before you know it, you'll be at level 2.

Level 2: In level 1, when you are relying only on artificial stimuli (the vehicles), the memorized material may seem confusing, disjointed, or even contradictory. When you reach level 2, you will have memorized enough and practiced enough that you'll begin to make some sense of the various vehicle meanings. Much more exciting, however, are the flashes you will begin to receive to help you bridge, or pull together, the information. These clips or flashes are your psychic flow at work. Psychic flow may seem to come from nowhere—like that cliché of a light flashing on in your mind. Suddenly, disjointed facts make sense! You may be looking at something (a certain palm line, for instance), not able to understand exactly what it means, and all of a sudden—pow!—you *know* what it means. Or your eye may be drawn to something unusual (even something not presented in the chapter, which, after all, is for beginners), and your *intuition* will tell you what it means.

The first time you experience an unexpected flash of insight is very exciting. It signals your entrée into level 2. It indicates that you've experienced a certain degree of proficiency. Of course, there are different levels of expertise even within this level, as you move toward level 3. But most people stay in level 2 for a long time, and some people do not progress any further. But believe me, level 2 is a hell of a lot of fun. While psychic clips don't come every time, you have gained enough trust in the meanings to do really good readings. And when those psychic flashes do come—watch out!

Level 3: As you continue to use your vehicle(s), the psychic flow will begin to come more freely and frequently. Eventually, you may realize that your psychic flow is so frequent that you no longer need the aid of a vehicle to stimulate it. You have entered level 3. At level 3, you actually become a channel for psychic flows. You are receiving information and dispensing it all at once. For example, while you are giving a reading, your mind may say, "This is . . . ," while your mouth says something totally different than what you were thinking. The information you spouted did not come from you or the artificial stimulus (your vehicle). You became a channel for the psychic flow. The information you received came from one of several sources: the subject, God, or the collective unconscious.

When you become a channel for psychic flows, it is not your job to censor the information, but to deliver it as given. Your *subject* will know what it means, even if you do not. In addition, even though you no longer need a vehicle to do a reading, you may find you prefer to use one to help your subject feel at ease. It provides something for him or her to focus upon and gives you a sense of stability should the reading go awry (usually due to an imbalance of energy bodies; see the chapter on cards).

Note: Contrary to popular belief, ESP cannot be turned on and off like a faucet. It surfaces at will: its will—not yours. The most you can do is be ready for it.

Because ESP is an unconscious ability, your control initially may be slight. You will have problems on some days. It might be that you just got up and haven't had your coffee yet, or you just aren't "on" and "cooking." If so, try, try again. Within a reasonable length of time, your hits will outnumber your misses, and your ESP abilities will continue to grow. (Some lucky people, like me, have ESP just happen to them. Others jump from level 1 to level 3. These are highly unusual occurrences, but if it happens to you, congratulations!)

TAKE A WALK ON THE WILD SIDE

You are obviously ready to learn more about ESP or you wouldn't be reading this book. You may have had some experience with ESP. These events could have been very small occurrences, but big or small, you probably thought they were kind of neat. I have ESP experiences every day, and I still get excited about them and want more to happen! To be honest, what have you got to lose?

You can begin the process of learning ESP by starting with the simple exercises included in this book. As you begin to learn, you will be excited and will want to share what you've learned. I have seen a family gathering of about thirty people turn a normal Thanksgiving dinner into a palm-reading party. The reader was a rank beginner, but no one cared; they all laughed and had great fun! The ESP bug bit everyone there, even Great-Grandma. Believe it or not, people will be disappointed if you don't continue to share your knowledge.

I cannot promise that this book will make you a Carole Kennedy. I have been practicing ESP all my life, after all, so I have a little head start on you! I can promise you, though, that your abilities will increase. All you will have to do is to try it. Take the case of Julia, who'd had no previous ESP experience. I recently attended a big meeting where I was supposed to convince the people present that ESP is easy. I chose to demonstrate psychometry, the art of gathering facts from an object about its owner by touching the object. A young lady named Julia reluctantly volunteered to be my student. She had never tried psychometry before, and was nervous and unsure of herself. I sat her down, explained the rules, and gave her a ring from my finger to read. I told her to close her eyes and start yakking. At first, she was giving me descriptions of the ring: metal, hard, and so on. To make her zero in on the object's vibes, I began to snap my fingers and told her, "No, tell me what you see, tell me what you feel!" Immediately she began to zero in. She described the dresser in my bedroom that I kept the ring on, then the room itself, down to the wallpaper pattern. All information was accurate with the exception of a roll-rack for clothing that she called a closet. Not bad for a first attempt!

If you want to use your new ESP abilities for more than just fun, you'll be able to do that as well. Becoming ESP-sensitive can help you lead a better, happier, and more trouble-free life. It can change your whole perception about life and living it. It will be a subtle change that happens over a period of time. It won't hit you like a bolt of lightning. But becoming an ESP-sensitive person will change you because it changes how you deal with your business associates, your spouse, your child, your child's teacher, your neighbor, and your friends. By becoming more in tune with yourself and the people around you, you begin to understand them better. You also begin to learn how to work with people in a more compatible way.

Beckie Woodmore is a great example of how using knowledge gained through ESP can help a person deal with personal problems. Beckie had always put her two children's welfare at the top of her priority list. Usually, this is a wonderful motherly trait. Beckie, however, was overdoing it with one of her sons. This son was an underachiever, and that worried her. She came to me for advice, and I saw that all he needed was a good leaving alone! Because the reading I had done for Beckie had been 95 percent accurate, she followed my advice. Sure enough, she left him alone, and his grades and attitude soon improved. This son had felt the pressure, even though it was unintended, and had simply balked. Beckie says the main difference in her new ESP-sensitive life is the trust factor. She follows her intuitions and feels more freedom and peace about her decisions. Once she has made a decision, she doesn't worry about it.

For when ESP does surface, and it will, it prompts you into immediate, direct action. For instance, you may feel cold chills run down your spine, and that prompts you to turn your head to see what is happening behind you. A car could be pulling out of a parking space and coming straight for you as you attempt to cross the street.

Once you become ESP-sensitive and begin responding to the information that you are given, the responsiveness bleeds over into your daily life. ESP will help you to be prepared for all that life hands you. Your attitudes will change a great deal. Following your ESP can sometimes be hard to explain, even to yourself. It may not be easy to do either. In fact, you may find that your ESP ability may sometimes cause problems for you. Conflicts may arise involving timing, values, and choices that you'd prefer not to deal with. You will find, however, that it does become easier. Why? Because most of us can use all the help we can get, and ESP is a big help.

Most people will agree that you need to be prepared for anything in this life. In our information-hungry culture, education and survival skills *must* include being ESP-sensitive. And because our advances as a civilization have been so geared toward technology, we have become lost in our own technological advances and blunder through life and relationships without guidelines. Many people want more; they want access to the untapped resources within their brains. They want to go beyond the physical sciences and make up for lost ground. ESP is the ultimate form of communication, and everyone should want to become proficient. For example, everyone has heard the rumors about the Russians' research and laboratory experiments regarding ESP. They are testing ESP-sensitive people to see if they can learn to use their abilities to control or manipulate events and conditions. One possibility is the use of ESP to divert incoming missiles.

Going beyond all the new information about body language, positive thinking, effective management training, active listening, and the like, ESP broadens your overall communications base to its highest potential. ESP is the top of the ladder. It is the most complete information-gathering process available to humans. It will become, like computer knowledge, a required course for all people.

You don't necessarily have to believe in ESP, or that ESP will work for you, or even that you have any ESP abilities. You just start doing it, and it works. Sounds simple, right? I can't convince you that ESP is easy, though, until you try it for yourself. If you're ready, then use this book and let's get started! You may have a few false starts to begin with. So what? Give yourself time, and you will soon get results.

2
BEHIND THE SEEN

EVERYONE KNOWS THAT mothers have "eyes in the back of their heads." Have you ever heard of "women's intuition"? Do you play your hunches at the race track? These are acceptable behaviors to us because we have been exposed to them all of our lives. Termed "intuition," "instinctive behavior," or "folk wisdom," they are not considered spooky or supernatural. These commonly accepted phenomena are nothing more and nothing less than part of the ESP framework.

You have been unconsciously using your ESP ability your whole life. It was probably on a *very* minor scale; you may not have even noticed it. I want you to be able to accept ESP as easily as you accept your own business hunches.

Since people tend to fear the unknown, or anything new or different, we often reject things like ESP, especially if it might cause us to be ridiculed. This chapter asks you to stretch the limits of your belief system. The ESP exercises will work for you whether or not you understand (or even fully believe in) ESP, but you'll be more comfortable and have a better success rate if you put ESP in the context of your life. The fear of the "unknown" will be eliminated. And once you've had a few good experiences, you won't care what anyone else says, anyway!

YOUR OWN PERSONAL CUE CARDS

ESP itself is known by many names: premonition, twinges, chills down your spine, intuition, or just a hunch. It really doesn't matter

25

what you name the occurrences. I don't care if you say, "My synapses have fired right off the board!" All these events are based on the same kinds of occurrences. Nothing here has a "supernatural" flavor. All ESP occurrences, and all hunches, work through sense impressions. I call them *body sensors*. Body sensors are similar to a radar scan, because they scan for information.

Body sensors are the attention getters in ESP. They are your symptoms, if you wish, to make you sit up and take notice. Just as fever or pain tells you to take care of an impending physical problem, body sensors tell you of impending events.

You have been preprogrammed to ignore these feelings. To be fully successful in using your ESP skills, you must raise your awareness level. You may have to be deprogrammed—or reprogrammed.

You might start with an understanding of what ESP stands for: extra sensory perception. Broken down, *extra* means more, larger, or better than what is normal. *Sensory* means connected with the reception and transmission of sense impressions. *Perception* means insight or intuition. So ESP is the process of gaining insights or intuitions through sense impressions that are larger or better than normal.

As you know, humans are generally considered to have five senses: sight, hearing, smell, taste, and touch. Each sense tells us something different about the world around us. We use our five senses more or less automatically, making decisions—like when to cross the street—based on the information our brains receive from our senses. It is only when one of our senses is lost—even temporarily—that we fully appreciate it. If we lose our sight, our balance is thrown off. The same is true of hearing. If you've ever had an inner-ear infection and stumbled around, bumping into walls, you know what I mean. It is only when deviations to these sensory information-gathering patterns occur that we completely understand how automatic our responses actually are. If you're still not convinced, imagine yourself making a phone call to a friend. No big deal, right? Now imagine doing the same thing—but with your eyes closed. Think it's easy? Try it. Or try to imagine dialing (or pushing) the right numbers without a sense of touch. We depend heavily on our five "accepted" senses.

There's something else you should know about your senses: They function on two levels. The first level is the conscious level. If

I say, "Smell this onion," you lean over (if you're a willing victim, that is) and take a big whiff. The second level is the unconscious or semiconscious use of these senses. When making a phone call, you don't think about it, but you could well be using at least four of your senses (five if you're munching on an apple while you gab). The obvious ones are sight for pushing the buttons, touch for picking up the phone, hearing for listening to your friend. Why do I say you're using *four* senses?

Smell. While you're chatting away on the phone, you could smell the scent of the person who last used the phone. Or you might realize that you need a shower. Or you might smell the fish cooking in the apartment next door.

The interesting thing about senses is that we're not always conscious that we're using them. You could be smelling yesterday's hamburger in the drapes and not even notice it—because you're preoccupied with other things, because you're used to the odor, because a stronger scent overpowers it to the point where you notice only the stronger scent. Or think of thousands of visual stimuli you receive each day, thousands of little pictures. Of these, you are conscious of only a small portion, and of this small portion, you remember only a tiny fraction.

All of the sensory stimuli you receive without consciously requesting them such as looking at a sunset, smelling a flower, or listening to music comprise the second-level sensory experiences. Your body sensors, like little radars, work all day, every day, and overtime, giving you a constant flow of information about the world around you.

Sometimes this information seems extraordinary. Your great-aunt comes to visit, and you can smell her violet sachet. No one else has the faintest idea what you're talking about, but Aunt Nancy allows as to how, yes, she does keep a little bit of sachet in her underwear drawer, some with a violet scent. Or you're driving along a dark road at night, and your friend sees the barely lit road sign that everyone else in the car missed. These are instances of what is literally extra (ordinary) sensory perception—although these sensations would not be considered psychic. Body sensors are working overtime, especially well, to provide you and your friend with information.

To understand the mechanics of body sensors, think about teenagers who tell their parents they have to "feel" the music in order to dance. Body sensors work together beautifully, in perfect balance, usually without our conscious awareness. When we are aware of the balance and the stimuli are positive (an outdoor concert and picnic on a breezy evening), the combination can be breathtaking.

ESP is your sixth sense. ESP works, just as the other five senses do, through body sensors. You "see" something you normally wouldn't be able to. You "feel" chills up and down your spine. These experiences are not coincidence, nor are they easy to explain away. When you physically experience a stimulus, that stimulus is *there*, even if it is something you cannot easily explain. Think, for example, of having a cold. You didn't get that runny nose out of nowhere, but for centuries, no one understood what caused colds. Now we know, however, that:

1. The brain senses a foreign substance (virus) that is causing a deviation from the body's normal balance.
2. The brain sends white blood cells to restore balance by attacking the virus.
3. You react by getting a cold; only now do you have the symptoms of illness and become consciously aware of the virus that has been with you for days. *Even though you didn't sense it, the virus was already acting on you.*

Psychic phenomena work the same way. They are around us and acting on us all the time—it's just that we are usually unaware of them. Our body sensors record these minute deviations—not all the time (remember that you have a cold virus well before you know you have a cold), but regularly. For example:

1. In the cosmos, information is being made available to you. (This gets into the spiritual side of ESP, which we'll discuss later; just take my word for it for now.)
2. Your body sensors pick up on something different and alert your brain.
3. If you are unaware of the power of these body sensors, nothing happens. But if you are naturally sensitive to what your body sensors are telling you, or learn to be sensitive, your openness to psychic flow will allow your brain to react by bringing these stimuli to the conscious

level. The hair rises on the back of your neck (sense of touch), you hear a voice (sense of hearing), or you see something unusual (sense of sight). You become *aware* of the psychic stimuli.

This instinctive reaction might appear during an occurrence of "instinctive fear." There is no logical basis for your reaction; your body simply responds automatically. If you sense danger or feel fearful, you turn your body to where the danger is. Let's say you are walking in darkness, but in familiar territory. You are having a good time looking at the stars. All of a sudden you stop dead in your tracks. You look around carefully, and sure enough, barely discernible in the dark, is a big chuckhole. Had you kept walking, it could have caused you a serious fall. You stopped automatically because your body sensors told you that danger was near.

If you have never analyzed these types of occurrences, it is because they are normal. You were probably so unaware of what actually happened that it did not even register with you. You have been reacting automatically and unconsciously.

The sixth sense that governs these occurrences is your *ESP base*. Your body sensors signal you, you receive the signal, and you follow through. I spoke earlier about your ESP equipment. Your body sensors are that equipment. You were born with it.

REALITY: THE BIG QUESTION

Now that you understand the logical flow of ESP occurrences, ESP probably doesn't sound like much of a mystery. It is just another function of your body. Once you conclude that ESP is a normal function of your physical body, you will realize that some bodies function better than others. That is OK; we all can't be Olympic gold medalists, either. You may always stay within the range of "small occurrences." So what? Even a small amount of ESP ability could be the key to your success. ESP may help you in making quicker and better personal and business decisions.

As you can see, I am asking you to bridge the reality gap into the mechanics of ESP, for there is a dual reality existing in our world. The two realities are what *appears* to happen and what *really* happens.

The term *reality* implies a total understanding of the world and the events that are predictable daily occurrences, facts, and truths. But many things are not as they appear to be. For example, we talk about the sun "coming up" and "going down." Now, we *know* better, but we say it anyway, because that is how it appears to us. Scientists have verified that the earth rotates and revolves, and they can plot the earth's movements with highly technical equipment. We trust scientists and their equipment, and we believe in data, so we accept their findings.

We have not had to give up any of our beliefs to accept the dual reality concerning the sun. This gives us comfort—we can still talk about what we perceive. It is OK to say that the sun comes up or goes down, because saying so does not change what we know to be true. Together, perceptual reality and scientific, data-based reality show us that what we perceive is only part of an overall picture. Both types of reality are valid, but even more enlightening when considered together.

IN THE BEGINNING

There are also several different ways to perceive the ESP reality. One premise is "man as animal." As many animal lovers will tell you, many instances of unusual behavior in their pets suggest ESP of one type or another. Parapsychologists, notably J. B. Rhine, report that "homing" or "trailing" cases are the most common examples of unusual animal behavior.

The most famous case of trailing involves a cat named Sugar. Sugar was left behind when his family moved from California to Oklahoma. Sugar crossed deserts, rivers, and mountains to find his family again. No one can explain how he found his way. Parapsychologists explain these cases as examples of clairvoyance—the ability to perceive things that are not in sight or cannot be seen.

Some animal behavior suggests precognition or foreknowledge, including awareness of danger. Skippy, a small beagle hound who loved to hunt rabbits, refused to join his master on a hunt one day. Despite his efforts to hide or run away, Skippy was forced to go along on the hunt. He was accidentally shot and killed during the course of the hunt. Did Skippy foresee his own death?

The Rhine studies show that humans, too, have ESP. Where does it come from? Is it hereditary? If so, does it go back to evolutionary beginnings? Is it possible that ESP is the property of all living animals?

We willingly accept these cases of unusual animal behavior as fact. We also accept "instinctive" behavior in cave people. We accept instinctive behavior in modern humans, within a certain framework. We accept women's intuition, hunches, and Mom's "eyes in the back of her head." But we haven't typically put these instincts into the arena of ESP occurrences.

Scientists (rather proudly) acknowledge that the human animal's large brain helped humans to develop in ways other animals have not. The primitive human's creative and inventive thought processes led to the use of fire for cooking and heat, to the use of the wheel to move objects, and finally to verbal communication. But how did cave people communicate before they had a verbal language? Jean Auel, in her novel *The Clan of the Cave Bear*, poses an interesting theory. She hypothesizes that cave people initially used grunts and sign language to some extent —but mainly communicated by mental telepathy.

People still communicate by telepathy. Telepathic "bonding" is common between family members and even between good friends. One set of female friends of mine can no longer play partners in games. They feel as if they are cheating because the communication is so strong that they can't be beat! They said it was funny for a while, but a sense of fair play finally won out. This pair also finishes each other's sentences and gets a big kick out of sending each other "messages" telepathically.

Mother-and-child bonding is also very common. Many stories have been told about mothers knowing that their children were sick or in danger. One such story involves a woman named Karen Brown. Karen was at work, busily involved in her typing assignment. Suddenly she felt as if she needed to go to her daughter's school. The feeling persisted and gained intensity. Karen couldn't shake it off. She finally gave in and decided to call the school, just to prove to herself that all was OK. As she dialed the school's number, Karen prepared herself for the reaction she was sure she'd get; she was certain that she would be treated as an overprotective and bothersome parent. But she was wrong. The school secretary didn't even let Karen finish her first sentence before she told her that she was so glad that Karen had called. Karen's daughter had been hurt on the playground, and they were just getting ready to call Karen. Again, this was a telepathic message: Karen's daughter had "called" her.

The people involved in these incidents seldom put a name to the occurrence, or even understand what has happened. They just know what they felt, and they knew that they had to react.

If you accept "man as animal" as a theory about ESP, you believe that ESP is an instinct that every living animal and human has. You also believe that it started out as instinctive and protective intuition. You believe that it was a means of communication before speech and still exists in all animals, including humans.

As they evolved, humans developed all sorts of advanced communication systems. Beginning with the spoken word, people progressed to the written word. In time, they developed mail, telegraph, telephone, and computer services. Perhaps, in the process of becoming modern, civilized, verbal communicators, humans forgot, through disuse, their instinctive, intuitive, and telepathic communication skills.

A LINK TO THE SUPREME BEING

Another idea or theory of ESP as a form of communication is that people communicate intuitively and telepathically, not only with one another, but also with the Supreme Being. According to most religions, our intuitive skills were meant to be the direct link with the Supreme Being. We are told that we were meant to be in constant communication with the Supreme Being—to keep the channels open, so to speak. Most religions teach the ultimate importance of this communication.

Many religions use ritualized prayers or incantations to open these lines of communication. The methods used by Buddhists may differ from those used by Catholics, Protestants, Jews, or Moslems, but they all have a common purpose: to allow men and women to converse with their higher power, or Supreme Being.

Many legends of prophecy and psychic occurrences have been passed down through the centuries. It's not difficult to think of the religious prophets as psychic or having the gift of "sight." They had visions, heard voices, experienced prophetic dreams, or possessed healing powers. A perfect example of this would be Moses, who not only had visions and performed miracles, but also had direct audio communication with his God. Father Alois Weisinger, a well-known writer on Catholic themes, traced visions to "the original spirituality of the soul . . . that still exists in a latent dormant state in all of us."

These rituals also involve some form of meditation. Meditation is supposed to clear the mind of day-to-day clutter. It is supposed to open your mind to the Supreme Being. Then and only then can he speak directly to you. Confucious, too, taught the importance of "keeping in touch"—he said you can't hear if you don't listen. To put this another way, prayers are only one method of communicating with the Supreme Being. Meditation helps you to *hear* the answers. Communication between man and this Supreme Being is believed to be the key to understanding and knowledge. We are told that we just need to listen and obey.

The Buddhist religion teaches that this communication is not realized by perception and recollection of facts, by speculative knowledge or the power of reasoning. True knowledge cannot be gained by any intellectual process, but it must be attained through intuitive knowledge, which can be attained through meditation.

In Hinduism, the major objective is to be united with God. This union is achieved by prayer and yoga. A meditating yogi, in the highest state of meditation, does not see, feel, hear, taste, or smell anything. He is one with God. To put this very simply, practicing meditation will, over a period of years, bring enlightenment. Mohammed teaches that the substance of the Islamic religion includes five major truths: faith in Allah, the one Supreme Being; submission to His will; trust in his foresight; prayer and meditation; and alms giving as the only requirements of worship.

The substance of Judaism includes a supreme living God, and His providence and moral laws. Ritual prayer, as set down in the Torah, is the heart of the religion. Devout Jews pray every morning and evening of their lives. Prayer, canting, and blessings are the principal parts of worship.

Putting a special emphasis on prayer, Christians acknowledge one God, and a savior, Jesus Christ, and deepen their faith by practicing the sacraments—such as communion, baptism, and prayer. They believe that all people have the potential to be united with God through belief in Jesus Christ and the gift of the Holy Spirit.

As you have probably noticed, the major religions have similar themes. All religions are paths to the same goal and have the same core. All of them supply answers to the mystery of life, help believers to bear sorrows, give instructions on how to live, and offer assurance in regard to death. Religions tell us that inner knowledge, gained through prayer and meditation, should assist us in making better decisions in leading our lives correctly. No matter what doctrine or method of worship one follows, communication with one's God is paramount.

Many people would assume that a conflict would be involved in a religious person's acceptance of ESP. Not true. If you accept the premise that ESP is simply a communicative tool, given to people for their benefit, then where would the conflict be? You don't have to give up any of your religious beliefs to believe in ESP.

AND THEN THERE'S SCIENCE

People in general seem to be proof-oriented. We want ideas validated scientifically, with years of research and data to support them. So, for you skeptics, parapsychology is the study of *para*normal psychology, or deviations from the normal psychology. Parapsychologists study and observe behavioral deviations that produce unexplained insights. "Proof" of their observations is considered scientifically documented only when it has been repeated (or seen) many times by many people.

At Duke University, a scientist named J. B. Rhine sought to document ESP occurrences. This research began when the public requested him to explain some very unusual incidents. These incidents had no apparent explanation and fit into no known category of research. The cases presented to Dr. Rhine suggested that ESP did exist.

A very encouraged Dr. Rhine began carefully controlled experiments. The basis of the research was to satisfy his curiosity about how and why ESP occurs. As in all scientific studies, a control group was set up to show what would have occurred in any case and to discount the possibility of coincidence. Once the data base began to build, Rhine felt that there was such overwhelming evidence that ESP occurs that it ruled out any statistically significant possibility of coincidence. Based on thousands of case histories, the Rhine studies included testing a single individual, two-member teams, and larger groups. Major areas of research included testing for clairvoyance, general ESP, and precognition.

J. B. Rhine, based on this research, concluded that psychic ability is a reality. According to his wife, Louise Rhine, in her book, *PSI*, this is "a simple scientific conclusion. This conclusion has the same kind of basis as that of any other field of science. It has been established just as they were, by experiment and the statistical evaluation of results. PSI ability does not fit into the physical materialistic-mechanistic scheme . . . clairvoyance is not confined to the immediate surroundings, precognition invades the future, telepathy makes possible even the awareness of thoughts in other minds. . . . It may well be that PK [ESP] is an ability inherent in life itself."

"All things, whatsoever ye shall ask in prayer, believing, ye shall receive." Matthew 21:22

I don't know what your world is like. I don't know how you will incorporate ESP into your own reality. But you *do* know how. With all the information given in this chapter, you can come up with a way. To believe, you merely have to find the thread that connects all the explanations given here. You will surely find an explanation that is comfortable to you.

The inner-core consciousness or voice of ESP triggers the physical body, along with the mind, to prepare us to listen and respond naturally—in a nonrestrictive manner—to receive the messages. These inner-core messages will never send us an incorrect emotional message. If you believe that your creator or the connecting "force" in the universe is omnipotent and his perfect will is in effect, then you will have a sense of security, to be worn like a protective cloak. Once you fully understand that this comes from God—whoever God is to you—you'll realize that ESP and information derived through ESP won't hurt you, and that it comes to you for a reason.

3
VALIDATION

NORMALLY, IT TAKES years, with the ESP perceptions coming in on a regular basis, before one begins to trust and respond to those perceptions. Journalization and sharing should help speed this process along. To develop your ESP most effectively, you should begin to build your own personal data bank. This is done through journalization. Why do you need to journalize? Well, ESP is not real for anyone unless that person can "prove" what has occurred. No other validation process exists. If you don't write down events or tell someone about them, your rational mind will try hard to convince you these events didn't happen.

If you journalize as an event you have documented occurs, you have a system to check yourself with. You can then say, "Look here, husband, see . . . I wrote this on June 16, 1981. It is now June 16, 1984. And look, it has happened! It took a while, but it happened." And your husband says, "Yes, sweetheart. Where's supper?" Sooner or later, you'll document something that wows him, too.

The primary reason for documentation, then, is to reassure you that what you're doing is totally real. A secondary reason is that journals help with the interpretation process. Comparing or combining events with other events may help you make sense of them. If you hear a man's voice before you get a big raise, you might look for another raise when you hear that voice again. A third reason to document your ESP growth is that the journal will tell you how and why ESP happens to you. Patterns will develop.

Specific things may remain constant. The time of day or the place may be significant. A fourth important reason to use a journal is to be sure that you don't forget the information, as it can take months or years for a specific event to occur. Another (and important to some skeptics) reason is for later validation by friends, relatives, police, or other people. This will give you credibility. But most important, you will be proving to yourself that ESP exists *in your life*.

If you don't keep an ESP diary, you will never be able to properly interpret the events or gain adequate validation. In other words, you will not learn and grow . . . and neither will your abilities. In addition, it helps your psyche if you keep a diary. Once on paper, the feelings of uneasiness, the twinges, the insights, the symptoms will all be recorded for your review. A journal will allow you to *release* all your feelings, insights, and occurrences so you can forget about them and get on with a "normal" life. It frees you of the beginner's hurdle of overinterpreting these new twinges. Better still, it frees you to experience more ESP events!

Another thing you should know about ESP is that psychic occurrences are not governed by time as we know it. The psychic world knows no "now," no today or tomorrow, because, on the psychic plane, everything is occurring at once. Time is not relative. While this is sort of a difficult idea to grasp, it helps explain precognition (knowing about something about to occur) as well as psychic insight regarding the past. It also explains the perennial belief that time travel is possible. Journalization will help prove this to you; the more ESP occurrences you document, the easier it will be to understand. While scientists, particularly physicists, are fascinated by this phenomenon and research it widely, those of us familiar with the psychic plane accept without question the fact that, on a psychic level, past events and events to come are all occurring, now and forever. Once you make the leap of faith to this belief, you may experience the kind of spiritual awakening that can come with ESP awareness, and which I'll cover at the end of the book. Documentation is crucial to this awareness.

You can document or share your experiences in one of three ways. The first way is to tell someone, anyone, that you trust. The second way is to use a tape recorder. The third is to write your experiences in a journal. I prefer a system of checks and balances; I use a journal *and* I tell someone. But initially, you will probably prefer a journal or diary. This diary does not have to be a permanent fixture in your life. After a period of time, you may gain enough credibility for yourself and others to put it aside.

Journalization is not hard, but it is exacting. It is worth the time and effort it takes, though, as it will be interesting and fun to watch your own progress. You will need to include thoughts and insights that occurred during the experience. All the "symptoms" or "feelings" that you have are important and must also be included. For example, you may say, "I just felt excited—for no reason . . . ," or, "I felt a sense of foreboding . . . ," or, "I just felt sad, and my eyes teared up . . . ," or, "I felt disappointed."

WHAT TO JOURNALIZE

Journalization is used primarily for dreams, telepathy, and clairvoyant occurrences—any event where you don't get immediate verification. Psychic information is received in flows, and you may not have instant verification of an ESP flash. So you need to journalize to keep a record of what has happened and when the experience occurred.

You will not need to journalize psychic information resulting from using cards or palms, as you usually get immediate validation from the client. Because you have instant verification, psychic flows are not interrupted, and the client *is* your validation.

HOW TO JOURNALIZE

Buy a spiral-bound notebook—the kind students use to take notes. Number the pages. On the first four pages, copy down the information requests from Illustration 3-1, the sample journal worksheet. (After this, you'll remember what to write.) Allow two whole pages for each occurrence, as it will encourage you to enter everything relevant.

To properly journalize any ESP or unusual occurrence, you must write down all key information in a manner that you will understand long after the event. This is not a good time to invent your own system of shorthand! Be explicit with your descriptions, as later on a failing or faulty memory may not dredge up any further information. Be sure to fill in *all* the pieces of information asked for on the journal sheet, as patterns may develop. I have

ILLUSTRATION 3-1
SAMPLE JOURNAL WORKSHEET

1. Date (month, day, year, day of week): _____

   _____

2. Time Experience Occurred: _____

3. Record of Experience: _____

   _____

   _____

4. Body Sensors (Sensations) Involved (beginners may not
   always recognize the signals; put down what you think):

   _____

   _____

   _____

5. Emotional Response (sense of joy, dread, etc. after

   occurrence): _____

   _____

6. Did You Follow Through on What You Felt You Should Do?
   Did You Tell Anyone? _____

   _____

   _____

7. Additional Information: _____

   _____

   _____

ILLUSTRATION 3-2
SAMPLE JOURNAL ENTRY I

Date: _10-14-87 Thursday_

Time: _6:30 a.m._

Experience: _Woke up—startled—as if the phone just rang. I listened, but it didn't ring. Then the alarm went off—I got up._

Body Sensors: _Thought someone or something woke me up. Felt strange, but not scared. Didn't really feel alone. Sensed someone's presence._

Emotional Response: _Not scared or uneasy—just felt as if someone needed me._

Follow-Through: _I didn't do anything or tell anyone—I didn't know who to tell._

Additional Information: _6:30 a.m.: When I woke up I felt a strange sense of being needed by someone. I even listened to see if the phone was ringing (along with the alarm clock). The feelings were intense but not uneasy, really. I had no way of knowing how to follow through on the feeling—so I just noted it here._

10:00 a.m.: I have gone around all day waiting for the phone to ring and someone to tell me what they need from me! I have also found myself looking over my shoulder—expecting to find someone there. I didn't leave the house all *day because I really did feel as if I would be needed—for something.*

6:00 p.m.: I've cooked dinner and cleaned up. As I was cooking I wore myself out looking over my shoulder!

11:00 p.m.: After I finally gave up on anyone calling, I took my bath and got ready for bed. Not 15 minutes later, the phone rang. As soon as I answered— Sue told me that she'd been trying to call me all day—but her phone was out. She then told me how she needed me!

included two sample journal entries to give you an idea of what journal entries can look like (see Illustrations 3-2 and 3-3).

If you have neglected any areas on the journal sheet, you will have an incomplete picture of your personal patterns. You may, for example, be more apt to have ESP occurrences in the afternoon or in the bathtub. But how will you know this to be true if you have been slack with your journal information? As you learn to journalize, you will find yourself filling in details in order to form a more orderly scene (or setting). This will give you the information you need to cross-reference with the actual event. You will be able to see how close the perceptions were. Later, you can note when an anticipated event occurred, and how long after the experience of the original perception it took for the event to actually occur. This gives you an idea of what pattern your ESP cycles will follow.

HOW TO VALIDATE

People often ask me, "How can I be sure I've had an ESP experience?" When you will know depends upon which vehicle you choose to use. Some of the vehicles do not produce instant gratification or verification. Here are a few examples:

- Cards (relatively complex) produce immediate validation of what the subject's past or present activities are. Future

ILLUSTRATION 3-3
SAMPLE JOURNAL ENTRY II

Date: _5-2-86 Sunday_

Time: _4:30 a.m._

Experience: _Dreamed I was in large house—felt it was mine, I kept going up and up and up the stairs—but never got to the top. It was a blue house—lots of light—I had to get to my roommate upstairs—even though I knew I needed to warn her—I couldn't yell— my voice was really tiny—she never heard me, and I never got up the stairs—then I woke up._

Body Sensors: _I was cold, and my heart was racing—I felt very high energy._

Emotional Response: _I was scared and frustrated—because the stairs never ended and I never got up to my roommate—that I'd somehow failed her._

Follow-Through: _I told my roommate about the dream— and told her to be careful (why I don't know). She said she would be._

Additional Information: _None._

events, of course, will be validated later by the person you are reading for.

• Palms (with an overwhelming amount of information to assimilate) produce immediate reactions and responses, especially about past events, current transitions of character, and health cycles.

- Clairvoyance (easiest to do but hardest to wait on) does not always actively involve or invoke an immediate response, as you may not know the people involved or will have to wait until the event occurs. This is true for both audio and visual clairvoyance.
- Visualization and meditation (easy to do but hard to believe) involve concentrated discipline over a period of two weeks minimum.
- Psychometry is easy to do, but it is hard to bridge or interpret the information given.

How do you know if you've had a psychic experience? There are several clues. First, you will probably experience an unexplained emotional response—a chill, a tingling, a racing pulse, a raising of the hairs at the back of your neck. These are all examples of body sensors at work. Second, you will find yourself the proud owner of some new information. You might have seen, in your mind's eye, a train crashing. Or "heard" a friend crying for help. (It is important, of course, to be sure that these experiences are, indeed, extrasensory. While hearing a faraway neighbor call for help may require the use of some highly developed body sensors, it is most likely not a "psychic" experience in the true sense.) Sometimes, if your psychic flow is going strong, you may not be able to isolate one of your senses as the conduit of the information, but you find you are absolutely *sure*—say, that your boss will call in sick tomorrow, or that your mother's plane will be late (hey, no need to rush!). A third way to know is that *you will have little doubt that you've had a psychic experience*. If you find yourself asking, "Was that a psychic experience?" it probably was not.

Of course, our ability to overanalyze enables us to convince ourselves that a perfectly lovely psychic occurrence didn't happen at all. I've had students who were so excited by one little clip of psychic information that they talked about it and blew it out of proportion. By the time they were finished, they were sure they imagined the whole thing! For the most part, you'll *know* when you've had a run-in with ESP. If in doubt, *write it in your journal*. As mentioned earlier, the journal will help document what is psychic and what is not, and alert you to patterns and the times of occurrence, your emotional state, your reactions.

Occasionally, people with highly developed imaginations and very strong wills "imagine" that they've received psychic information, or allow their imaginings to run rampant, effectively blocking out any real psychic flow. If you suspect this is happening to you, be sure to do the meditation exercises in the next chapter, particularly the one that helps you tune out your mind chatter.

One more important thing to remember is not to analyze a psychic experience while it is occurring. Enjoy it. Ask for more information if you wish. Listen. Later, when it is over, you can attempt to interpret it.

The real validation, of course, occurs when something comes true. For example, your psychic flow tells you that you're going to learn a foreign language. Your initial response may be, "No way, Jose!" You immediately dismiss the information; however, one year later you are living in another country and speaking a new language. You realize that your psychic flow was correct.

BUILDING TRUST

The next stage in your development is to start building trust in the information you're receiving. This is the hard part. Trusting totally in your intuitions will cause you some inconvenience and problems. For instance, you may have a busy day scheduled: doctor's appointment, a PTA meeting, pants at the dry cleaners, or a business trip planned. Something tells you not to drive your car. But if you don't do what you're supposed to do today, you know you're going to catch it. So, now what?

Sit down, drink a cup of coffee, and wait until everything calms down. In other words, don't drive your car until the feelings of unease have passed. They may not pass for quite a while; you might be late or have to save an errand until the next day. No big deal. At least you are safe and have another day available to you.

One of my students actually had this "car won't start" incident happen to her. She says, "I was on my way to a business meeting, and my car wouldn't start. I called a mechanic, and he had the car running smoothly in no time flat. But as soon as I got behind the wheel, it quit. It would not start again. I was frustrated and angry and embarrassed about calling the mechanic again. I was afraid he would think I was really dumb! Then I remembered what Carole had told me once. She said that all things happen for a reason . . . find the reason. I felt that I wasn't meant to go anywhere at this time and went back into the office. Shortly thereafter I received an important phone call from someone I had been trying, unsuccessfully, to reach for weeks. Had my car started, I would have driven off and missed the call. Later, my car started easily, and I had no further trouble with it. I jokingly told people that my car was having 'hot flashes.' "

These are the first steps in trusting ESP. You respond or react to the information given without really questioning why. You prepare yourself for whatever flack you will have to take because of your decision. You understand that ESP is an information source. It is a source of protection for you. As mentioned previously, ESP will not hurt you, it will only help you.

Most of my students will agree that they benefited much more than they thought they would from opening themselves to ESP. One student said, "I really never thought I would become intuitive, but I do find, now that I'm paying attention, that I had much more ESP ability than I ever dreamed! Mainly, I have tried to become more 'people smart,' and in my business you need that!"

Another adds, "My attitude has changed very much. I now find that I don't have to try to make myself like everybody; that sometimes I was right when I had a bad first impression—some people are jerks! I trust my handshakes to tell me a lot about a person, and if I get a bad feeling, I try hard to be on top of the situation—I watch that person like a hawk!"

Some students simply say that their relationships are much more rewarding now, and this is because they are now fine-tuned to their ESP signals and symptoms.

INTERPRETATION

Because of our educational processes, from childhood to adulthood, we have been taught and retaught to analyze every scrap of information before we're able to categorize and fit the information into what we've been taught.

Scientific documentation has been a miraculous tool and terrible curse. The process by which we arrive at scientific documentation has taught us to overanalyze data and has provided understanding of how things work, giving us a belief in cause and effect. But this doesn't allow for the intangibles in life; for example, it won't answer the question "What is love?"

Some areas of our lives only deal with the intangible things that defy application of scientific methods. We have been taught, in dealing with those areas, to accept what is. Love exists, as do many other emotions and concepts too numerous to mention. These things or concepts are incorporated into our reality. In some cases our ideas of reality are subject to change. For instance, we all have a fantasy of what marriage is. After we marry, reality forces us to readjust our fantasy of marriage. In the same way, we must adjust our concept of reality as ESP experiences occur.

Some things, however, we just have to take on faith. ESP, like love, must be accepted into our sense of reality even though we don't fully understand it. In other words, as Louise Rhine puts it, ESP "connects the personality to the world around it *without a mechanism*, or at least, without any mechanisms sufficiently like those of the physical world to make it [ESP] in any way similar [to things we can prove]."

Psychic information is not meant to be overanalyzed; it is supposed to cause a reaction. If you are not getting a clear idea of what the psychic information means, you may need to just file it away for later use. You may, on the other hand, simply be trying too hard, which in turn sets up a resistance to psychic flow. In this case, you just need to relax. You might also be subconsciously resistant to the information. But, in any case, the psychic information will keep coming back to you until you *do* react. In other words, if a message is meant for you, something inside of you will react to the information eventually.

If you are puzzled by psychic information, it makes sense to discuss it with friends or relatives. For all you know, the information has no relevance to you whatsoever, and was given to you so you could relay it to someone else. It is important that you not assign your values to either the information or the person receiving the information.

It will also help if you avoid judging information relayed to you. Let's say, for example, that you have a recurring dream that you have a job sweeping floors. As you will learn from reading the section on dreams in Chapter 5, recurring dreams often impart psychic, rather than psychological, messages. You find it impossible to believe that you will lose your prestigious job as office manager at a toy manufacturing plant. You unconsciously judge the dream, therefore discounting any message it has for you. You might be surprised when, three days later, your son slides on some pebbles on an unswept floor and breaks his arm!

Because you cannot always know *exactly* what a psychic clip means, *forbid yourself* to dwell on it, or to give it all sorts of meaning, or to try to make it logical. Accept the information for what it is, keep an open mind, and go on with your life. Eventually the meaning will be made clear.

HOW TO TALK TO OTHERS ABOUT ESP

For an ESP event to become effective in your life, it must be put into usable terms. You must share it. For even though a particular event may not mean anything to you, it may click for someone else. The ESP information may not make any sense to you at all, but your friend may identify with the information immediately and know exactly what it means. This is when ESP becomes real. The event you've experienced means something to somebody.

This is not to say that I advocate telling everyone about everything you experience. But if an ESP event has no meaning for you, it's worth checking with family and friends to see if it clicks with them. As you do this more often, you'll become better at knowing for whom any given information is useful.

Sooner or later you will have to make a decision concerning the sharing process. You can either say, "I won't talk to anyone about this," or you can say, "Let me take the risk and talk about my ESP ability. And let me see if I can validate my ESP experience." The talking about ESP gives positive reinforcement to that occurrence.

Sharing involves two people (at least), hopefully to the benefit of both. If you share an ESP event with someone, you have not only distributed the facts of your experience but have also contributed to the other person's storehouse of knowledge. You may have, by the way, created a convert, or at least increased someone's interest level.

The first decision you make based on an ESP occurrence may be a bit hard to explain. When one tries to explain something new or novel to others, it *is* very difficult. The words are hard to come by. You may not be certain how to convey the idea to someone else. You may be tentative with your approach, because you aren't sure how you're going to be received, and people, in case you haven't noticed, do not like rejection. You can make it easier by using your sense of humor. You may say something like, "Well, you know I'm as crazy as a bedbug, but let me tell you what happened to me the other day." People can laugh and be more accepting of what you are telling them. You may be frightened that you aren't good at ESP just yet. That's OK, no one is great at a new activity. A novice seamstress may keep a tea towel she has made hidden for a long time. She thinks that maybe someone will say "ugh!" when they see her first attempt. One day she puts the towel out for display. No one screams or laughs. So much for her fears. Most things *are* acceptable if they are not hidden.

Until ESP becomes a natural part of your personality, you will find it hard to talk about and will tend not to discuss it. You will know you're ready to discuss ESP when you've based a decision upon your ESP intuitions and someone asks you why you acted "out of character." You may respond, initially, that a little bird told you to do it but will own up to the intuitive process when pressed. When people you know begin to accept that some of your decisions are based on intuitive flow, they will incorporate this into their perception of your personality, thus accepting your intuitive base.

How do we know which people are susceptible to ESP? There's an old saying that "birds of a feather flock together." There is truth in that statement. People gravitate toward people with like interests. This is accomplished by body sensors and those unseen mechanisms we spoke of earlier. Trust implies faith, and faith is the fiber of truth.

Exposure to ESP, along with growth and improvement, helps produce faith, which directs you concerning when and to whom you can express your psychic information and expanded beliefs. An example of trusting psychic information when confronted with a skeptic or nonbeliever is the case of Joe. Joe was an employee of a very large corporation who felt that his position with the company was secure. After all, he had been employed there for seventeen years. I didn't know Joe, but we were in a social setting, and the psychic information I was receiving just kept on coming stronger and stronger. Finally, Joe gave me the opportunity to tell him, "You will be changing your job within five months, to a totally different company and environment." His immediate response was one of utter disbelief. He had a good laugh. As he was laughing, I also told him that along with the new job he would receive a $10,000 salary increase—at which point his wife quipped, "Oh boy, I get to drive a top-of-the-line car!" Five months later, Joe came by to tell me I had been right. Joe still says he is a nonbeliever, yet he checks with me regularly to see if he *might* be looking at a job change or salary increase. By the way, his wife got her top-of-the-line car!

FREE WILL

Many people, when they first learn about the mysteries of ESP, get a little scared. "If everything is predestined anyway," they say to themselves,"why do I bother making an effort or, for that matter, even getting up in the morning?" That's because they don't understand the role of free will.

In the previous example, Joe didn't immediately react to the information I gave him. Later, however, he was more open to psychic perceptions while still remaining skeptical. He exercised his prerogative of free will.

You exercise your free will every day. You know you're supposed to be at work by 9:00 but you routinely arrive at 9:15. Or you decide to come in early to get things done before others start their day.

On a psychic level, free will works much the same way. Your palm, for instance, may have no writer's mark. You might be "destined" to be a singer. But for some reason, you want to be a writer, so you exercise your free will and decide to become a novelist. As you practice your craft, several things can happen. You can fail terribly as a writer and decide that you'd make a whole lot more money using your voice. Or you can write for a while, decide it's not for you, and make a midlife career change—it just feels more comfortable singing. Or you can continue to exercise your free will. Destiny, after all, is only what will happen if you don't decide to change things. If you do decide to make a change, destiny will follow your lead. If, for instance, your will prevails and you become an excellent, even successful writer (or even a bad, poor, but determined one!), your palm will change to reflect your free will. You are, in fact, able to change destiny.

It is for precisely this reason that ESP awareness is so important.

After all, how can you change your destiny if you don't know what it is? The more you know about your inherent tendencies and the direction in which fate is leading you, the more able you will be to decide what you want to change and what you want to keep. If you are unaware that the plane you are about to board is going to crash, you cannot change your fate. But if you know, through precognition, that it will crash just after taking off, you can exercise your free will not to board the aircraft.

Now, some people feel that it is wrong to avoid fate. "It is fate," they say of a couple who marry after a whirlwind courtship. "They're meant to be together." But if, five years later, he beats her, is that fate, too? Because of my religious background, I believe that our free will, our choice, is our greatest gift from God. As any Horatio Alger story will show you, *anything* is possible. If we look at our natural desire to grow and change, it's difficult *not* to believe in the power of free will. Instinctively, we make choices. We desire self-improvement. Because fate isn't always good and we naturally and quite rightly want the best for ourselves, we have no choice not to exercise free will. Without it, our lives would be meaningless.

Of course, it is not always easy to exercise free will. Many of the bad things that go on happen as a result of a failure to make that choice. If a man is born with a predisposition to murder and he does not choose to exert his own free will, he will kill.

I knew one woman who chose not to exert her free will, even though she was told it meant she would die. When I spoke with Mary, I told her that, if she returned to her home, her life would be in danger. However, she had animals that needed to be fed. Even though a police officer who was with her told her that she should call someone else to feed the animals, she chose to override the psychic instructions and insisted that she be allowed to return home to feed her animals. Thinking she could have it both ways, she did respond to the information I'd given her enough to allow the law officer to accompany her home, assuming he could protect her. She sent the officer to feed the animals while she checked her house. Her estranged husband, who had been hiding in wait, seized the opportunity to shoot her with a .22-gauge rifle.

The decision not to accept the reading but to try to manipulate the conditions cost Mary her life. While few of the decisions we make are that important, it is impossible to overemphasize the importance of free will in ESP. For without free will—the ability to change our situations—ESP would be nothing more than a bizarre form of torture. What good would it do to know you were going to trip and fall if you couldn't use that knowledge to prevent the fall? Why would we get the information in the first place?

As I've mentioned previously, ESP can never hurt you. It is there to help. The good forces in the universe, or God if you prefer, gave us ESP as a gift. We can choose to accept or reject that gift, as well as the information it allows us. Either way, it's our choice.

You are probably wondering at this juncture if I'm saying that everything in our world is predestined. The answer is *no*. We always retain freedom of choice and freedom of personal will. You may receive or be told ESP information, but you have the choice of whether to accept it and act upon it, accept it and *not* act upon it, or ignore it entirely.

For example, imagine that you are given a bit of information concerning a friend's health. In this case, your friend could prevent, or at the very least, postpone the health problem by seeking medical attention now. By sharing your ESP information with this person, you may influence the final outcome, but your friend still retains freedom of will and freedom of choice. It is up to that person to either use or discard the information. In other words, the cause and effect of this situation are entirely up to your friend.

ETHICS

Each of us has a type of ethical code by which we live our life. In formulating an ethical code relating to the proper use of ESP, we must understand that ESP is for the common good, not just for our personal benefit.

People usually apply their ethical codes and spiritual understanding to their use of ESP. In the case of Judeo-Christians, for example, the Golden Rule will apply. Your own spiritual base will give you the checks and balances needed to deal with the ethics of using ESP. If your spiritual base is in tune with the laws of the universe and your values are also in place, then you won't risk misusing your psychic abilities and you will promote common good.

If, on the other hand, you consciously decide to use your ESP abilities for illicit ends or personal gain, then this is negative. *As a result, your ESP abilities will be jeopardized, lessened, or even lost.* Remember, all psychic flow stems from the Creator or source, and you, as a psychic channel, receive knowledge or information not by your will, but by His or its grace and mystery. If you do not use ESP correctly, the Creator or source will take it away.

When you first begin to impart psychic knowledge to another, in any type of setting, your role subtly changes. This subtle change takes you personally out of the picture, and you become a counselor—impartial and with no value assumptions in place. The person receiving has also undergone a subtle change. That person has gone from being a friend or confidant to a client. As you assume the role of a psychic counselor, your responsibility increases and your influence becomes more apparent. A good reader will be conscious of this, as it is extremely important not to make any value assumptions or moral judgments concerning your client's nature or activities.

A counselor goes beyond the mere telling of information to help the client reapply the information in a more beneficial manner. For example, an emotionally distraught, bankrupt client of mine was seeking a solution. The reading indicated that this person's economic situation was too severe to be helped by a mere monthly salary. What was the solution? The reading suggested three general options, which I outlined for him. He left. Some weeks later, he called to tell me he had followed one of the options given and was on his way to financial security. (This client did so without robbing banks, running drugs, or undertaking any other criminal activities. It is important to point out, however, that my morals can control only my conduct, not my client's.)

In other words, a reader just feeds out information; a true counselor helps the client by explaining the alternative options that may have come to light in the reading. The client *always* retains free will and chooses to accept or reject any or all of the reading.

Money Matters

It's OK to make a living with ESP ability. It's not OK to take advantage of the circumstances by manipulating them for your personal gain. For example, let's say that I decided to use my ESP abilities to gamble in Las Vegas and "broke the house" in several casinos. So now I'm supposedly rich. What have I really gained, though, if I lose my psychic ability, my power to help others or make a living? Money will be spent and gone, and I will be left with nothing.

The unwritten cosmic law states that the universe supplies. You must, however, replace or give back that which you take out. What goes around comes around, as the saying goes, in this never-ending cycle.

The whole purpose for psychic flow is the common good—to share with others. Therefore, even though I charge a fee for my services (which provides my living), I give away more than I receive. In other words, I give back to the universe that which was given to me.

A Good Reader

A good reader treats each client as the reader would like to be treated if the roles were reversed. With empathy and caring concern, good readers live by the following ethics:

- They will treat feelings softly and tenderly.
- They will not lie about their perceptions (because they will hold no moral judgments).
- They will not take advantage of emotional problems or distress, or request additional money for solving a problem. (Example: For $300 you can have candles burned to bring your estranged loved one home to you.)
- They will not give any absolutes. Rather, they will explore the options open to the client in any given situation.
- They will not request that clients return regularly. In fact, each reading should stand on its own, and the choice to return should be left up to the client. A truly good reader will give counsel (like the wise men and women of old) based on his or her perceptions.
- They never place their values, morals, prejudices, or judgment upon their clients. The reason is that a reader can jeopardize his or her abilities by trying to play God and allowing his or her heavy influence to hurt the client.
- They will explain to the client his or her ability to use free will to make choices.

4
GETTING STARTED

HUMAN BEINGS WERE designed to need a lot of rest. Despite our efforts to avoid rest, we cannot; after too long without physical and mental relaxation, our bodies put on the emergency brakes. If you suffer from stress, fatigue, or illness, you know what I mean.

Our hearts and souls need rest, too, so we can put our lives back into perspective. Many years ago, people got their rest through living closely with nature and talking with God. Today, we need to specifically set aside time to replenish our spiritual energy and thereby get in touch with the forces in the universe that help us feel whole.

The relaxation and focusing techniques provided here not only promote psychic flow, but will also help center you for better functioning in your day-to-day life. If you are tempted to skip this section, DON'T; you will shortchange yourself.

These exercises will also help you select your natural ESP vehicle(s) more easily. You can use these exercises to help in the selection process and to facilitate the bridging that comes with psychic flows. In other words, doing the exercises will help ESP become one fluid, consistent motion for you, because meditation fully prepares the body to receive psychic flows. Adequate relaxation will help you to put your life in order, too, by giving you the tools to set goals and go after what you want.

The first step toward getting in touch with your best self is to understand positive imagery. Positive imagery will lead you through the steps to becoming what you want to be. Almost all

55

When attempting to create psychic flow, *relax*. The harder you're working, the less likely something is to occur.

---

people have the desire to "remake" themselves, and you can.

Personal attitudes govern whether you view situations or circumstances negatively or positively. If you think good things will happen to you, they will. For example, take a sudden decrease in income. For years you have made *x* dollars, and you have adjusted your lifestyle to that amount of money. For some reason, the money flow stops. In your eyes, you are destitute. What do you do? If you become depressed and decide your life is over, it probably will be, because your attitude will prevent you from looking for new sources of income or adjusting to your problem. If, on the other hand, you can say, "Well, this looks a bit grim. Let's see what we can do," you open up lots of good possibilities.

Through positive imagery, we can confront our circumstances and view them as challenges. Yes, you have to cut down on expenses and luxuries, but through creative planning the bills can be met; the children will get fed; the roof will be repaired. You experiment and try new things. At Christmas you might end up making your gifts in your home instead of buying them; you may learn to sew to supplement your wardrobe; you may even be able to

---

It is usually best not to lie down when you're hoping to receive or send psychic images (unless you're trying to perform dream programming!). Instead, you want to get in the habit of having psychic experiences as you go about your daily life. It just wouldn't do for you to lie down in the middle of a party while sending come-hither signals to that sexy thing across the room!

---

author a book titled *6,372 Uses for Hamburger*. And while being poor is not the American dream, you may discover that it's not so bad. Necessity has become the mother of invention, and you have learned to use new skills to expand your thinking. Since you've had to work harder to achieve results, you can take extra pride in your accomplishments. In other words, you have fulfilled the old adage, "When life gives you lemons, make lemonade." Congratulations, and many thanks to positive imagery.

You will also find you have a new-found positive self-image as a direct result of positive imagery. This positive self-image will be a great help to you, and you may find that it, in turn, helps to resolve your problems. You may even find money coming your way!

Positive imagery will help stimulate psychic creativity. The new ideas that come to you to reverse an adverse situation or answer a perplexing question are actually psychic flows. If, on the other hand, you spend your time worrying and wailing, then your psychic flow is cut off and cannot help to provide you with effective solutions. If you're interested only in more positive outcomes, then this next section is for you.

You can also try to change your self-image directly. Even if your entire character is made of nothing but character flaws, this is where you start. Your quirks, flaws, and characteristics are your uniqueness. These are the things that make you different from everybody else.

In addition to our genetic heritage, our character is a combination of bits and pieces of personality traits we've adopted from the people who have influenced us throughout our lives. Teachers, friends, relatives, neighbors, television or political heroes, the butcher, the baker, the candlestick maker—whoever—end up being role models. Put all these influences into a pot, stir well, bake for fifteen, twenty, or thirty years, and out pops a personality.

Sit down and face yourself honestly. Remove all self-doubt, and examine the influences, the people who have shaped you into what you see as you. Some are positive, and some are negative. Once you've learned some things about yourself (maybe some of them you never wanted to admit before), you're ready to mold the clay that will become your self-image.

Now the positive imaging comes into play. Which of the characteristics do you want to emphasize, and which do you want to throw out? If you've always admired Cary Grant and have always wanted to project a suave and sophisticated image to others, it's time to stop gargling in public and belching in mixed company. And hey, maybe the sneakers aren't right for that job interview.

Maybe the image you want to project is more like Oscar, the slob in "The Odd Couple." Fine, but the point is that *you* are in control. You can project into reality whatever image of yourself you want.

With your honest self-evaluation, you can take negative characteristics and replace them with the positive images you want to project. The way we tie these together is by putting a goal or dream on paper. Break it down into its component parts. List the component parts you know you can fulfill at the present time, then list the ones you're not sure about, and list why. Then you need to decide how you should approach the problem areas on your list. Set up the scenario through visualization. You visualize yourself achieving your goal, and at the same time you are accumulating the resources for that goal. In the end, you will be successful in achieving your goal.

GOALS AND DESIRES: THE SEEDS OF SUCCESS

Each of us sets goals every day, but we rarely give conscious thought to the goals we set. Goals are the objectives of living. Goals, however, can completely alter our living and behavior patterns. Several examples of daily goal setting are: pick up the kids, do the laundry and housework, complete a report, search for a new job—the list goes on and on. Consciously we may not consider these to be goals. They are simply things we must accomplish in our day-to-day living. In fact, this is the definition of a goal.

To make commitment goals, you need to explore the hidden needs, wants, and desires that we all possess but are fearful to release into our conscious thoughts and actions. Before you can motivate yourself, you need to understand what goals and desires really are. To desire is to wish for or long for something. Most of us wish for lots of things but are not always willing to do what will bring about what we want. When we do try, the direction in which we move to achieve our desires is a goal.

How do you go about goal setting? You must be honest with yourself, about what you want and how far you are willing to go for your desires. Then you must make a commitment to achievement. You must also understand the motives behind your goal. Many people make the mistake of attempting to do things that they think others want them to do, and this merely produces frustration from setting what may be unrealistic goals.

Take the example of a client of mine who found himself in a very negative job situation. This man, Mr. B, came to see me for a reading. During the course of the reading, it became obvious that he was fearful of losing his job, yet he was very unhappy in that job, as it interfered with his family life and was causing him to have serious health problems. As we worked together, he commented that he had always wanted to have his own business so he could have hours more suited for his and his family's needs, but felt he did not have the oomph to go through the process of breaking away from that regular paycheck.

I suggested to him that he take a legal pad and, beginning on Monday, list all the occupations that he was interested in, without regard to whether or not he had the skills to fulfill the job description. On the next day, he was to list all of his likes and dislikes in the area of hobbies, and why. On Wednesday, he was to list all of the places he felt that he would like to live, and why. On Thursday, he was to go back to the first page and look at what he had written, and see if he still felt the same way about job fields. On Friday, he was to do the same with his list of hobbies. Saturday, he was to rethink the locations where he might want to live. During those days, he was to list the topics in order of priority, and to evaluate his feelings without considering how his family might respond to the items.

He was to leave the listing alone for two weeks, then redo the process by adding or deleting items or by rearranging them to reflect what was necessary for him to function within these occupations or locations. This revised list was to include the dollar amounts needed, materials needed, and even educational requirements. Then he was to put away his sheets again and wait two weeks. During this time he was to let his subconscious mind seek what his direction was to be.

It was several months before Mr. B called again for an appointment. When he came back, he told me that he had followed the procedure, and that he had had several offers for employment that he had not even solicited. He was very excited, as one was in a location that he had dreamed of but never felt was a possibility. He asked my advice, and I again instructed him to follow the same process for help in deciding. After he spent several weeks wrestling with his decision, the people again contacted him. They offered him professional standing, at which point he accepted the job and moved. I hear from him regularly, and he is doing well above his original expectations and is considered to be a leader in

If you feel you need help with goal setting or some other decision making, you might want to try the exercise Mr. B did.

Monday	List options you would consider if the reality of getting what you wanted were not a problem (such as marrying a gorgeous movie star).
Tuesday	List skills, people, interests, hobbies that you see as pertinent to your goal area. (If you are thinking about a relationship goal, for example, you'd list your relationship likes and dislikes, friends with whom you have fun, people you think might introduce you to a mate, and areas of interest you would like to share.)
Wednesday	List all the places you would be happy fulfilling your goal. (Would you move to Florida for love?)
Thursday	Rethink Monday's options. Do you still feel the same way? Reprioritize.
Friday	Do the same for skills, people, and interests. List them in order of preference.
Saturday	Do the same for places.

Put the list aside for two weeks.

After two weeks have gone by, repeat the original process, this time making note of what you'd need to make your goal become reality. If you're goal setting for relationships and think you might want to try to marry Mel Gibson, you'll have to make note of the need to move near to where he lives, meet people who know him, or write him a letter. Be honest about the financial, emotional, and physical tolls each goal possibility will take on you.

Put the list aside for another two weeks, *while consciously willing your unconscious mind to work on the problem*. If necessary, repeat the process. Be open to ideas and answers that pop up. They may not be what you expect.

---

his community. In addition, his wife and children are more settled and happier, as they have more time with him and are allowed to travel with him.

This process can work for you as well. It is the first step in learning to secure for you and your family the type of success you want. Your dreams can become your reality once you learn how to define the desire, the goals, and the needs, and to visualize.

Steps to Achieving Goals

1. *Identify your goal:* Examples are stress relief, end to procrastination, appetite control, headache relief.
2. *List priorities involved in achieving your goal:* Categorize the priorities that are directly involved in the goal achievement. (In the example of Mr. B, the priorities were family, job, social life, resulting in lack of time for self.)
3. *Options for achieving goal:* Mentally list all options that you could put into a structured form for reorganization. In the example, the options might have included several methods of organization, change of lifestyle within the family to include more time together, a job that allows more productive use of time—and even time for oneself!
4. *Recategorize and solve using psychic flow:* Through the process of meditation, you will benefit in two ways. The first will be a regeneration of body energy. The second benefit is that psychic flow provides insight into your problems, generating answers, options, and solutions.

VISUALIZATION

Visualization is the advanced art of learning to remove yourself from the now and to transport yourself to where you would like to be in the future, with every detail indelibly imprinted in the desired scenario. Imagine being so well acquainted with a fantasy that it becomes reality! A word of caution: the fantasy is not necessarily of the Harlequin Romance variety, but one in which you live out your scenario by practical application.

Like the other practices described in this book, visualization involves a definite method you can learn and use to produce the desired results. This method is not difficult but will require a little time to perfect. It is best to start with something simple.

To learn visualization, follow these five steps:

1. Set aside fifteen minutes when you can be comfortable and no one will bother you. Be sure to choose a place where you will not be interrupted, and one that produces a relaxed state for your body. I personally do rather well in the bathtub. Ordinarily no one bothers me, it is private, and the water feels great.

2. Instruct your mind to become blank. That may sound difficult. It does require concentration, because as adults we are conditioned to believe that we are always supposed to produce thought. Try closing your eyes, but don't go to sleep.

3. Be aware of your body and the sounds around your body, and let your mind wander at will. Try to identify the sounds around you, and visualize how the sounds you hear may look. To do this you must form a mental image. For example, listen to that running water or a drippy faucet. (Don't consider calling a plumber until you learn to visualize it in a serene way.) When you find yourself able to recall the faucet in total detail, how the drop looks before it drips, the way the water looks as the drop hits it, the area surrounding the sound, all articles close to the faucet, and the total room, you can go forward to the next step. Remember where you left off when recalling the detail.

4. Check for accuracy. Did your visualization work?

5. Repeat until you get it down pat.

This process will take a couple of weeks before you really solidify the technique. The second part to this wonderful experience, and it *is* good, is learning to do something well through visualization. An example is learning how to make a cake. Folks, this may be difficult—particularly if your mother-in-law never measures and her cakes are always perfect, yet yours tend to be snubbed by the family pet. Maybe you have tried all kinds of cake mixes, and they are still rejects. You had your mother-in-law, bless her heart, even walk you through making the cake, and the results still produce pity. This example is the basis for the following script. It does not attempt a wedding cake, but a mere two-layer iced cake that has no lumps or bumps (or valleys!) and is well browned to a golden hue.

The script shows you properly attired—nice clean clothes; a starched apron, which never gets soiled; hair in place; and all of the cooking equipment gleaming in an immaculate kitchen. You first see yourself in the setting, reading the instructions carefully. Not only can you read them, you understand them. You turn on the oven, measure the ingredients, proceed to mix well, and then prepare the pans to receive this glorious cake. When you have

There are ten keys to success that, used with visualization, will produce a more successful person. However, the definition for success is not an absolute. It is what the individual determines success to be.

The successful person:

1. Releases all negative fears.
2. Believes in the impossible.
3. Is able to laugh at him- or herself, to help keep a proper perspective.
4. Perceives obstacles as challenges.
5. Is persistent and consistent.
6. Has patience, does not give up too soon.
7. Learns to be flexible.
8. Learns how and where to find resources.
9. Is not embarrassed to admit lack of knowledge or ask questions.
10. Has faith in his or her ability to carry through to completion what is started.

greased and floured the pans, without scattering flour upon the surroundings, you open the preheated oven, insert the cake gently without burning your forearm or fingers, gently shut the door, set the timer, and see yourself preparing the icing. You see and hear the timer, smell the aroma, hear the soft sounds radiating from the hot oven, and (if your oven has a glass door and light in it) you watch your success become a reality in your mind's eye. You go through the process of checking for doneness, cooling the cake, and icing it. No sweat!

Repeat this exercise until you get the courage to actually go into your kitchen and produce a cake that is excellent, even in your mother-in-law's opinion. Since you have visualized this so many times, when you find yourself in the kitchen, you actually set the same scenario and reproduce the activity, at which time your success will be astonishing. Practice *does* make perfect.

Your positive mental attitude provides you with the stimulus you need to see accomplishment in even the smallest step, as a way to the end result. At the end of the mental scenario, you see yourself being rewarded, which in turn opens other doors, helping you to project positive mental images onto other areas of your life. You become, in effect, what you mentally see yourself as. Now, remember this won't change your foot size, but will help you to choose shoes that fit. The exercises are simple, but faith and consistent application are more difficult. Don't get discouraged. Take small steps first, then graduate to larger projects.

This same technique can be used for practical application of stopping smoking and losing weight. Granted, it may take more time, but the results have definitely been proved (and some people will charge you a small fortune for seminars to help you to do it. Once you learn the basic principles (remember the faucet and the cake), you can visualize your way to anything. Believe!

Visualization for ESP Skills

Let's say your goal is using ESP. To do this, follow the same procedures that you used for achieving other goals, except substitute the desire to use ESP skills for the desire to increase knowledge and happiness for yourself, your family, and your loved ones.

To use ESP in your mind's eye, see yourself relaxed and centered. Picture yourself receiving psychic information in such a way that there is no question of its validity. See yourself moving from one scene to another, sharing the ESP information and receiving smiles and hugs. Imagine yourself getting instant validation for this information.

MEDITATION

Meditation is for everyone and can be done by anyone. It is not difficult or complex, and is always beneficial. Many books have been written on the benefits of meditation with a whole range of topics, so read them if you desire additional keys to preparing for the knowledge of the inner spirit. Meditation is not an invention but merely the rediscovery of the human experience. It teaches discipline through concentration and having to live *within* life.

Once you have mastered the discipline, you will discover that your awareness levels will increase and your conscious senses are at peace with the universe. You will be much less affected by anxieties and frustration. Meditation helps you find, and accept, yourself. It is probably the perfect thing to do before you start any type of ESP exercise or before you begin to work with a vehicle. To send or receive correctly, you must be ready to listen and, at the same time, be prepared to share what you received.

The secondary result of meditation will be that your body's actual physical condition improves. Meditation can increase the longevity of energy, lower blood pressure rates, and for some people on medication, enable the meditator to decrease the dosages. The deep breathing done during meditation helps bring the body's mechanisms into proper balance. It gives the body the opportunity to release inner tension, relax muscles, and release toxins. Oxygen is supplied to the heart and lungs in larger quantities, thus stimulating emotional responses. This creates a sense of immediate understanding of your emotions. There is an old saying, "Be still and listen to the quiet, still voice from within." Meditation is listening to the quiet.

As doctors of medicine learn more about the beneficial results of meditation, they are beginning to appreciate it as a useful medical tool. They are recognizing in their patients who meditate regularly a change for the better in attitude and self-esteem, as well as less of a tendency toward self-criticism and criticism of others. Stress levels decline, patients have improved coping mechanisms, and their body regulators begin to take over. Patients begin to want the foods their bodies need, which improves diet, and patients often realize the need for regular physical exercise.

The most important aspect of meditation, though, is that your thoughts become the living reality. Meditation has been said to go beyond time and space to the world where time is not relative. Meditation alters your perceptions in such a way that the conscious is only aware of what is, rather than what should be. This produces a state of altered consciousness. Reasoning does not have to play the same role in meditation as it does in your daily living, in the conscious reality of here and now.

Techniques of meditation help prepare you for understanding your inner-core consciousness in relationship to the physical and spiritual worlds. I have often said that meditation is the flip side of prayer. When we pray, we are sending our supplications to the Creator. When we meditate, the Creator is sending us His responses (see Chapter 2 regarding this relationship to ESP).

Before you begin the meditation process, you will most likely want to list some of the expectations and goals you have for the meditation exercise. You can list these expectations or goals either mentally or in writing. It may be best, initially, to have a written list to keep you on target for that which you are seeking. If you chose a mental list, remember that the mind is not passive but active, and it can always retain more than one thought at a time. You'll learn.

Your goal for meditation can be as simple as keeping your body in good balance with physical, mental, and emotional equilibrium. It can also be as complex as you wish. For example, your goal can be to quit smoking, or to snare someone who attracts you. Either way, you set the scenario and goals.

Meditation can help you solve the stress of day-to-day living. It provides insights into what is really needed in any problem-solving scenario. Meditation, by stimulating psychic flow, will help you to solve problems or to set or achieve goals.

Meditation, which is important in preparing to receive psychic flow, is also good for goal setting. Let's set a sample scenario; say your main goal is stress relief. You have stress up to your ears! Your family is clamoring for more of your time, your boss is handing you endless deadlines, and your social life is nonexistent. You never seem to have time for anything you want to do. Your time off is spent running kids to soccer practice, attending school events, and juggling dental appointments. Your spouse helps out, but you still feel as if you need to be two people to get everything done. What can you do?

The first few times you meditate, your goal may be just to become "centered." During the process, you concentrate on one goal. You center on this goal. You begin to relax, which relieves stress and opens your mind to what your priorities really are. Once open (even if it's only a crack), your mind will expand and ex-pound on the problem area. You are now centered, on target, and open—enter psychic flow. You begin to realize that you could play ball with your son on Saturday afternoons if you did your project research on Thursday night instead of watching TV. PTA or school events would be less tiring and stress producing if you ate out. You could alleviate your job deadlines and pressures by buying a word processor. That would enable you to use the repetition of processing reports to your benefit. You can apply the same process to any number of goals. You can elaborate on the theme; insert your own scenario.

One of the goals of meditation is to start a flow of thoughts. (It would be better for you to make a mental note of the thoughts without breaking the meditation setting and act on them, should you so desire, later.) I like to refer to this process of thoughts entering and leaving during meditation as the "filtering" portion of the meditation cycle.

Meditation by relaxing you and significantly reducing your stress levels, will make it easier for you to obtain insights about any problem or concern you have. By stimulating psychic flow, it will help you tap into these insights; by relaxing you, it will enable you to sit still long enough to benefit from the psychic flow.

Procedures for Meditation

Many types of procedures can be used in the process of meditation. Each person will eventually choose a method that will work best for him or her. This chapter will give you some techniques to get started. You are welcome to rework them to suit your purposes. Each technique listed will incorporate some of the same types of beginning settings. The processes are also similar. The wording or purpose, however, can be different.

Now for the actual steps in doing beginning meditation. *Please remember that this type of meditation, unlike pure meditation that you may be familiar with, has been primarily designed for ESP. Remember, too, that the most important part of attempting any new process is a willingness to try. Without this desire, nothing will be accomplished.*

1. Choose a time of day and set aside fifteen to twenty minutes.
2. Choose a quiet place to sit in comfort. It is best to have a tall chair where you can relax your head.
3. Do not cross your arms, legs, or ankles.
4. Breathe normally.
5. Now breathe deeply three or four times, without consciously controlling your breathing cycle.
6. As ideas come into your mind, acknowledge them and let them go. Continue until you are relaxed, easily releasing thoughts, peaceful.
7. You are now ready to repeat the affirmation or litany. Following are two to choose from. (You are free to insert your own if you wish.)

Litany #1: "I call upon the universe to supply all resources needed to achieve [insert your goal here], and I ask that the universe grant the resources needed through happy and legitimate means."

1. Breathe at will. Feel energy replacing any drained feeling you may have. Relax.
2. Repeat the litany a total of three times
3. Arise and go about your daily activities.

Litany #2: Mantra is a form of chanting that produces a resonate sound and helps one learn to achieve single-minded focus. It is a good beginning point in learning deep concentration.

1. Sit in a comfortable chair.
2. Mentally chant "God is love" or some sound that is pleasing to you.
3. Begin chanting out loud.
4. Do nothing else.
5. Chant for fifteen minutes.

As you put more inflection and feeling into the chanting process, you may find yourself moving in a rhythmic pattern.

A possible side effect from any meditation process is the increase of psychic flashes or occurrences. This is not, however, the primary goal of meditation. Its basic concept is to discipline the mind to do only one thing at a time, so concentrate on the litany.

Some persons find it helpful to tense and relax the muscles in their body while doing the breathing exercises. You can begin with your feet and work your way up the body to your neck and head. You will feel an immediate relaxing of all the muscles in your body. NOTE: This works so well that if you aren't careful, you'll find yourself snoring, not meditating!

After meditating you will feel a new surge of energy. Always remember to thank the universe for what it has supplied you.

What I've just given you is a simple form of meditation. The next method takes more time, but is worth it.

The Mental Retreat

Each of us has a secret dream place, or retreat, or at least some-place where we would like to go "to get away from it all." By using this retreat as a beginning point, you can close your eyes and mentally transport yourself to this setting. Using the meditation process to relax and relieve yourself of tension, begin to set up the retreat scenario. For example, let me share my retreat with you. You might want to try something similar.

> I see myself sitting on a low branch of a tree in a field located on a cliff near the ocean. The sounds and music of the universe permeate my whole being. I happily drag my bare feet through the silky-feeling soil. I see and hear myself talking to a person who is there with me. This person, my spirit guide, and I are discussing whatever I have to say and what he feels I need to hear. I then remain there and let the pleasant feeling wash over me. Soon, I arise and retrace my steps back to my daily world. Just before I leave, I always say, "Thank you for being, and thank you for loving."

In this short time, around three to five minutes, I feel totally refreshed and ready to resume my day.

Few people are really ever able to comprehend all there is to know at a single sitting; meditation needs to be done regularly in order to increase knowledge. Hence, the Life Source gives the

---

Note: Remember to keep the details and sequence of events exactly the same each time you meditate.

---

student only what he or she is ready to absorb. Once the student has absorbed the knowledge, the student will incorporate it into his or her life without being consciously aware of doing so.

Meditation is one way each of us can connect to the Creator. This is always an act of faith, and the meditator fully expects some type of message or information to be revealed during this process. You won't be disappointed, but the message may not always be what you expect. Meditation is learning to accept, and *like,* silence. It is during the process of learning to be silent/quiet that you can be a channel for the Divine.

Some meditators feel that meditation is the remembrance of all that we already know, but have forgotten or chosen not to utilize.

As such, meditation becomes one of the prompters that stimulates the creative flow of psychic insights. This is because meditation puts you in the ESP mind-set, which transcends time, space, structure, and all human boundaries and concepts.

Once you have opened up and are receptive to the eternal message of love through the meditation process, you begin to develop a sense of belonging, of being at one with your world. You will begin to see nature as an extension of yourself. The universe will become part of you. Even a beginning user will feel a wonderful sense of peace. Soon you will move forward to an understanding of complete love, linking you to other people and to the center of creation. This love relieves the fear and darkness in your life with the light of universal love and truth. This truth will never hurt you.

HOW TO CHOOSE YOUR ESP VEHICLE

How can you choose a vehicle? While I can't pick your vehicle for you, I can tell you with certainty that meditation is the way to gain the answer to this question. It leads you into the necessary awareness level at which you will be able to narrow the choices. The ultimate free-will decision still remains yours to make, of course, but at least you will have a starting point.

Since meditation and visualization promote ESP flow, it seems to be a natural progression to use the same method to pick a vehicle. This book has provided several vehicles from which you can choose, though of course there are many more than those listed herein. One, for example, is Bible scrying. With this vehicle, you open up the Bible at random, and the first scripture your eyes fall upon will contain a message applicable for you at any given time.

One person will have a natural affinity for one vehicle, while others will gravitate toward another. Some are fascinated with hands and their movements, while others feel more comfortable picking up cards. Those who work from tactile information will most likely choose psychometry, as that is exactly what psychometry is.

Before entering the state of meditation, ask yourself which vehicle will be best for you. While you are in the state of meditation, the answer will come. Listen carefully. If your vehicle is palms, for example, it may not be the entire hand, maybe only the fingers, mounts, or lines—whatever is relevant to your needs as a beginner.

Perhaps you prefer not to go through all of the mechanics to choose, as you know intuitively which is right for you. This vehicle, then, is the one with which to begin. Or maybe you do not feel particularly drawn to any of the vehicles. For you I suggest the "parlor tricks" in the chapter on palmistry, or try psychometry, described in Chapter 5.

In the beginning, you may make several tries with different vehicles before one clicks for you. One of the vehicles in the book will work for you in some fashion. As the vehicles listed in this book don't begin to scratch the surface of vehicles available to you, however, you may need to keep on searching as you gain more experience. While you are searching, though, have fun! Out of each vehicle tried and discarded, you will retain some valuable knowledge. You can apply this knowledge to your overall development of ESP psychic flow.

5

THE LAZY PERSON'S APPROACH TO THE USE OF ESP

THIS CHAPTER IS called "The Lazy Person's Approach to the Use of ESP" because the exercises here are very easy to do and quite often produce immediate results. Certain vehicles, such as palmistry, cards, and numerology (all covered in later chapters) call for quite a lot of time and energy. However, psychometry, dreams, and other vehicles discussed here can be used successfully with little practice and without special equipment (with the exception of one set of cards you can make yourself).

If you are skeptical about ESP or your personal ability to use it, or are really at a loss as to where to begin, I'd suggest starting here. You're bound to have luck with one of these vehicles. Even if you're one of those people who feel they don't have the time to really study ESP, you'll be able to use the exercises in this chapter to glean exciting psychic information within minutes.

It's always more fun to try a new activity with another novice or "partner in crime," so to speak. It's comforting and, if nothing else, you can laugh together over your faux pas or lack of success. If, on the other hand, you are successful, then you are immediately validated and have gained a partner for life.

A word on choosing partners: It is important to choose as a partner someone who will take ESP seriously. He or she doesn't have to be a scientist or the next Ruth Montgomery, but your partner should not be a confirmed skeptic determined that ESP does not exist. In addition, he or she should be someone you trust and someone with whom you feel you have a good rapport. Last, your partner should be a person you feel has a strong emotional or spiritual side, someone for whom pushing the "ESP buttons" will not be too difficult.

It is also important to understand that there are many names for the ESP vehicles covered in this chapter—clairvoyance, precognition, telepathy, and so on. While I will discuss each of these, don't get hung up on the words. ESP is a catchall for *every* kind of psychic phenomenon and, in the deepest sense, all ESP vehicles and phenomena are just different ways of getting at the same thing: truth. Furthermore, various ESP elements often occur at once, making it difficult to distinguish exactly *how* information is relayed. If you have an exciting ESP experience, it really doesn't matter what it's called; the names, after all, were developed by people who felt the need to "prove" and categorize ESP, and to make it palatable to others. But words are words, and the mystery and beauty of ESP transcends them all.

PSYCHOMETRY

Psychometry is the practice of "reading" an object that belongs to another by using the magnetic field that radiates from the object. The nice thing about psychometry is that you get instant validation.

Take the case of Cecilia Bond, who was going to try psychometry for the first time, on a lark. She asked her next-door neighbor to be a willing victim, because they barely knew each other. Cecilia felt this would be a good test because if she picked up any information, it would be strictly from the object she was using in the experiment. The neighbor, Barbara, offered Cecilia a ring from her finger to psychometrically read.

Cecilia tells about the experiment: "I took the ring from Barbara and held it first in my right, then in my left hand. It felt warm at first . . . then, I couldn't believe it! The first thing I knew, I was watching a scene taking place, much like a video clip. There was Barbara dressed in a white lace dress, at what looked like a lawn party. The outdoor scene was filled with tables decorated with white linen and floral arrangements. It looked like a wedding reception. I felt the ring was given to Barbara on the day of this event, and that it had been given to her by a man.

"I opened my eyes and laughingly told Barbara what I'd 'seen.'

Barbara's face sure was fun to watch! To say she was surprised would be a vast understatement. She told me that the ring had indeed been given to her by a man . . . her brother, on the evening before his wedding day at the rehearsal dinner. She had been wearing a white eyelet dress for the occasion, and the ring had been presented as a little gift to her. The scene, including her dress, was correct! Only my interpretation was slightly askew.

"Well, I was very excited about my first try at psychometry and couldn't wait to try it again. I now use it mainly during hand-shakes to help me form a more accurate first impression of some-one."

Everything in the universe is surrounded by a magnetic field that radiates a unique level of vibration. When we combine an object, such as a ring, with the magnetic aura of our own bodies, these two fields merge into one, thereby assuming the vibration levels of both. When a psychometrist holds an object that belongs to another person, he or she can read the combined magnetic fields for information about the object and its owner.

The art of psychometry employs the sense of touch, along with the sensation of vibration levels, which permits the reader to tap into the core of the object and the connection between the object and the individual being read.

The psychometrist's ability to hold an object, and to penetrate the fields that merge to center, enables him or her to surpass barriers of time and thereby view the origin of the item and describe personality traits and events in the life of the owner.

If the object doesn't belong to the individual who is requesting the information, the reader is able, however unusual it may seem, to give a description of the owner, which may include physical, emotional, or mental conditions. This ability is actually an exten-sion of the five physical senses, but obviously touch is the key when handling the object and receiving its vibration levels.

In some ways, the act of psychometry envelops the reader in much the same way an actor is enveloped in a role. For instance, when using psychometry for the purpose of crime solving, the reader "becomes the victim." From this perspective, the reader may be able to re-create the scene and even the action of the event exactly as it occurred, by scanning a photograph of the victim or the crime scene. Scanning is a simple method; one merely moves the hand closely above the photograph.

You may try this yourself with any photograph. Maybe you have an old picture of, let's say, your great-grandmother. This will prove satisfactory, not to mention fun, if your grandmother or anyone else who knew your great-grandmother is still living. You may read the picture using the following procedure:

1. Hold the picture in your hand, or lay it face up on a flat surface.
2. As you hold it or look at it, scan it lightly with your left hand, in much the same way a blind person reads a page written in Braille.
3. When you're done scanning, you should record any mental images you received, so that you will be armed with information that can later be validated.

Remember to begin with the obvious, such as dress and background, then allow your mind a free rein. You may be very pleasantly surprised indeed. For some, psychometry takes only a few passes of the hand, for others more time and/or concentration is required.

In the beginning you may feel you are not receiving correct information, particularly if the person with whom you are working is a friend. You may even feel you are picking up information that conflicts with what you believe to be factual. If at first you don't succeed . . . .

You can send as well as receive information. When practicing psychometry, you actually invade the electrical space of another, and in doing so you become a part of that space. As you become good at psychometry, you will be able to consciously leave your mark on objects as well.

Reading an Object

Initially, at least, you should begin with someone unfamiliar. This person can act as the observer and also supply the article to be read by psychometry.

1. Choose an item of personal value to your subject: a ring, watch, bracelet, wallet, even a small article of clothing. This object must be something that the subject wears or uses often—every day, if possible—and the person must

have worn it *recently*. It should not have been worn recently by anyone else.

2. Take the object and place it in either hand. (You will soon choose one hand over the other. This will be the hand that receives the most "vibes." Once you choose a hand, you need to stick with the choice.) Take the object in your hand and just let it lie there while you become very relaxed, allowing mental images to float before your eyes. After a few moments, begin to verbalize those images.

3. Have the subject start to snap his or her fingers. This sets up a rhythm, much like a metronome, and causes you to zero in on the object and produce quick, spontaneous information.

4. Either the reader or observer can write down the information coming through, but it's helpful to have a third person do it. The person you choose should write down your *first* impressions and sensations, and one-word clues, as well as any "pictures" you see. Have the subject validate the information you give. You'll be amazed at your results!

DEVELOPING CLAIRVOYANCE

This section discusses the phenomenon known as clairvoyance, both audio and visual. Clairvoyance incorporates both audio and visual telepathy (the sending of messages mind to mind) and precognition (foreknowledge of events) from all sources, and their many combinations. Again, it will sometimes be difficult for you to distinguish one from the other. Don't worry about "defining" your ESP occurrences for now. As your experience gives you knowledge, you will be able to differentiate between the types of occurrences, should you so choose.

In the world of yesteryear, clairvoyant vision was referred to as "second sight." It was also thought that one could not have second sight unless one was the offspring of the seventh child of the seventh child, or veiled at birth. No one has ever proved or disproved this theory, yet those who are the seventh children of seventh children (or veiled at birth), do seem to have a higher degree of clairvoyance.

This may cause you to think that the modern miracle of birth control is preventing the birth of clairvoyants, but not to worry.

Today's information boom regarding ESP makes clairvoyance a good possibility for anyone wanting to *learn* it—the world will no longer have to count on people born with "the gift" to have ESP. Furthermore, clairvoyants can pass on their own inborn skills to another, if they want, which they usually do before they die. When I die, for example, I will pass on my skills, and the lucky recipient won't even have to practice ESP—it will be as if he or she was born with it, as I was. Of course, this will mean that I will lose my skills, but then, I won't be needing them anymore where I'll be going!

But you don't have to count on someone passing his or her skills on to you. There is a resurgence of interest in clairvoyance, and many of those who experience visual or audio clairvoyance of information are more open to helping others understand what it is and how it works.

Recently there has been much ado about the validity of clairvoyance. Researchers at Stanford Research Institute have concluded that clairvoyance does exist. They don't quite understand all of its components, but they have accepted that there are people who do have these skills and use them effectively. It was during these studies that the term *distant viewing* was coined to help explain exactly what clairvoyance is.

Clairvoyance is the receipt of information that cannot be explained by normal means, yet it is true and its message is clear. It could be described in terms of thoughts being sent from the Universe and received by a person and implanted with great clarity in that person's mental eye, so the clairvoyant person can then repeat what he or she has "seen" in great detail. Skill in clairvoyance, like a TV, allows a person to receive information or signals that we are constantly being sent. TV signals are emitted for everyone, but only those who turn on their sets will get a picture. So it is with clairvoyance. Clairvoyance has also been defined as the ability to perceive as mental images the energy of thoughts that travel in waves.

I enjoy the example that Bill Cosby uses in his video. He talks about his little girl, who was told she could not have a cookie. He then put the cookie box high on a shelf and left the room. Moments later he heard the paper in the cookie box being rattled, and asked the child if she was in the cookies. Of course she was, but, as Mr. Cosby so adeptly put it, "The child did not realize that sound

travels." We are like that child in some ways; what we have personally experienced we don't forget, but at the beginning we may not
realize how thought travels. You see, there are no barriers in time
or space. Thoughts or energy can go forward or backward in time
(according to the usual conception of time) without any visible
problems.

In essence, the ability for clairvoyance is a highly developed level
of telepathy, because it circumvents our ideas of time and space.
For the thought waves to be received, the receiver should have an
intensely emotional personality with an openness to the mystery
and wonder of the world. Thought patterns are transmitted to the
magnetic field around the receiver's head. Studies such as those I
have previously mentioned have shown the best receptor is a
receiver whose brain is in the alpha state (attained by meditation,
certain sleep patterns, and yoga, for example). Dreams can be
clairvoyant, too.

Clairvoyance has two distinct patterns of transmission and
reception: visual and auditory. The only real difference in the
process is that one receiver "hears" the message, while the other
"sees" it. Joan of Arc is said to have had audio clairvoyant occurrences—voices told her to raise an army and fight and how to plan
her strategy. Sometimes audio waves come in so vividly that more
than one person in the same room will "hear" a voice and turn to
see who called, yet no one is visible to the naked eye. The audio
clairvoyant will be able to repeat the message clearly without
grasping for words. A professional clairvoyant can, and usually
does, experience both visual and audio information regarding
these occurrences.

Exercise to Increase Telepathic Clairvoyance (Visual)

Try this exercise to increase your visual telepathic clairvoyance.

1. Find two willing people to help you.
2. All three must agree upon a place, a day and one-hour
   time period for the test to be conducted.
3. Ask friend A to select three images (drawings, clippings
   from magazines). Have the images placed into separate
   envelopes.
4. Each of you go to the prearranged spots to rest and relax.

Your friends (A and B) should not be in the same room you are. They can be as far away as you want (be careful if you cross time zones to set your time carefully!)

5. Have friend A give friend B the first envelope. B begins to concentrate upon the image and thinks *only* of the image and your name. Remember, this involves sending mental pictures, not words.

6. After twenty minutes, friend A gives friend B the second envelope and friend B concentrates on the new image and your name.

7. After another twenty minutes, friend A gives friend B the last envelope. Friend B repeats the process followed in steps 6 and 7, with the new picture.

8. At the end of the hour, tape record the image flashes that have filtered through your mind.

9. All three of you reassemble (or talk on the phone) to check whether the images sent were the images received.

If this was accomplished successfully, great! If not, try again until the images sent are received. Switch roles. Try sending instead of receiving. Some people are natural senders, others natural receivers. Keep practicing; you'll get better!

Exercise to Increase Telepathic Clairvoyance (Audio)

Audio clairvoyance can be practiced in the same manner but by sending music rather than an image. In using music, the receiver must *definitely* be at a physical distance, lest strains of music drift into physical hearing range. It is easiest if friend A and friend B agree upon the *type* of music (rock, classical). Either a song or just a few bars of the music may be sent.

Children seem to be able to do audio clairvoyance well, especially if they don't realize they are being checked, so keep it fun.

Card Exercise for Clairvoyance

This exercise uses a homemade set of cards with symbols. The symbols are as follows: square, cross, circle, triangle, and rectangle. To make these cards, use cardboard—so the symbols will *not*

ILLUSTRATION 5-1
CARD SYMBOLS FOR CLAIRVOYANCE EXERCISE

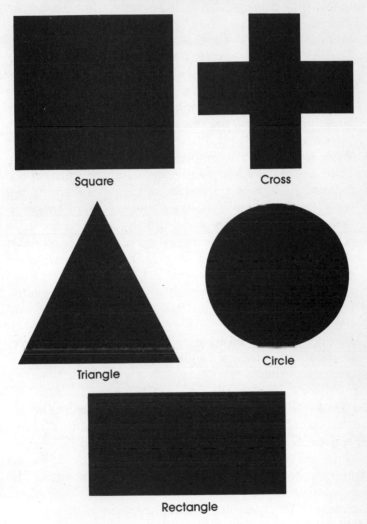

Square

Cross

Triangle

Circle

Rectangle

show through on the back—and a black felt-tip pen. Draw each symbol on its own card, and then fill in the design to form a solid symbol (see Illustration 5-1). You will need to make four copies of each symbol, or twenty cards in all. You may also use a regular playing card deck in this exercise.

Alone (For Precognition)

To improve your precognition skills, practice this exercise.

1. Sit down at a table with pencil and paper.
2. Shuffle your cards and lay them face down on the table.
3. Draw the first card from the deck, holding it in one hand with the symbol facing away so that you can't see it. Use your left hand if you are right-handed, and vice versa. Generally, the hand you use least often will be your "receiving hand."
4. Write down your first impression of which card it is.
5. There are two ways to do this step. You can either flip over the card right away, for instant validation, or go through the whole deck before checking yourself. Some people feel that knowing how they're doing helps them to focus; others, particularly perfectionists, get so disappointed that they turn off psychic flow entirely. These types are often people who need a few runs to get warmed up (that is, to relax!) as well. Be honest with yourself when beginning this exercise, and if the method you chose does not work, try the other.
6. If you are having problems, *stop thinking*. Relax. Don't worry about getting it "right." Just write down what comes to mind.

Do this for fifteen minutes a day. If you have trouble, be sure to meditate before starting the exercise. Soon your "hits" will outnumber your misses.

You may notice that, instead of "guessing" the card you are holding, you consistently hit the *next* card in the stack. This is called *anticipating*, and some people tend to anticipate whenever they have an ESP experience. This is just as valid as if you guess the card itself, and you will learn to take your anticipation skills into account when requesting psychic information.

Once you become proficient at this, you can increase the length of the exercise. Or you can try it using a regular deck of playing cards.

With a Partner (for Telepathy)

To do this exercise for telepathy, you follow the same steps as in the previous exercise, only you use a partner or two.

With two people: The "sender" picks up a card, visualizes it, and "sends" it to the receiver, who either writes down what he or she saw or speaks it aloud (see step 5 of the previous exercise). Since some people are better senders than receivers, and vice versa, it is important to try switching roles.

With three people: This is really the optimum situation, since the third person can do all the record keeping, and the sender and receiver can work without interruption. After the exercise is over, the record keeper can report on the success of the exercise. It is also useful to have a third person around if it turns out that the first two are both receivers, or both senders. Furthermore, a third person can add extra psychic energy to the proceedings.

DREAMS: THE ART OF THE MIND

A dream is an involuntary mental image experienced during sleep or when one is in a type of trance. These images are a channel for psychic awareness. They can provide insights into life conditions, help to solve problems, and promote a clearer understanding of oneself. Dreams can be telepathic, precognitive, or just plain "clairvoyant."

Dreams have been a source of mystery for centuries. In early history, it was thought that dreams were the direct link between the Creator and people. The Christian Bible is full of references to how dreams told of coming events, and how God chose who would interpret those dreams (see Daniel 6:12 for an example). The Greeks, Romans, and Egyptians placed such importance on dreams that the social structures of their civilizations were greatly influenced by the dreams of their rulers.

The course of history has been changed more than once because of visions witnessed in sleep. One extreme example is a dream that young Corporal Adolf Hitler had one night in the midst of World War I. He dreamed that the trench in which he lay was hit by enemy fire, and he was entombed beneath earth and molten iron; he was injured and was bleeding from a chest wound. When he awoke from this terrifying experience, he was lying unharmed in his trench, and all was quiet not far from the French front.

However, the dream troubled him. He left what he considered to be the security of the trench and, in an almost trancelike state, walked into the open area between the two armies, knowing that at any moment he could be hit and killed. Suddenly he heard a barrage of enemy fire and felt an explosion so intense it knocked him to the ground. He struggled to his feet and rushed back to his trench, only to find a huge hole. Everyone who had been in that trench had been buried alive. Hitler took this to mean that he had been given a mission of great importance and destiny. This belief spurred him on in his goals, and he did indeed alter world events. Dreams can safely be called the triggering agent of the mind to forecast a precognitive event.

Many authors and poets have drawn from their dreams and woven the results into some of our greatest literary works. One outstanding example is Mary Shelley, creator of *Frankenstein*. Samuel Coleridge dreamed of the splendor that resulted in his classic poem *Kubla Khan*. Another notable nocturnal creation is *The Strange Case of Dr. Jekyll and Mr. Hyde*, by Robert Louis Stevenson, who did most of his writing in bed. Charlotte Brontë drew from her dreams for inspiration, as did Gothic romance writer Ann Radcliffe. Writers are usually quite in tune with their dreams.

In the areas of science and technology, similar events have also occurred. William Lear dreamed about his future Lear jet, and Jonas Salk had recurring dreams enabling him to perfect his polio vaccine. These are but a few examples of how dreams have influenced our lives and altered the course of history.

In today's society, dreams have come to symbolize how we relate to our own inner consciousness or feel about ourselves. Dreams are the language of the unconscious. When Sigmund Freud, the father of modern psychology, wrote *The Interpretation of Dreams* in 1900, people began to look at dreams in a whole new light. Freud however, in his rigidity, tended to bend dreams in order to make them fit his theory (and anyone familiar with Freudian psychology knows he would have had a field day with that last statement!). However, Freud is credited with the discovery of the relationship between dreams and the mental and physical health of the person.

Carl Jung, who was initially a disciple of Freud, later became disenchanted with his mentor, and vice versa, for a number of reasons. Jung was infinitely more flexible than Freud in his interpretation and philosophy of dreams. One of his most interesting theories is the concept of "collective conscious." Jung believed that humans inherit not only physical traits but also traces of memories, which have their origins in the earliest human experiences. Hence, the mind contains bits and pieces of all ancestral experiences. People can therefore call upon these experiences in their dreams. (According to the study of palms, these same ancestral memories are stored in the palm, within the Mount of Luna. In palms, the Mount of Luna is the personal unconscious center for knowledge but doesn't necessarily relate to actual personal experience.)

As long as people have been on earth, they have wondered whether they can interpret the future through dreams. Evidence suggests that, sometimes, at least, we can. Hitler was saved for bigger, if not better, things by a battlefield dream. Abraham Lincoln, only days before his assassination, saw himself "laid out" in the East Room of the White House. Samuel Clemens (Mark Twain) dreamed the death of his brother in an explosion on a river boat shortly before it happened in reality. Try arguing with anyone who's had a precognitive dream!

Today, many scientific sleep study clinics dot the globe. Included among these are some that study the possibility of telepathy and clairvoyance through dreams.

Sleep studies have proved what we already knew to be true. The body requires sleep to produce balance. The same studies have proved that dreams are an integral part of the sleep process and necessary to restore our physical and psychological balance. Often, psychic knowledge can't reach us during the waking state, because we are too easily distracted by external stimuli.

From a psychic standpoint, the function of dream analysis is to penetrate the contents of the dream—common events, concerns, and problems that occur in day-to-day living—and to provide information and direction to the dreamer. Thus, some dreams clearly give "psychic equilibrium."

It is important to pinpoint the sources and solutions of imbalance. The analysis is found within the dream, and only the dreamer can interpret it, as the dream provides knowledge about the dreamer. Dreams also provide knowledge about others to whom we relate, as well as information about our roles in particular situations. Our dreams project the need for wholeness of the personality, and are mostly forward projections, not hindsight as some believe.

Dream Interpretation

If dreams are in fact mental pictures, and if pictures are self-explanatory, why is it so hard to interpret their meanings? One reason is that any natural ability to interpret our dreams has probably been suppressed by parents, spouses, even our too-busy selves. We place so much importance on the meaning of words—our language—that we often ignore other languages—the language of love, the language of color, the language of dreams. If you want to learn another language (Spanish, Greek), you must learn the symbols and clues that give the language meaning. In much the same way, you can learn about the language of art symbolism or literature. If you want to understand your dreams, you must learn the symbols that are the language of the dreamer.

When you begin this process, of course, your dreams may appear to be a collection of unrelated symbols, words, and disjointed images. It is only through practice that you will recognize what your dream symbols mean and will be able to understand your individual dream patterns. Simply put, you learn a new language. When you learn to relate your dreams to your waking reality, they will begin to provide you with information that will fill in the gaps in your life.

Remember that each of us operates in our own little world, in our own personal perception of "reality." For example, Alice may see herself as fat, even though her doctor says she is anorexic. Which scenario is the reality? Thus, the first clue to interpreting your dreams is your conception of who you are, as it has direct bearing on your dreams.

The second clue to understanding your dreams is how you perceive, in your waking state, the people you dream about. Are they people you admire? Do they make you fearful? Do you consider them to be of value in your life? The value you place on people, places, and objects in your waking world will be the value you assign to them in your dreams. For example, if a woman in Afghanistan fears Russian soldiers, dreaming of a Russian soldier will express her fear.

The third clue to analyzing your dreams is the motivational forces that are inherent in all of us—the "what makes me tick" concept, if you will, or how you feel about or relate to the rules by which you live. What happens when you bend or break the rules? Do the rules seem to express what you feel or think? In our waking reality, we constantly explain our actions. For example, in our society, the rule is you don't kick someone when he's down. In dreams, this and other societal rules do not apply.

The fourth clue in dream interpretation is how you perceive conflicts. How do you attempt to resolve conflicts? Do you feel conflicts between what you think you should do and what other people tell you that you should do? Are the conflicts in your dreams the same as those you encounter when awake?

Dream Programming

Isn't it amazing that science has at last discovered what we in the metaphysical world have known all along? You can preprogram your dreams to help you live more effectively. This technique is called (you guessed it) dream programming for problem solving. The technique was arrived at through countless studies, originally designed to ascertain that each of us has dreams, whether we remember them or not. Studies have shown without a doubt that most of us dream at least three to four times a night, and that dreams are necessary for the proper maintenance of health and well-being.

During sleep, a person goes through what are known as Rapid Eye Movement (or REM) stages, when the eyes move under the lids. Sleep stage studies have found that it is during the time of REM that people dream, and that if a subject was awakened just after a REM period occurred, the dreamer could recall the dream much more clearly than if the researchers let him sleep through it. If he was allowed to sleep through the majority of the REM periods, the dreamer tended to vividly remember only the dream of the last REM period. Researchers also found that dreamers tend to edit their dreams to form coherent dream stories, or themes. Over a period of time, it became obvious to researchers that the subject's waking attitude affects his or her dream state. If for example, a subject seemed to have more happy experiences while awake, the subject was more likely not to recall his or her dreams. A subject who had more turmoil while awake experienced dreams that reflected this agitation, and the subject was much more likely to recall more of his or her dreams.

In these studies, the subjects began to report that, after they had been awakened at the end of a REM cycle, they could resume a dream and finish it, having taken a sort of a commercial break. The researcher called this activity *serialized dreams*.

This was a great help to researchers dedicated to analyzing dreams for therapy. They found that people tended to dream serially about things that were important to them, and that each dream revealed a little more. Researchers were then able to relate the dream theme to the subject's present ability to rebuild his or her world. This has been especially helpful in teaching patients how to cope after a loss of a loved one, a position, or a station in life. While only the dreamer can actually interpret a dream, the therapist has a clue at least of where to begin in attempting to heal the hurts. The therapist takes the theme and relates it back to current conditions, helping the dreamer recognize what is bothering him, and helping him to look for alternative methods of resolving the conflicts. As a result, the individual who takes his or her dreams seriously can better recognize in advance conditions that he or she needs to work through mentally. The patient will even be less fearful of confrontation in the future.

After researchers had collected hundreds of dreams, over a period of time, and had thoroughly examined these dreams in the context of the personality who dreamed them, they came to recognize the importance of record keeping as part of learning about dreams, their meanings, and the person who dreamed them. You already know, from Chapter 3, how important it is to record experiences.

But can you also redo your dreams *as you sleep*? This has been called lucid dreaming. When you sleep, you are not totally unconscious, or unaware of your surroundings. How else could you explain that a parent can hear a sick child turn over in bed two rooms away? I'm sure you've had dreams in which you incorporated actual events (a street noise, needing to use the bathroom) as they occurred. Or have you ever tried to tell yourself to wake up at a certain time and been able to do it, without an alarm clock (try it—it works!) If you have done any of these types of things, then you will be able to redo your dreams to your own specifications.

Start by programming your dreams one night a week, and then increase the process as desired. If you're a novice, begin this process on the weekend, when you aren't under pressure to jump right out of bed, because it takes a little time to properly record a dream. Here's how to do it:

1. Have a pencil and paper or a tape recorder at the bedside.
2. Before retiring, choose a topic that you would like to dream about or a problem you would like solved during the dream state. You must write down these thoughts. In the beginning, stick to one topic for dreaming or for problem solving. Use your top priorities.
3. Tell yourself that, yes, you will remember the dream, and that you will be able to apply it to your next day's activities. State the questions that you want answered or the topic of the dream you want to dream. This step may be uncomfortable for the beginner, but as you practice, it becomes easier and more comfortable. Eventually, you'll be able to create and enjoy your own dream movies!
4. Just as you feel yourself drifting off, still aware of your surroundings, continue to hear the room noises, but do not allow them to have an impact on you. This is when you are most suggestible, and when you should restate your dream program or goal. For example, you might repeat in your mind, "I am going to dream about a solution to my financial problems."

Note: In working with the dream serial, the process is the same, but it may take several more tries before the serial is completed. It is especially important to record serial dreams, so you won't lose the sequence. Some persons who tend to have serial dreams have programmed themselves to wake after each REM cycle and record the dream parts immediately. The next morning, they fit the dream theme into day-to-day living experiences.

If all this programming seems a great deal to do before you retire, and you are very weary, don't worry. After you've been practicing serial dreaming a while, your body will understand the process very well, and it will take over for you. You will awake at the right times and remember the dream theme and details.

5. Enjoy your dream!
6. Upon awakening, lie still and keep the dream images in your mind while still relaxed. After all, dreams are the visual and sensory images of the mind. This will provide more time to familiarize yourself with the process.
7. Record the dream in your journal. Don't forget to include these items, as they will be important in determining what the dream says to you:
   • Note the date and time you awoke.
   • Indicate whether your dream placed you either in the past, present, or future. Determine this by surroundings, events, and clothing.
   • Describe the events of your dream.
   • Describe how you feel about the dream. Did it disturb you, or did it make you feel light-hearted? In the dream, were you acting as you normally would, or were you depicted in a bad light? What role did you play? What was your mood or the mood of the dream? Did you like the role assigned to you? Why or why not?
   • Indicate whether you were self-motivated in your dream. Did you do what you wanted to do, or were you following someone else's orders?
   • Discuss any ways in which the dream was connected to a past activity you were involved in (such as the place or role of an old job) or a current role in your waking life.
   • Analyze your dream for messages that you may be blocking in your waking state. If you were programming for a specific dream, did you get what you wanted from it?
   • Await validation of your dream, if it is prophetic.

A wonderful aspect of dream programming is its potential for healing. By using these simple techniques, people who have incurable diseases can actually dream their cure, such as a cancer growth being reduced in size or toxic waste being filtered through the liver. Other dream programming includes preventative medical care by seeing yourself in the dream in a constant state of being well physically, mentally, and emotionally. I refer to these processes as the healing cycles of dreams. Healing dreams have also proved helpful in the management of stress.

By the by, dreams of health and healing can be used not only for ourselves, but for our loved ones or anyone about whom we are *genuinely* concerned. For those who are familiar with "the laying on of the hands," this is the same process.

It is amazing to think you can just list the questions in written form, say, "I want specific answers," then let your mind and body take over. But it works!

Over a period of time, your self-confidence will increase. You will be willing to tackle more difficult issues. You will be amazed to see how the relationship develops between your dream analysis and your dream programming, as well as their application to day-to-day life. This technique will bring immediate results for some, but for others it will take more time. Don't give up. If it takes a little extra time for you, it's worth it.

Dream Analysis

In interpreting your dreams, remember that your subconscious mind is relating messages, sometimes important, sometimes not, regarding people, situations, or feelings that you have been unable or unwilling to deal with when awake. Again, remember that each dreamer's dreams are unique to that person.

Dreams about oneself are the most difficult dreams to interpret. Not only do you have to deal with your own dream psychology, but you may be hindered by wake-state fears, or your subconscious resistance. But if you dream detailed information about another person or a world event, it is easier to tell if a dream is psychic.

While most psychic dreams recur in a distinct pattern, certain dreams, particularly about events that are not directly related to you, can be psychic even if they occur only once. These tend to be dreams in which your recall of the dream is so thorough, and your emotional response to it so strong, that there is no doubt in your mind that it did actually occur. It was as if you were there. This type of dream isn't just a scary nightmare, or one of those dreams where "it seemed so real." In this type of psychic dream, your mind does not make the weird leaps it does in normal dreams (the way you see a house that you know is your house but it looks nothing like your house), but rather occurs in the same time and manner as real events. Such dreams are rare, but if you have one, you'll know it. Examples of this type of dream are a dream of an imminent plane crash, or a dream that solves a problem of world-wide proportions (a disease cure).

These dreams may be classified as telepathic, clairvoyant, precognitive, or all of the above. These dreams don't discriminate; they have no respect for race, creed, sex, or age. Psychic dreams occur when they want to occur, not when you want them to occur.

Dream telepathy, sometimes referred to as shared dreams, is direct mind-to-mind communication. Usually, the stronger the personal attachment between the receiver and the sender, the clearer and more frequent the occurrences will be. Such sending and receiving of messages can occur between humans and animals, as well as between humans. One example of telepathy is a child at a distance needing some type of help; the mother is asleep, but wakes up and calls the child. The child says, "I was just hoping you would call. I need you."

Dream clairvoyance occurs when the dreamer experiences an event in detail, so that the dreamer obtains information through the dream that could not have been attained through normal means. The Old Testament contains numerous examples of clairvoyant dreams that foretold events to come.

Most people are fascinated by their dreams. The best way to learn about them, however, is not by reading, but by exploring the world of dreams, by delving into your own dreams and yourself. Of course, you can read dream studies (if you're interested), but if you are the type of person who likes to see and do for yourself, then start recording your dreams to learn what you can about yourself.

Prophetic dreams occur for several nights in a row or in some other regular pattern (on the first of the month, on Tuesdays, on significant days). The dream is essentially the same, people play the same roles, mental images and colors are in the same pattern, and the message is clear, even if you do not know the characters in the dream or have never been to the place where the dream is set. Be sure to watch for patterns. A repeated dream may only be a signal that you are beginning to have psychic flow. If a pattern develops, the dreams are themselves prophetic. *Any* repeated dream, however, is a sign that psychic flow is about to begin.

The second clue to whether or not a dream is prophetic is that the event will most likely come true within two to three weeks. (This is not to say that some dreams do not delve further into the future, because they may.) You must journalize the dreams for validation of prophetic dreams; otherwise, unless the dream was emotionally stressful, you will forget it.

The third clue to decide if the dream is prophetic is how clearly you have received the message. Of course, if you aren't sure if a dream is prophetic, you can ask for the meaning of the dream to be given in terms that you will understand, and it will be given. If the answer isn't provided, the dream cannot be classified as prophetic.

There is a fine line between what I call the psychology of dreams (including dream programming) and "psychic" dreams. For those who are scientifically oriented, even the psychology of dreams may seem a little weird (but remember, scientists are studying it!). For the intuitively minded, like me, there is such a strong connection between our minds, our souls, our inner core, and our oneness with the universe that it is difficult to care about exactly *where* exciting and helpful information originates. I do understand that it can be difficult to make this leap, but faith in the unseeable is what this book is all about.

While it is possible, and not unlikely, to dream about an actual event (car crash, death) as it occurs, it is far more interesting to have a prophetic dream. You can then use free will to avoid bad events, plan for good ones, or share your dream to help someone else.

Dream Symbols

Dream symbols are but the surface level of a person's identity, the tip of the iceberg, so to speak. When you examine your dreams, you are just beginning to scratch the surface in the search for your true self, the deeper core of what you really are.

You need to look at your dreams as the beginning rather than the end of the process to understanding a message. If you relate the dream to yourself and open your psychic channels, you will be provided the needed help to understand the deepest sense of who and what you are.

These psychic channels are like the elusive smell of a perfume that floats in and out of your awareness, catches your attention, and is dissipated so quickly that you can't locate its origin.

Dreams, with their symbolism, are one of the ways you can "trap" the elusive essence of ESP. By relating the dream symbols to your personal life you can explore and actually grasp the information that is trying to capture your attention. Once you begin to corre-late your dream symbols with the standardized symbols in dream dictionaries, then you have started the process of stripping away the layers to penetrate the essence of the real you.

Look for dream patterns. You might wake up at 4:00 A.M. on four days in a row. In this case, the time of awakening triggers your attention to the fourth day. On this fourth day an unusual event may occur.

Color

Color is one of the easiest symbols to interpret, as it always pertains to an upcoming event. By checking a dream dictionary to find the code or definition of this color, you can identify the type of event and its significance.

Assume that you tend to dream in shades of medium to navy blue. You are wearing the color, but the color has dominance throughout the dream, is even worn by strangers. According to the following dream dictionary, the color blue denotes business activities will be involved. Therefore, in your waking state, you'll be especially aware of what is occurring in business, such as in a seminar that you'll be attending.

Connections between colors and days symbolize the astral levels of the calendar. Those who associate these colors with their dream themes will in most cases be able to accurately predict the day of the event dreamed.

A dream that has many colors, either in the background or found in clothing, indicates that many changes are to occur, and the changes are for the better.

If a dream is all one color, then the dreamer needs to make changes but is overly cautious in making those changes.

If the dream is primarily dark in hue, then it indicates the dreamer has many conflicts to resolve and needs to confront and challenge the conflicts within.

If the same colors appear regularly in a dream, then the colors become an extension of the personality, and this person will, in the waking state, tend to wear the colors or decorate with them.

Dream Dictionary

COLORS

Color	Definition
Red	Health, strength, and energy; Tuesday; Aries, Taurus, Virgo, or Capricorn.
White	Purity, truth, sincerity; also Monday.
Blue	Hope, money; business; Thursday; Cancer.
Rose	Sweet disposition.
Violet	Intelligence; Scorpio, Aquarius, or Pisces.
Lilac	Freshness; Scorpio or Aquarius.
Black	Sadness, loss, confusion; also Saturday; Virgo, Libra, Scorpio, or Capricorn.
Yellow	Falseness; also Sunday; Cancer, Leo, Virgo, or Capricorn.
Purple	Pride; also Wednesday.
Orange	Luxury, stimulation, attraction; Taurus, Gemini, or Capricorn.
Light blue	Tranquility, patience, understanding; Cancer, Scorpio, Sagittarius, Aquarius, or Pisces.
Dark blue	Depression, impulsiveness; Cancer, Scorpio, Sagittarius, or Pisces.
Green	Finance, fertility, luck; also Friday; Virgo, Libra, Scorpio, Capricorn, or Pisces.
Gold	Attraction, persuasion, charm; Leo.
Brown	Uncertainty, hesitation; Virgo or Capricorn.
Pink	Love and honor; Aquarius.
Silver	Cancellation, neutral; Cancer.
Green-yellow	Anger, jealousy, sickness; Virgo or Capricorn.

If you have, over a period of years, been dreaming predominantly in one color, and you find you are beginning to dream in another color, you should check the new color's meaning to see what changes are about to occur in your life, as this kind of color shift always signifies a change in your life.

Numbers, Letters, and Other Symbols

Dream symbology is very exciting, because it gives important clues into our psyche and can be a strong connection to the

Dream Dictionary

NUMBERS

Number	Definition
1	Ambition, unhealthy, automobile, travels.
2	Acquisition, ants, beautiful, final conclusion.
3	Affliction, arm, religion.
4	Power, powerful emotions.
5	Happiness in life.
6	Perfection in projects.
7	Efficient effort.
8	Conservation of life.
9	Uneasiness in one's environment.
10	Secure in future.
11	Law, all things pertaining to law.
12	Excellent taste in all areas of life.
13	Contemptuous.
14	Losses due to family.
15	Will have love and compassion for others.
16	Love, universal understanding.
17	Shame and fear of own doing.
18	Tired, bone weary, worry.
19	Anger and unhappiness.
20	Strict in action and thought.
21	Smooth plans.
22	Mystery is solved.
23	Revenge is reversed.
24	Learning.
25	Birth.
26	Good business.
27	Intelligent mind, practical use.
28	Receives love and affection.
29	Wedding.

psychic plane. Like all of the vehicles we are discussing, dream symbols are interrelated and, to a psychically aware person, are completely interchangeable. While dream symbols can be gathered from many vehicles—primarily astrology and numerology—they all ultimately get at the same truth.

To make it easier for you to interpret your dreams, I've listed the symbols and their meanings in a few different ways: by numbers, letters, months and days, and other terms. As you are trying to interpret, keep in mind that many symbols are interchangeable; it is up to you to figure out which applies to your particular situa-

30	Star-is-born attitude, receives fame.
31	Personal qualities are good.
32	Expression by action, spoken word.
33	Honest.
34	Glory seeker.
35	Good family health.
36	Special, child's birth.
37	Shared love by dreamer to others.
38	Desires gained in life.
39	Envy.
40	Wedding reception and party.
41	Loss of reputation.
42	Trip, event or events plagued with delays.
43	Church service.
44	Will meet a prominent person.
45	Sexual encounter.
46	Productive in work or avocation.
47	Long life span.
48	Court activities.
49	Secret admirer.
50	Forgiveness.
100	Divine intercession.
200	Danger due to indecision.
300	Will meet or work with philosopher.
400	Long, distant, and productive journey.
500	Will win.
600	Will be rewarded for work well done.
700	Strength to carry through and to overcome trials.
800	Head of project, affairs, state, position, or government.
900	World hunger.
1,000	Will receive desired escape.

tion. Only the dreamer can interpret what the symbols ultimately mean. Of course, for those who play numbers in games of chance, if you dream a number, then you should play it the following day. Use your intuition to guide you to meanings; sometimes a letter or number is clearly meant to be taken as is, and other times it should be interpreted according to one of its other meanings. If you dream of any symbol on a regular basis, you should use it in a constructive way to help you make decisions. By the way, any time you dream of a single letter, it is a positive sign.

Number	Letter	Letter	Definition
1	A, J, S.	A	Ambition, 1, 5, 40.
2	B, K, T.	B	Beautiful, 2, 8, 29.
3	C, L, U.	C	Christian charity, 3, 9, 46.
4	D, M, V.	D	Danger, 4, 8, 16.
5	E, N, W.	E	Eager, 5, 22, 25.
6	F, O, X.	F	Faith, 5, 9, 16.
7	G, P, Y.	G	Gentle, 9, 40, 57.
8	H, Q, Z.	H	Honest, 9, 47, 69.
9	I, R.	I	Illness, 5, 9, 17.
		J	Joy, 7, 19, 50.
		K	Kirk (the name), 38, 46.
		L	Love, 27, 69, 38.
		M	Mercy, 7, 16.
		N	Notoriety, 27, 13, 72.
		O	Opportunity, 57, 21, 91.
		P	Postpone, 3, 20, 28.
		Q	Quarrels, 12, 60, 61.
		R	Scandal, 16, 43, 27.
		S	Society, 19, 38, 56.
		T	Truth, 60, 69, 74.
		U	Useful, 11, 14, 39.
		V	Victory, 10, 15, 44.
		W	Wealth, 15, 26, 69.
		X	Stubborn, 6, 13, 43.
		Y	Loss, 1, 8, 25.
		Z	News, 3, 19, 27.

MONTHS AND DAYS

Numbers in parentheses, while not primary numbers, are also associated with these months.

Month	Definition
January	Long life, 15 (19, 55, 63).
February	Wealth, 11 (13, 16, 75).
March	Thrift, will overcome problems, 45 (7, 15, 20).
April	Health is less than good, 1 (4, 7, 20).
May	Losses and ruin, 73 (2, 4, 6).
June	Success in love, 22 (3, 6, 9).
July	Secrets, 17 (8, 16, 42).
August	Carelessness in money, 8 (6, 17, 41).
September	Success in business, 61 (5, 9, 40).

October   Misfortune, 78 (8, 42, 62).
November   Troubles in life, 62 (7, 9, 63).
December   Contentment, 12 (8, 16, 79).

Day	Definition
Monday	Treachery, 1.
Tuesday	Riches, 2.
Wednesday	Surprise, 3.
Thursday	Disagreeable, 4.
Friday	Friend, 5.
Saturday	Property, 6.
Sunday	Scandal, 7.

Holidays	Number Definition
New Year's Day	4
Martin Luther King's Birthday	63
Washington's Birthday	73
Easter	33
Independence Day	65
Columbus Day	1
Thanksgiving	10
Christmas	22

THINGS, FEELINGS, ACTIONS

Term	Definition
Abroad	Going or being in a different country, good sign.
Abuse	Business disputes with close associations.
Acquaintances	To meet them is a good sign. To fight with them means death of dreamer.
Adder	You may acquire riches through marriage.
Adultery	If committing, great temptations and great inner struggle. If you resist the temptation of adultery, then you will escape danger.
Almonds	Either picking or eating indicates business or personal financial difficulties.
Alms	If you refuse it, you will succumb to poverty.
Altar	Joy and gladness, especially in family units.
Anchors	Unexpected elements of good luck in business.
Anger	Rival near you.

Angling	If you catch a fish, then good news from afar.
Ants	Trouble brewing or sickness. Flying ants means journey or potential accidents on travels. Common ants signal fertility.
Anxiety	Someone will help you achieve your desires.
Apparel	To be dressed in white, good. To be in black, unhappiness. Blue means good business prospects. Yellow means jealousy of a sweetheart. Red, good energy and, if new, hostile feelings. If you appear well dressed in the dream, then good fortune. If shabbily dressed, then poverty.
Arms	If male arms grow longer, then wealth. If married woman dreams of arms, then husband is due to be successful. To dream of losing the right arm means death of a male relative. A left arm amputated means death of a female member of the family.
Ass	Foolish quarrels.
Attorneys	Authority and that you will have authority.
Bagpipes	Trouble and strife.
Banquet	Prosperity.
Ball or ballroom	Joy and happiness.
Barn	If full, good. If empty, a sign of poverty.
Bathing	Clear water means joy. Dirty water means disappointments.
Bats	Ill health or illness approaching.
Bees	Success, profits, gains. If stung, may loose profits or gains.
Beets	Growing or eating them means more freedom to do things.
Bells	Lovers that are true.
Birds	To hear them singing, joy. If married children see the birds flying, indicates travel. To catch the bird, good money.
Blindness	Needs to check events in personal life to see if things can be corrected.
Blood	Losses of all kinds. Could mean short illness for the dreamer.
Blossoms	Great joy.
Boat	On smooth water, happiness. On rough water, business troubles.

Boots	If single, a sweetheart. If married, meeting with friends.
Bridge	If damaged or washed out, indicates business obstructions.
Burglar	If he steals something personal, sorrow is coming.
Candle	If lit, health and fortune. If not lit, sickness.
Cakes	Great happiness and pleasure from friends.
Cards	Favorable for lovers.
Carrots	Profits and endurance.
Cats	Vexation, watch out for enemies.
Chains	Marital troubles.
Cheeks	Plump, rosy ones indicate good health for a woman. Pale, lean ones imply sickness.
Cherries	Ripe, red cherries mean enjoyment of some type of deceitful activity.
Cheese	If eating, good home life.
Child	If a female dreamer is childless, dreaming of a child means she will become pregnant soon.
Children	To those who wish children, denotes great care and concern for others. To those who have children, indicates happiness in children.
Church	Praying there, good for joy and happiness. If talking in church, mend your ways.
Climbing	Honor coming your way.
Coffin	Death of a close friend or relative.
Combing hair	Combing your own, change in affairs for the better. Combing others' hair, change of residence.
Cooking	Marriage will occur. If already married, domestic happiness.
Corn	Profits and riches in material possessions and personal life.
Crocodile	Deceit around you.
Crutches	Walking on them indicates an accident.
Cucumbers	Hopes unfulfilled, but will have good health.
Dancing	Good news on the way.
Darkness	You are blinded by your situation and can't find the way out. Also indicates fear.

Death	Marriage. If you are married, birth of a child.
Death of a mother	Emotional independence.
Death of a father	Independence of action.
Devil	Contrary to popular belief, a sign of good luck.
Dice	Unexpected inheritance of money. To dream that you lost while playing dice means additional losses.
Disease	If you don't have a disease, then it means promotion in job or career.
Dogs	Luck. Barking dogs mean bad business but for the short term.
Dolphin	One that is swimming indicates change in weather. If the dolphin is beached, it indicates a death of a friend.
Dragons	Investment that will be better than your wildest expectations.
Drowning	Visitors approaching.
Drunkenness	Loss in business but luck in love.
Eagle	If the bird is high up in the sky, it is a good omen for the soldier and indicates protection. However, if the eagle lands on your head, then your life is in danger. It may even signal death.
Earthquake	Unsettled affairs. If married, marital quarrels.
Eating	Arguments with friends.
Eggs	If unbroken, good omen for success in endeavors. If broken, then disappointments in friends.
Face	Secrets that you will learn.
Falling	To the unmarried, means a breakup. To the married, means new domestic articles.
Feast	Disappointments in job or career.
Fighting	If you lost, means the opposite of the dream.
Fire	Good health.
Fish	If dressing the fish, it means peace of mind.
Flies	Enemies are around you.
Flowers	Happiness and joy in work.
Fox	Sly person around you, so beware.
Friends	Good omen and pleasant tidings.

Fruit	Profit.
Apples	Success and health.
Apricots	Prosperity and good marriage.
Cherries	Love squabbles.
Currants	Happy married life.
Gooseberries	False witness nearby.
Grapes	Success in new business venture.
Lemons	Patience will be needed in affairs.
Oranges	Need to put affairs in order both at home and in business.
Peaches	Lucky in love.
Pears	Good omen for the lonely.
Plums	Caution in business.
Raspberries	Happiness.
Strawberries	A good time had by all. Social gathering.
Games	Playing games shows good news on the way.
Garden	Poverty in the future.
Geese	Comfort in life.
Gifts	Giving one means loss. To receive means happiness.
Glass	Caution in love affairs.
Gloves	A gift from a friend.
Gold	Success in endeavors that are on the dreamer's mind.
Guns	Danger.
Hat	A new hat means trouble with co-workers. To lose a hat means unexpected gift.
Heaven	Peace of mind.
Horse	Adventure.
Hospital	Good omen for health of family members.
House	If house has many rooms, conflict within the dreamer.
Hymn	To sing one signals business ventures will be hindered.
Jealousy	If someone is jealous of you, then you are truly loved. If you are jealous, beware of friends' gossip.
Jet	Travel and romance.
Jewelry	Gift from an unexpected source.
Journey	Travel to strange areas.
Jumping	Change is indicated in home areas.
Keys	Prosperity. Only one key means true love. To lose keys indicates loss of temper or quarrels.

Kite	To dream of flying one means escape from danger or implies escape from strife in domestic affairs.
Kissing	Luck in romance.
Ladder	Climbing one indicates success. Falling or descending from one indicates a warning on projects undertaken.
Land	Good marriage and one that is fruitful.
Letter	True friends. If you send one, it indicates a gift from a sweetheart.
Lettuce	Affairs will be difficult to manage.
Lightning	Without thunder, indicates a change in residence or job. With thunder, indicates domestic unheavals.
Logs	Splitting them means a visitor is coming, most likely a stranger.
Losing teeth	Growing up.
Lost	If you are looking for articles, you are anxious and suffer tension and indecision.
Mail	If you deliver the mail yourself, you will have many friends and business associates and be well liked.
Marriage	Success in persuasion.
Mice	Good luck in school.
Money	Increase in money.
Monkeys	Beware of false friends.
Moon	Fulfillment of wish.
Mother	Good news and parties.
Music	News of a friend's happiness.
Nails	Element of good luck in learning new skills.
Needles	Prepare to deal with a quarrelsome person.
Nuts	Wealth. Eating them means loss of friends.
Office	If working in a large office, many friends.
Owl	Sadness.
Oyster	Decisions that are difficult.
Pearls	Tears.
Quarrels	Unexpected pleasures.
Queen	High position and wealth.
Rainbow	Bliss and comfort in home area.
Rats	New associations that can bring conflict between good friends.
Raven	A death of a friend.
Roses	Picking or smelling them means good luck to the dreamer.

Running	Trip will be taken soon.
Seat	Falling out of a seat indicates loss of job. Getting back into a seat means recovery of the lost job.
Sickness	Unemployment.
Silver	Loss through deceit.
Snakes	Healing or warning.
Snow	If snow is bright, then good news is on the way.
Soldiers	Troubles.
Spiders	Psychic world.
Strangers	If among strangers, you will have a total change of environment.
Swans	For married couples it foretells of children.
Sun	A sunrise means good news. A sunset means sorrow.
Thirst	Ambition, success in endeavors.
Teeth	Worry and disappointments in life.
War	Peaceful days ahead.
Washing	Definite change of address.
Water	If hot, accidents.
Wool	Good luck, especially to those who are unwed.
Worms	Worries.
Wrestling	Strife with people.
Zebra	A warning that you will deal with a person who is not what he or she appears to be. Use caution.

FINDING YOUR SPIRIT GUIDES

A spirit guide is the essence of the conscious energy mass of one who does not live in our physical, earthbound plane in a form that we can (usually) see. Simply stated, a spirit guide is the incarnation of a person who has passed from this plane to the "other side." (Some people feel that death is just a passing from one existence to another, whereas others believe that a person's spiritual soul or mass goes either to a heaven or a hell, for eternity.) Just as people here on this plane have many shapes, forms, and personalities, so too do spirit guides.

Each of us has a spirit guide. Some people refer to them as guardian angels; others refer to them by their proper names. Some people believe that spirit guides are the essence of the Supreme

Being's love for us and are given to us with no conditions applied. Your spirit guide's job is to help you develop an understanding of yourself and the world at large. He or she is placed here to guide you through times of growth and conflict. Above all, spirit guides are to serve you and love you unconditionally.

Spirit guides are a topic about which even confirmed New Agers have only a smattering of knowledge. Some people have a tough time with this. All I can tell you is that you *do* have a spirit guide, whether you acknowledge it or not, and that a spirit guide is nothing to be afraid of. If you don't fully believe in your spirit guide, try to at least keep an open mind.

Great! But where do I get one, how do I get one, and what's his or her name? One of the easiest ways to contact your spirit guide or guardian angel is to ask that he contact you through the process of meditation or dream programming. Now, your spirit guide may not appear immediately upon request. It may take several times before he presents himself. Usually, the spirit guide will introduce himself to you a little at a time, in ways that you will understand. You will have a sense of what he looks like and what his personality is. This is a process of building rapport and getting to know each other. If you ask, your spirit guide will tell you his other earth names, where he lived, and the circumstances by which he came to be in the spirit world. If you choose to pursue it, this information is verifiable.

Spirit guides are arbitrarily assigned to us in most cases. They normally are not departed members of your family or anyone you have known on this plane. There are exceptions to most rules, of course, and a spirit guide in special cases can be someone that you had a special rapport with in life, or even a loved one. Sometimes a familiar spirit guide remains in contact because you have special needs or circumstances. In these special cases where a spirit guide was known to us on this plane, it provides proof of the existence of the other side, since it establishes a trusted source of communication with the other side.

Remember that spirit guides are here to help guide you through the learning experiences, acting as open channels to provide needed insights, relieve fears, and give information that is meant to be shared with others. Spirit guides have many ways of communicating with you. They can alert your body sensors to their presence, contact you through dreams, work with you through meditation and visualization, or use you as a "channel" for their vision. Your spirit guide will fit his or her message into your vocabulary and often will provide solutions to problematic situations or circumstances.

You may have as many as three or four guides. All will do their best to help you, but you'll probably find you prefer to deal with one more than the others. He or she may have a better sense of humor or work more quickly.

Your spirit guide is there, ready to help you, encourage you, and to love you. In fact, he or she is already doing these things—you are just not aware of it. Your spirit guide will help you even more, however, if you ask for his help, and become aware of his efforts on your behalf. Help may come in unexpected ways, and it may not be the help *you* think you need. But it *will be exactly* what you need. As an example, I asked my spirit guide for help in writing this book. He suggested I listen to my editor, because she had suggestions that would help the book flow more smoothly. Because of his input, I was more patient, more willing to learn, and the book went smoothly. Had I not listened to him, I might still be working and reworking the first chapter! Now, he wasn't telling me what I wanted to hear (I wanted to write the damn thing without help), but what I needed to hear.

Don't forget. If you don't ask your spirit guide to help you in a way you will be aware of, he or she will not. You'll continue to get help, but not in the most powerful manner. To get in touch with your spirit guide, just talk to him as you would talk to yourself in your head, or the way you have imaginary conversations or the way you talk to God. *Listen.* Try not to have any specific expectations. Before long, you'll have a new friend.

AUTOMATIC WRITING

Automatic writing is the communication between the upper-level spirit world and our present-day environment. In our world, there are many levels on which we can operate, though most of us choose to operate on only one. In developing our psychic abilities, we can call upon the spirit world of the cosmos, as spirits can help direct or guide our movement in our world.

Automatic writing is one good way to communicate with the lower levels of the astral planes, most usually our spirit guides. It is a natural extension of interest in tuning in to the cosmos to seek direction. It is just one of the steps along the way that can help us move from one level of consciousness to the next.

Automatic writing is a skill that some people find very easy to do, while strong-willed people have trouble with it. It requires patience and the ability to let the pen and hand move by their own direction.

The art of doing the writing is considered by some to be a form of mediumship, or channeling. To do automatic writing, one must want to communicate with a more advanced entity, or the writing will not take place. Perhaps you have heard of Ruth Montgomery, the metaphysical writer who uses this method when writing her books on the metaphysical world. Her spirit guide is Arthur Ford, who was a well-known psychic before his death. He chose Ms. Montgomery to be his instrument.

When you are involved with automatic writing, as with any psychic phenomenon, you will need more energy than usual to produce the information. You may feel drained afterward.

In the beginning stages of automatic writing, you will feel excited, since you may see immediate results, but remember it will take time for the rapport to be established between you and your guide. At first the information coming in may not be clear enough for you, the writer, to totally understand. Given time, the writing will be coming through clearly, and the message will be complete.

The process used in automatic writing is similar to that used when one works a Ouija board. Here is what happens: Physically you may feel a tingling in your arm. Your wrist is limp. You may feel a general numbness of the arm. You will be amazed to see your hand begin to move. Other symptoms may be constricted muscles and an active and alert mind. Remember, your arm is merely an involuntary instrument for communication.

The style of writing depends upon the guide, but the guide will generally accommodate him or herself to your manual abilities. The script may change as the different guides appear. It may seem strange, but it will not be your handwriting, but theirs. Once you and your guide(s) are familiar with each other, these skills may be transferred to using the typewriter or word processor or to audio clairvoyance.

To try automatic writing, practice it the same time each day to establish a regular scheduling of visits. Here's the procedure:

1. Say a prayer or do some meditation before starting.
2. Find a quiet place in which to work. Have plenty of paper and pens.
3. Place the pen in your usual writing hand, point to paper.
4. Close your eyes.
5. Let the feeling take over.
6. Stop if you find yourself manipulating the pen. Relax.
7. Talk to your spirit guide if you need help.
8. Rest afterward so your energy levels will be replenished.

Without your realizing it, you have just become acquainted with the basic concepts of ESP. You have probably tried, or are now more knowledgeable about, psychometry, telepathy, precognition, dreams, clairvoyance, and automatic writing through spirit guides. You have used these techniques within the exercises to begin to turn on your psychic flow. If you're ready, move on to some of the more demanding—rewarding—vehicles.

6
CARDS

CARDS IN ONE form or the other have been in existence since early recorded history. Tarot cards, dating back at least 500 years to Egypt, are generally believed to be the oldest and most mystical of cards because of their pictures and symbols. ("Tar" means path in Egyptian, and "ro" means royal—suggesting that these cards were either a favorite of the ruling class or a tool so special that they were believed to be a key to heavenly destiny.)

Reading tarot cards requires you to concentrate. They are considered by some to be difficult to read, interpret, and bridge (interpret various cards together to come up with an overall reading). Some people are frightened by the pictures found upon these cards, and there is a lot of superstition surrounding the tarot deck. One of the superstitions is that one cannot purchase a deck for oneself, as it can bring bad luck. If you wish to read tarot and are superstitious, you must be given a deck of tarot cards, preferably by a reader who intends to pass his or her wisdom on to you along with the cards.

The next oldest known deck is the gypsy deck, which gypsies (a nomadic people of eastern Europe) evolved as a shortcut method of reading the tarot. Twenty-six cards were removed from the traditional tarot deck of seventy-eight, leaving fifty-two cards (sound familiar?). The meanings of the twenty-six discarded cards were integrated into the cards that remained. Gypsy cards, though similar to the tarot deck, tend to have more modern images that are less frightening.

Most experts feel that the tarot deck is the forerunner of our modern playing deck, perhaps by way of the gypsy cards. Though that old deck of cards you've had floating in a bottom drawer for years lacks the pictures and written interpretation found on individual tarot or gypsy cards, it is a powerful tool for tapping into the psychic world. This "regular" deck that we are all familiar with has four suits, numbers, and court figures, like the tarot and gypsy decks, and lacks only the astrology portion of the tarot deck.

The beauty of using standard playing cards is threefold. First, it's cheap, and you've probably got them already. Second, because the cards aren't as sensitive as tarot or gypsy cards, they don't require as much special handling. And third, you and your subject are already familiar, even comfortable, with the deck. It's not scary or strange.

Before you can read for yourself or others, you must have the proper attitude toward the cards. As with any new tool, you will have to practice before you have a finished product you feel good about. The "rules" you will learn in this chapter reflect centuries of study; over the years, the meanings of cards have been codified by psychically gifted people, enabling people without any psychic skill to tap into the great knowledge beyond our plane.

But these truths are only the beginning. In working with a tool of the occult, you have a real advantage; once you get some of the basic concepts down, your psychic ability will begin to take over. You'll be amazed when it does. Bridging will no longer be a "conscious" activity. You'll be able to quickly scan the card layout and synopsize the information given, using your here-and-now senses as well as your extrasensory expertise. You'll get quite accurate information on your subject's personality, habits, and concerns, as well as clips on events in his or her life and how he or she relates to the spiritual and physical worlds.

SETTING

The setting you use must be comfortable for both you and your subject. Trust your intuition to help you find the place in which to work. You'll need a clean, uncluttered, flat surface, two comfortable chairs, a pen or pencil for you to use as a pointer when referring to specific cards, paper and pen for the subject to take notes or for the reader to write down information for the subject, and whatever else helps you work in comfort. I drink coffee, so I keep a big mug handy. This way I don't have to leave in the middle of a reading to get a refill. If a subject likes, you can tape the session so he or she can keep a record or check for accuracy.

It goes without saying that for a reading of any type—cards, palmistry, psychometry—it is best to have relative quiet and to be somewhere where there will be no interruptions. While readings will work at parties and in noisy locales, a reader's psychic flow is less likely to begin if he or she is disturbed or interrupted by noise, activity, or even the curiosity of others.

PROCEDURES

Cards are not mystical themselves. They are, rather, ingenious tools for reading auras, the vibrational fields of energy that surround every object, animate or inanimate. During the time of the reading, the cards, which are inanimate, take on the vibration of the stronger, animate, aura. It can be said that the cards "capture" your aura and put the information there into a clue form that can easily be read. Once you know the "rules," you can break the code and decipher the "message." This works very nicely with a self-reading, but becomes a bit more complicated when you realize that, in a third-party reading, the reader's aura also comes into play.

The reader's duty is to concentrate upon the cards and to relate only the information given by the cards and their layout formation. Sometimes, however, there is a conflict in vibrational fields, as the cards pick up the subject's conscious or unconscious resistance or blockage. Sometimes the subject's body vibrations want to invade the reader's body space, which prevents a smooth merging of the magnetic aura fields into that oneness needed for a viable reading. If this happens, it is imperative to take a few deep breaths and let your mind go blank (sometimes known as retreating into your subconscious aura field) so that the cards will come back into balance. This will reestablish the correct mental attitude in the reader and give her the mind control she needs to concentrate upon the cards.

It is best, however, to prevent this resistance altogether. It is helpful to follow the procedures outlined in this section closely while you get used to the differing experiences and feelings you can have during card readings.

As you read for a subject, you are both giving up bits of your aura. It is best to set up barriers to help reduce the chance of untimely invasion of body space. After all, you are opening channels to and from your own energy body. For these reasons, sit back from the subject by at least a foot, if you can, during the reading, and try not to touch him or her.

Before you read for someone, it is best to prepare him for the fact that the answers he seeks might not be easily recognizable, or what he wants to hear. If for example, a subject thinks he is worried about his job, that worry may really be about money. If the reading shows a death of a relative (and inheritance), the subject may not view the information positively and may, indeed, find it a confusing answer to his question about his job. For that reason, it is crucial to tell the subject *before* the reading to keep an open mind, but also that the cards don't make judgments. Some view death as bad, for example, while others think of it as heaven. In cards, whatever is is good.

When you are ready to begin your reading, decide which method you want to use—the thirty-six-card layout or the astrology method. If you or your client likes or knows a lot about astrology (which, despite what you see in papers and magazines, is a *very* precise science), I'd recommend the latter. I use the thirty-six-card layout most often, because people seem to like it and it's simple. If you're using the thirty-six-card layout, remove the 3s, 4s, 5s, and 6s from the deck and set them aside.

Shuffle the cards, using either the Las Vegas shuffle or the slipping motions used by magicians and tarot readers. This shuffling will cleanse the cards of any fields that may remain and will assure that all negative vibrations have been removed. There is no hard-and-fast rule for how long the reader should shuffle the cards. Just do it until it "feels" right, just as you do when you play cards. Hand the cards to the subject, then, and ask her to shuffle the cards long enough to be sure she's touched all of them. At this point, both your aura and the aura of your subject have been imparted to the cards.

During this period of shuffling, try to discourage conversation between you and the subject, as it breaks the concentration of both the subject and the reader, and can cause a disjointed laying of the cards, which in turn will produce a disjointed interpretation. As you gain experience, you may notice that the cards feel different from reading to reading. Sometimes the cards "run" smooth, jerky, or sticky. This is completely normal—it only means you're getting better!

Ask the subject to cut the cards twice with her left hand (which is considered to be closest to the heart of the soul and thought to transfer the honest desire for knowledge), dividing the deck into three stacks. These do not have to be of equal height. While doing this, the subject should concentrate on the question or questions she would like answered during the reading.

Next lay out the cards as shown in either Illustration 6-1 or 6-2. Since you are doing the reading, the cards face you. For a thirty-six-card layout, the top cards in the three stacks become cards 1, 2, and 3 in the layout. Be sure that card number 1 is the card that is from the first stack the subject made. Card number 2 is from the second stack, and so forth. Otherwise, when you pick up the stacks to do the layout, the order of collection is at your discretion.

Explanation of the Thirty-Six-Card Layout

In the thirty-six-card layout, the lead card is the first card that is turned up from the top of the deck. It is the predominant card and tells what is uppermost on the client's mind, reflects current conditions, and also sets the tone for the reading.

The top cards from the other stacks are turned up and placed in the second and third positions, respectively, next to the lead card. They relate to the lead card, giving additional information or explanations.

These first three cards are set apart from the other cards and placed above the card rows, on the top left, in what we will call the "indicator card" section. All three indicator cards will later be mentally transferred to the last positions in row 6. These will help you determine the final outcome of the reading, based upon which suit's or card's connotations apply.

The cards laid out in rows 1 and 2 (reading horizontally from left to right) deal with events or conditions that are either in your subject's past or will very soon become history. Rows 3 and 4 represent current events or conditions in your subject's present life situation. The last two rows indicate upcoming events or conditions, either in the very near future or several months or years from now.

Sectional brackets shown at the bottom of Illustration 6-1

ILLUSTRATION 6-1
36-CARD LAYOUT (Using a Regular 52-Card Playing Deck)

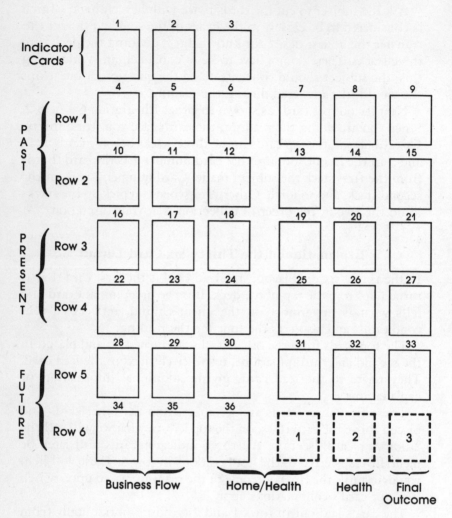

Business Flow   Home/Health   Health   Final Outcome

denote the definition of the vertical columns. Individual card meaning is derived from card position, as the area of concern will determine which card definition applies. The two rows on the far left are concerned with business flows and finances. This definition includes *all* business and financial concerns. The middle two columns express conditions and events within the framework of your subject's personal life—that person's home and hearth. Involvement with family, friends, and loved one(s) are indicated here. Health information is found in the next-to-last row. This can include emotional and mental, as well as physical health. This information can be personal or can relate to persons in the previous row. If an actual health card is found within this section, take note—it is important. Don't worry about a nonspecific health card in this section. The last row is the final outcome of the reading. It is an overview, or recap, of areas of concern. Remember to mentally transfer the top three indicator cards to their appropriate spaces and incorporate their individual card meanings into this summation.

Explanation of the Astrology Method

The Astrology Method of card reading is, as you might have guessed, based on astrology, the study of the influence of stars and planets on human affairs and earthly events. The positions of the stars and planets on the day you were born, according to astrologers, determines your inclinations, tendencies, and characteristics.

In using the Astrology Method of card reading, you have the chance to bridge the card meanings previously defined with the added information you can get from the astrological layout pattern of the cards. Even if you are not familiar with astrology, your card reading will work in the same manner as that of the thirty-six-card layout. Any added insights you garner will depend on the strength of your psychic flow and/or your knowledge of and comfort with astrology. As with any vehicle in this book, if you are uncomfortable with the astrological card method, choose another vehicle.

Astrology is an exact science; the horoscopes you see in the newspapers and magazines are only the tip of the iceberg. Astrology is based on the zodiac, a heavenly belt that encompasses all of the principal planets, which is divided into houses, represented by constellations. These constellations, from Aries the Ram to Pisces the Fish, move around the earthly sky, and the entire astrological area that they cover is home to different planets at different times (which is why you might have heard the phrase "ruling planet").

When someone says "What's your sign?," he or she is inquiring about your sun sign—that is, the sign that shows where the sun, or dominant influence, was when you were born. Other planets, however, are important as well, and, depending on their placement

ILLUSTRATION 6-2
ASTROLOGY METHOD (Using a Regular 52-Card Playing Deck)

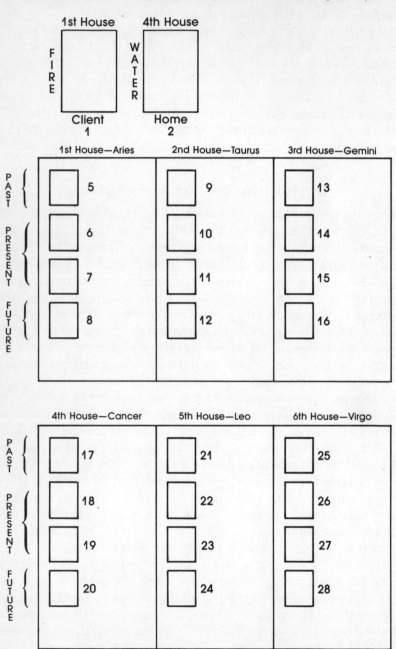

ILLUSTRATION 6-2 (continued)

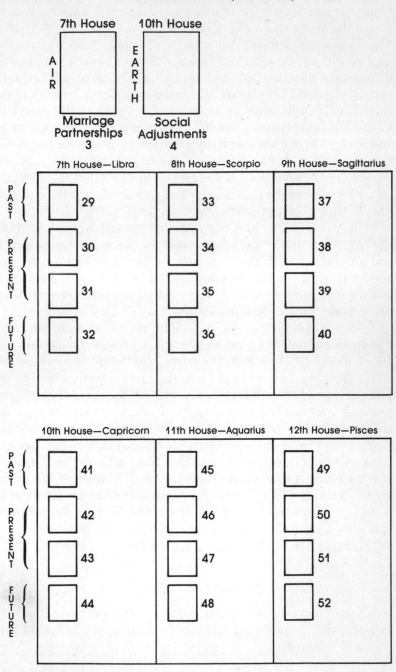

7th House

AIR

Marriage
Partnerships
3

10th House

EARTH

Social
Adjustments
4

7th House—Libra

PAST { 29
PRESENT { 30
31
FUTURE { 32

8th House—Scorpio

33
34
35
36

9th House—Sagittarius

37
38
39
40

10th House—Capricorn

PAST { 41
PRESENT { 42
43
FUTURE { 44

11th House—Aquarius

45
46
47
48

12th House—Pisces

49
50
51
52

and number, can sometimes be more indicative of your personality than your sun sign is. In addition, each sign has a strong link to one of the four astrological "elements"—air, earth, fire, and water. The air signs (Gemini, Aquarius, and Libra) tend to have the qualities of air; people ruled by air signs are usually people who focus on the mind and grasp ideas quickly. The earth signs (Capricorn, Virgo, and Taurus) are associated with characteristics of the earth, and people born under those signs are usually practical, nurturing, and "firmly planted." The water signs (Cancer, Pisces, and Scorpio) are linked with liquid qualities of change and movement, as well as depth. People born under a water sign are usually sensitive, emotional people. The fire signs (Leo, Aries, and Sagittarius) represent the purification and power of the sun. Fire sign people tend to be optimistic, even inspired.

Many good books have been written on astrology, describing the characteristics of each house and the planetary influences. If you are interested in astrology on its own, or in furthering your ability to read by the Astrological Method, I recommend *The Astrologer's Handbook* by Frances Sakoian and Louis S. Acker (New York: Harper & Row, 1973).

To do the Astrological layout, collect the cut cards in any order and lay out all fifty-two cards into twelve groupings, as shown in Illustration 6-2. As with the thirty-six-card layout, you will be able to see from the layout which cards refer to the past, which to the present, and which to future events. The top four cards (which, you will note, are not indicator cards here, the way they are with the thirty-six-card layout) represent the elements discussed above—air, earth, water, and fire—and will show your subject's "fixities" (this will indicate where he or she has strengths and weaknesses). If you have a queen of spades (warning card) in the first box of the layout, for example, it means this person should be careful not to overinspire, oversell, overadvise, or overdo. In the water position, this same card would warn against overzealous emotions.

Following are the meanings associated with each sign.

First House—Aries

Aries represents the self; including physical appearance, personal affairs, personal outlooks, attitudes, environment, health, changing, and beginnings.

Mars and Pluto are the ruling planets for the first house. Mars indicates energy, courage, passion, action, aggression and starts. Pluto indicates regeneration, transformation, insecurity, altercation, and the underworld.

Second House—Taurus

The second house governs your money, possessions, talents, power, income, gains, and acquisitions.

Venus is the ruling planet for the second house. This planet indicates love, affection, appreciation, and the artistic, as well as attraction, and the social aspects of life.

Signs of the Zodiac	Date Sun Sign Begins	House
Aries the Ram	March 21	1st
Taurus the Bull	April 20	2nd
Gemini the Twins	May 21	3rd
Cancer the Crab	June 22	4th
Leo the Lion	July 23	5th
Virgo the Virgin	August 23	6th
Libra the Balance	September 23	7th
Scorpio the Scorpion	October 24	8th
Sagittarius the Archer	November 22	9th
Capricorn the Goat	December 22	10th
Aquarius the Water Bearer	January 20	11th
Pisces the Fish	February 19	12th

Third House—Gemini

The third house governs all activities of your objective mind: communications, correspondence, news, messages, telephones, typewriters, minor changes and decisions, short journeys, close relatives, books, education, instructions, and writing.

Mercury is the ruling planet for the third house. This planet indicates metal processes, mental expressions, communication, and reasoning.

Fourth House—Cancer

The fourth house governs your home base—domestic and family issues, your property, family circles, foundations, the deeper-link parent (the one who exerts the greatest emotional influence on your life).

The Moon is the ruling planet for the fourth house. This "planet" indicates the personality, a reflector, inner emotions, feminine, and domestic issues.

Fifth House—Leo

The fifth house governs your creative affairs, affairs of the heart, recreation, love, courtship, pleasure, speculation (apart from the investment side), gambling, risks, entertainment, artistry, and children.

The Sun is the ruling planet for the fifth house. This "planet" indicates creativity, individuality, vitality, leadership, and power.

Sixth House—Virgo

The sixth house governs illnesses, therapies, hygiene, food, medicine, clothing, pets, animals, routine employment, servants, methods, and techniques.

Mercury is the ruling planet for the sixth house, as well as the third. This planet indicates mental process, expression, communications, and reasoning.

Seventh House—Libra

The seventh house governs mates, partners, opponents, open enemies and the public, opportunities, negotiations, transactions, marriage, divorce, settlements, contracts, and close friends.

Venus is the ruling planet for the seventh house. This planet indicates love, affection, appreciation, and the artistic, in addition to attraction and the social aspects of life.

Eighth House—Scorpio

The eighth house governs money of your mate or partners, payments, taxes, loans, insurance, legacies, gifts, money owed, losses, accidents, and surgery.

Mars and Pluto are the ruling planets for the eighth house. Mars indicates energy, courage, passion, action, aggression, and starts. Pluto indicates regeneration, transformation, insecurity, altercation, and the underworld.

Ninth House—Sagittarius

The ninth house governs major plans for the future, law, religious and spiritual interests, editing and publishing, long journeys, foreign lands, philosophy, insurance, and inspirations.

Jupiter is the ruling planet for the ninth house. This planet indicates expansion, joviality, generosity, religious concepts, luck, and philosophy.

Tenth House—Capricorn

The tenth house governs major projects and ambitions, attainment, achievement, accomplishments, reputation, status, prestige, honor, public standing, publicity, credits or discredits, profession, the employer, authority or authorities, and the outer-link parent (the parent exerting the most obvious authority over your life's direction).

Saturn is the ruling planet for the tenth house. This planet indicates discipline, a teacher, restrictions, contradictions, security, thrift, and cold.

Eleventh House—Aquarius

The eleventh house governs friends, acquaintances, circumstances, advisers, hopes, wishes, ideals, aspirations, clubs, associations, social ties, large scale events, and a universal love.

Mercury, Saturn, and Uranus are the ruling planets for the eleventh house. Mercury indicates mental processes, mental expression, communication, and reasoning. Saturn indicates discipline, a teacher, restrictions, contradictions, security, thrift, and cold. Uranus indicates progressiveness, inventiveness, independence, genius, awareness, and chaos.

Twelfth House—Pisces

The twelfth house governs potentials, undercurrents, the behind-the-scenes, privacy, seclusion, retreats, the unknown, the subcon-

Don't be put off by similar meanings in differing cards. Once you've got your cards set up in formation and begin reading, it will be obvious to you, in context, what the cards and placement—together—mean.

---

scious, preparation, exile, misfortune, self-undoing, secret enemies, hospitals, self-sacrificing, jails, institutions, detentions, betrayal, failure, and the health of your mate.

Neptune and Jupiter are the ruling planets for the twelfth house. Neptune indicates illusion, deception, intuition, inspiration, imagination, and the mystical. Jupiter indicates expansion, joviality, generosity, religious concepts, luck, and philosophy.

READING

Proceed with your reading using the card-meaning chart that follows. You won't believe how easy it is. Of course, you're ultimately going to try for an overall picture. But at first, you may have to go card by card. Take an ace of hearts (unreversed) in the fourth position on the thirty-six-card layout. Row 1 indicates the past; the first column means business flow (as seen on the layout chart); and ace of hearts means home, real estate, letter. Therefore I would take this to mean that at some point in the past, the subject had a favorable real estate transaction, most likely a home that she had gotten a good deal on or likes especially. There may have been some correspondence involved. See how easy it is?

Card meanings are the same for both the thirty-six-card layout and the astrology method. (Of course, the 3s, 4s, 5s, and 6s in the thirty-six-card layout are integrated into the other cards.) You can try to memorize these meanings if you wish, but I usually encourage students to refer to the meanings list during readings at the beginning. It's more fun learning this way, and I think the validation you receive will make it easier to remember what specific cards mean.

As with any art, you'll have to use your noodle to make bridges and connections, but it's hard to be completely off base. Bridging is easier in card reading than with other vehicles, but it can also be more complex. It is important to learn to read cards as a *whole* and to avoid overanalyzing. Some cards won't be particularly significant; that's OK. Don't try to force meaning out of them—if you're meant to have information, it will come. As you get better, "insignificant" cards will begin to have meaning.

For now, look for cards in the "proper" categories (a money card in the business flow area, rather than health—although, of course, it could be referring to medical bills, but you'll be able to tell, don't worry). If your health row has no significant cards in it, don't sweat it. It just means that nothing of particular import is going on in this area of life right now. Surely there's more than enough information to get you going in another area, though! Soon your psychic flow will come into play, and you won't need to concentrate so hard or think so much!

It may help at first to pay special attention to "lead" cards, cards that influence other cards around them. These are often the first cards in a row, for example, but they can also be cards your eyes are drawn to. It may be a health card falling in the health section. Trust your intuition. The character of a lead card will dominate that area.

You might not think of cards as "reversible," since they can easily be read upside down, but all number cards and aces have a "right" side (look at the suit symbols in the body of the card for the differences), and, if reversed, the meaning changes. Reversed face cards are determined by the first face card laid out. This lead card will have the "face" of the queen, king, or jack looking toward the left or right. Any subsequent face card looking in the opposite direction is reversed. Be sure, especially in early readings, that you're reading for the correct direction! Also, red cards often indicate a fair-haired person; black, a dark person.

Tips for a Successful Reading

There are several things to keep in mind when reading. The first is that you should not assign moral values to your subject or the events you see in the cards. *You are to read only what is given and not make value judgments.*

Second, remember that the words you speak may have no meaning to you, and that's OK. The information will have meaning, or will trigger a response, in the subject.

Do not be nervous when you read. If you are nervous, it indicates that you are too personally involved with the subject or the reading to do a good reading. Be friendly, but maintain a certain distance. Don't worry about how you'll do. The more quickly you

Card Meanings

Hearts	Meaning	Reversed
Ace	Home/real estate, letter.	Changes, don't own home.
King	Male/authority.	
Queen	Female/environmental surroundings.	
Jack	Male/news, information, April—white/pink,* May—red/yellow, June—red/blue.	
10	Cheerfulness, negates other negative cards around.	Birth, enthusiastic, lucky marriage.
9	Wish card, pleasure.	Loved one.
8	Friend/marriage, social invitations, furniture, fix-up.	Jealousy, social animal, new friends.
7	Domestic affairs, generally good, siblings, children, animals supporting Wish Card.	Drawers in a snit, jealousy.
6	Past pleasures.	Future, social duty.
5	Marriage proposal, present.	Company coming, home.
4	News, telephone call.	Complaining, griping.
3	Goals, time (man's time).	Papers, contracts, documents.
2	Love/affection, second marriage, calendar day.	Obstacles, departures.

*Colors and months are indicated with jacks. Surrounding cards should determine *which* months and colors are indicated.

Clubs	Meaning	Reversed
Ace	Papers, news, luck, letters, telephone calls.	Bad news, death.
King	No sex, wild card, enhancer.	
Queen	Lovers/infidelity/ personality traits.	
Jack	No sex, family ties, July—green/brown, August—red/green, September—gold/ black.	
10	Journey, short trips, good events.	Water.
9	Legal business, regular business.	Delays.
8	Friends, statements of a social nature, business meetings.	Papers, lots of talk.
7	Success, projects completed.	Worry over money, insecurities.
6	Present aggravation.	Lots of efforts, distractions
5	Dear loved one, talk.	Loss of action, fussy.
4	Pleasant news, match.	Delays, doesn't sleep well.
3	Caution, letters, news.	Attains desired position, read carefully.
2	Children, new people.	News, letter, move, invitation.

detach yourself from your own thoughts, the more quickly the psychic takes over and feeds you the information. Have your mind in control at all times.

Always be honest with the subject. Don't withhold information based upon your personal feelings. It is not up to any of us to decide what is good or bad for anybody else. God will not give us any information we are unable to handle. In addition, the subject always has the free will to take what she wants from the reading and reject the rest—or reject the whole reading.

Be prepared to counsel the subject a bit. Explain that the information given is only made available to the client to aid her in

Diamonds	Meaning	Reversed
Ace	Present, ring, money.	Money, news, letters, property, selling, profit.
King	Male, borrowed money or goods.	
Queen	Female, money, gamblers.	
Jack	Male, responsive concepts, January—blue/green, February—white/green, March—white/pink.	
10	Money.	Fire, pleasant outing.
9	Anger, separation, divorce, money, business.	Spontaneous fights, quick choices, logistics of day-to-day living.
8	Exercise, jewelry.	Disagreeable, clothes, major purchase.
7	Siblings, children, animal.	Picture, mail, gift, bored.
6	Optimism, pleasure.	Home troubles, delays.
5	Good fortune, legal settlement.	Legal litigation.
4	Society, friends.	Pleasant, not influential.
3	Business, friends.	Separation, quarrels.
2	Money, surprise.	Surprise, pleased, gossip.

making decisions. Again, death is an example. Death could be a blessing in disguise, or news of death can prompt better health care (exercise of free will). If one knows of the approach of illness, one has the chance to take precautions. The real goal of any reading is to help the subject see his or her options to make decision making easier. If the client takes the information in the right light, she can make changes in attitude, lifestyle, or health that can greatly improve the quality of life.

During the reading, do your best to relax. Don't try to "force" information. If your subject has questions the cards don't clearly answer, don't feel inadequate. Just state you don't know—after all, you're not God, just a card reader! Not everything will be an-

Spades	Meaning	Reversed
Ace	Business, building, selling, good luck.	Spiritual or physical death, illness, danger.
King	Close of life/past, present, future.	
Queen	Warning card, no sex.	
Jack	Either sex, money, depression, October—black/blue, November—brown/black, December—gold/red.	
10	Water, trips, distance, ocean.	Troubles, illness.
9	Loss.	Death, trouble.
8	Illness, depression, worry, Lack Card.	Gloom/doom, sadness, mental illness.
7	Change, agreements, leave.	Accidents, uncertainty.
6	The unexpected, travel over water, child/relative.	Surprise, difficulties.
5	Loss of a loved one.	Grief.
4	Loneliness.	Suggestions.
3	Arguments, tears.	Confusion, trials.
2	Friends, automobile.	Enemies, minor worries, mail.

swered in every reading. What you know, you know; what you don't know, you don't.

Much has been made of the words *past*, *present*, and *future* in readings. If you see an event clearly and your subject wants to know when this event will occur, don't sweat it. Although it is difficult for many people to understand, time as we know it just doesn't exist in the psychic world. What is happening now is happening in the past and future concurrently. Even when you *can* predict when an event will occur in time as we know it (as in palmistry, for example), it has happened before and will happen again, too. To a good reader, past, present, and future are all one vision. This vision may be a complete picture of your subject that you "see" in one flash, or it may be seen in the symbolism of the cards. The subconscious field of the mind and body contains internal and external imprints that have no beginning or end. So, as a reader, you've got to give your subject your best guesstimate of time. Generally, I find that events seen in the cards occur in a two-year period, unless a card definitely states a year number. (This is the exception to the rule, rather than the norm.)

Psychic Flow

While your goal as a reader, as you practice with the cards, is to get your psychic flow going (or going better), it is imperative that your goal *for each reading* be to help your subject gain information she wants. Don't wait breathless for your flow to kick in—you'll be distracted from your reading. To help you avoid this pitfall, here is what may happen when the psychic takes over. When it happens, acknowledge it and let it go (marvel over it *after* the reading).

One of the ways that you can recognize that your psychic ability is working is that you begin to sense tactile differences in how the cards are feeling from one person to another. Your sense of touch will be heightened, and you will be able to feel if the cards are sticking, or feel sluggish or blocked. This feel is important to the reader, as it is one of the first clues to an inward sighting of the personality that one is dealing with.

The second clue that your own psychic ability is taking over is that you will begin to feel and see clips of information about the person sitting across from you. Chances are, you as a beginner will not feel comfortable enough at this point to express what you are seeing and feeling, but your memory will retain this information, and at some point during the actual reading, your mouth will open and the information will fall out. The client most likely will give an expression of sheer surprise. You have just received validation.

Flashes can come in the form of smells, voices, mental pictures flashing across your mind, or a particular image that just won't release until it has been shared. A good example of this type of experience is a client of mine who came in for a reading. As he sat there quietly waiting his turn, I came out of my office with the previous client. In passing, I spoke with him and told him to go on back, I'd be with him in a minute. As I was doing this, a mental image, along with a sound, filled my mind. I saw him boarding an

CARD COMBINATIONS FOR THE MODERN DECK
Combinations are found in a straight line or diagonally.

Combination	Meaning
4 aces	Radical changes in thoughts and actions. Some danger is implied, as well as loss of money or love troubles. If one or more of the cards is reversed, it helps erase the negative meanings.
2 aces	If a heart/club combination, means a good union. If a diamond or spade combination, jealousy. In any of these combinations, one or both are reversed, it will produce less success due to uncontrolled passion.
4 kings	Good influences, possible honors, public recognition. Reversed: Less significance in public recognition or honor and awards.
3 kings	A seriousness is implied. Conditions taken in hand with good outcome. Reversed: Conditions taken in hand; outcome doubtful.
2 kings	Business good, honest conduct, and partial success. Reversed: an obstacle to be overcome.
4 queens	Social gatherings, associations. Reversed: Dull party, lack of entertainment.
3 queens	Friendly persons, visits. Reversed: Gossip, caution.
2 queens	Exchange of information, meetings between friends. Reversed: Inquirer, action based on questions of others will bring suffering. Only one of 2 queens. Reversed: Jealousy.
4 jacks	Noisy, happy-go-lucky people. Reversed: More sedate-acting people and associations.
3 jacks	Worries, concerns, possible slander, questioned honor. Reversed: Dealing with those less fortunate than the subject.
2 jacks	Losses, scheming. If both are reversed: Trouble in close proximity. If only one reversed: Trouble in the near future.

Combination	Meaning
4 10s	Good luck with money, success in undertakings. Reversed: Obstacles to overcome before success is achieved.
3 10s	Legal litigation, possible loss of lawsuit, caution. Reversed: Less chance of lawsuits and/or losses.
2 10s	Unexpected luck, change of jobs or career. If only 1 of the 10 is reversed: Time is close. If both are reversed: job change is a good time away.
4 9s	Accomplishment of projects, unexpected events. Reversed: Longer time before subject will feel success has been achieved.
3 9s	Health, money, happiness. Reversed: Lots of discussion, temporary money setbacks.
2 9s	Good money, fairly content in environment, especially relating to business, documents. Reversed: Small aggravations and worries.
4 8s	Mixed success/poor travel condition, new job position. Reversed: Good stability in the old position.
3 8s	Love/marriage, family ties. Reversed: A flirt, foolish actions.
2 8s	Short-term pleasures, boyfriend or girlfriend, gifts. Reversed: Disappointment in affairs of the heart.
4 7s	Intriguing or calculating personality involved. Reversed: Lessens those negative connotations.
3 7s	Loss of friends, illness approaching. Reversed: Slight illness.
2 7s	Shared love, unexpected events. Reversed: unfaithfulness in thoughts, not considering others' feelings.

Combination	**Meaning**
6, 5, 4, 3, 2	The values of these cards remain as previously stated; two or more together will either strengthen or weaken the meaning of the lead card, or the lead card will weaken the meaning of the subsequent card(s), depending on suit. (Example: Spade is the lead card and is followed by a heart; the spade weakens the overall good of the heart card.) Don't agonize over what a "lead" card is. As I said before, trust your intuition. The character of a lead card gives flavor to the region surrounding it.

airplane near a snow-covered mountain, and heard the roar of the engines getting ready for takeoff. I also felt the heavy anxiety that he was experiencing over this trip. When he was seated in my office, and after we both had shuffled the cards and he had cut the deck, I told him about what I had seen him doing, how I knew he felt anxious, and asked him what it meant to him. All of this transpired before I picked up the cards and laid them out. My client readily responded by telling me that he was scheduled to take a trip to see his daughter for the first time in a year, and she lived in a state that had snow-covered mountains. He was anxious about the reception she might give him. He was not sure he was doing the right thing in trying to reestablish a relationship with her. I responded by telling him that I felt a sense of pleasure and ease associated with the trip and encouraged him to go. I perceived it would produce positive results. He immediately felt better and promised to let me know of his reception. We then went on with the reading. Later he called to tell me his trip had gone exactly as I'd predicted. What great validation!

This kind of impression is very important and should never be discounted. It should always be included in readings. These visions and insights can be referred to as "side vision" or clairvoyance—call it what you will—but learn to listen and respond to it, as well as to trust it.

The third clue that your psychic ability is kicking in is that you will begin to be able to bridge the information you receive into vocal paragraphs that the subject can relate to, without stumbling or grasping for information from the client. This third clue is probably the most difficult to understand, as the reader is not always aware of the mental processes that are occurring at the time. These are an amazing combination of the feeding of information through the body sensors, the visual clips of information, and the physical responses of the client (which you as the reader are not consciously aware of).

Ending a Reading

As a reader, you'll feel a "natural" end of the reading; after a while, you'll have no more information to impart. I ask clients at this point if they have any more questions, and I guide the client gently toward wrapping it up. It's much like ending any other meeting— you have to signal that you're ready to move on. Don't forget, you can't force information that's not available. Tell the subject, if she is insistent, that you've given her what's there—if it's not there, you can't pull it out of the air!

After a reading is completed, recleanse and neutralize the cards and the area of the reading by shuffling. It is also important to move around between readings. Let the previous reading leave with the client; let your mind go blank so that you don't consciously remember what was said in the reading. By doing these things, you will heal your body's aura field and rejuvenate your energy so that you can continue with your day or move on to a second reading without being tired or ineffectual.

SAMPLE CARD READING
Thirty-Six-Card Layout

This sample reading will help you understand bridging as well as how to differentiate between the more significant cards and the less significant ones. The (R) means the card in question is reversed. You might want to do your own sample reading first (looking at Illustration 6-3 and the card meaning chart) to see how you do.

First 3 Cards	Meaning
Queen of Hearts	Female, environmental surroundings.
2 of Diamonds	Money, surprise.
Ace of Diamonds	Present, ring, money.

First Row	Meaning
2 of Clubs	Children and new people.
10 of Spades	Water, trips, ocean, and distance.
8 of Hearts (R)	Jealousy, social animal, and new friends.
Queen of Diamonds	Female, money, gamblers.
7 of Hearts	Domestic affairs, generally good, supporting wish card, siblings, children, animals.
Ace of Spades (R)	Spiritual or physical death, illness, danger.

Second Row	Meaning
Queen of Clubs	Lovers, infidelity, personality traits.
8 of Spades	Illness, depression, worry, lack card.
King of Clubs	No sex, wild card, enhancer.
10 of Diamonds	Money.
King of Spades	Close of life/past, present, future.
Jack of Spades	Either sex, money, depression (October, November, December).

ILLUSTRATION 6-3
SAMPLE
36-CARD LAYOUT

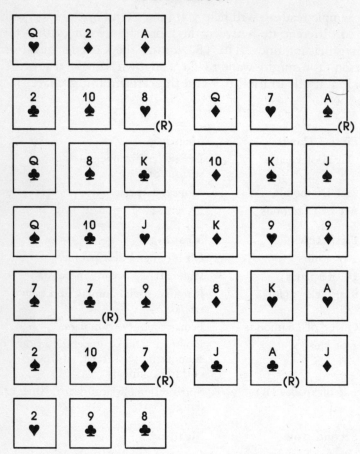

Note: (R) indicates a card that is reversed.

Third Row	Meaning
Queen of Spades	Warning card, no sex.
10 of Clubs	Journey, short trips, good events.
Jack of Hearts	Male, news, information (April, May, June).
King of Diamonds	Male, borrowed money or goods.
9 of Hearts	Wish card, pleasure.
9 of Diamonds	Anger, separation, divorce, money, business.

Fourth Row	Meaning
7 of Spades	Change, agreements, leave.
7 of Clubs (R)	Worry over money, insecurities.
9 of Spades	Loss.
8 of Diamonds	Exercise, jewelry.
King of Hearts	Male, authority.
Ace of Hearts	Home, real estate, letter.

Fifth Row	Meaning
2 of Spades	Friends, automobile.
10 of Hearts	Cheerfulness, negates other negative cards around it.
7 of Diamonds (R)	Picture, mail, gift, bored.
Jack of Clubs	No sex, family ties.
Ace of Clubs (R)	Bad news, death.
Jack of Diamonds	Male, responsive concepts (January, February, March).

Sixth Row	Meaning
2 of Hearts	Love, affection, second marriage, calendar day.
9 of Clubs	Legal business, regular business.
8 of Clubs	Friends, statements of a social nature, business meetings.

Special Combinations*	Meaning
2 Queens	Exchange of information and meetings between friends.
2 7s (R) (R)	Unexpected events, unfaithfulness in love, not considerate of others' feelings.
2 9s	Good money, fairly content with business.
2 Aces (R)	A good union, but may produce poor success due to uncontrolled passion.
2 8s (R)	Disappointment in affairs of the heart.
3 Kings	Seriousness implied; conditions taken in hand with good outcome.

---

*Combinations here are more specific than in the card definitions chart because we know what the suits are in these cases. We're beginning to bridge here.

Overall Interpretation

This reading was done by two beginning students. I had one of their work associates, about whom they knew very little, shuffle the cards. She then left. They weren't even told who the subject was. Their readings were based on the definitions given in the chapter, and they had to make assumptions according to what the cards indicated. Their interpretation of the cards seemed, to them, so exaggerated that they feared they had let their imaginations run wild. Little did they know, their interpretation was almost entirely correct. The reading was as follows:

The Queen of Hearts represents the client, a female. **1** She has money and romance on her mind, as indicated by the first three cards. **2** She has been encountering new people at work **3** and has developed a romance with a co-worker. **4** She is warned against talking, or other people talking, about her secrets. **5** There is also a travel card in the business sector that indicates a trip near water with this co-worker that is disappointing romantically. **6** This leaves the client depressed and may mean a breakup of the pair. **7** The client is also worried about money and work, which indicates that she is in fear of losing her job—probably over this romance (people obviously have been talking). **8** If she remains calm, and plays her cards right, everything will be OK, and back to business as usual. **9** The 10 of Hearts negates some of the trouble at work and makes the outcome slightly better.

In the home sector, there is a jealous male **10** (fair)— maybe her husband. There is also an indication of sepa-

---

1. Indicator row—first card.
2. Queen of Hearts, 2 of Diamonds, and Ace of Diamonds.
3. 2 of Clubs.
4. Indicated by Queen of Clubs (romance) in work sector.
5. Queen of Spades (warning) bridged with Queen of Clubs, combination (people talking).
6. 10 of Spades (trip near water) bridged with Queen of Clubs (romance) bridged with the combination of 8 of Hearts (R) and 8 of Spades (disappointment).
7. 8 of Spades (depression).
8. 7 of Clubs (worry over money, insecurity) bridged with 7 of Spades (change, leave) in work sector with Queen of Spades nearby (warning).
9. 2 of Hearts (love and affection "pleased"), 9 of Clubs (Good legal/business card). Later this was validated. She wasn't fired, but she became a partner in a new business (as also indicated by 2 of Hearts and 9 of Clubs).
10. Jack of Hearts.

ration with legal connotations related to this male and the jealousy. **11**   This will take place in April or May. **12**   Friends will keep talking. The situation is serious, as indicated by the 3 Kings in a row. **13**

At home there is worry about children, **14** specifically a male child with dark hair, as indicated by the Jack of Spades. There is a grave illness or possible death for this child, **15** and in October depression **16** will follow. There are legal documents attached to the child that will work out OK with the help of a male authority figure. **17**   This authority figure also ties back to the jealous male diagonally. They are all interconnected.

There is also a loss of family ties in the outcome. This will occur in January, February, or March. Money is also involved. **18**

When my friends called the "client," they received instant validation; she was flabbergasted!

***

11. 8 of Hearts (jealousy) bridged with King of Clubs (enhancer) bridged with Jack of Hearts (male) bridged with 7 of Clubs (leave).
12. Jack of Hearts (indicates month).
13. King of Clubs, King of Diamonds, King of Hearts combination in a diagonal line.
14. 7 of Hearts.
15. Ace of Spades (R).
16. Jack of Spades.
17. King of Hearts.
18. Jack of Clubs bridged with Ace of Clubs bridged with Jack of Diamonds.

Astrology Method

As with the sample reading for the Thirty-Six-Card Layout, this sample reading will enable you to practice your reading ability if you refer to Illustration 6-4 and the card meaning chart before looking at the actual reading. Check and see how well you did! Remember, (R) means the card is reversed. In the astrology method only, you may choose to ignore reversed card and read as if they were all straight up. You will get a balanced reading either way.

First 4 Cards	Meaning
6 of Spades	The unexpected, travel over water, child, relative.
6 of Diamonds	Optimism, pleasure.
6 of Hearts	Past pleasures.
10 of Spades	Water, trips, distance, ocean.

First House	Meaning
Ace of Clubs	Papers, news, luck, letters, telephone calls.
Jack of Clubs	No sex, family ties (July, August, September).
Jack of Hearts	Male, news, information (April, May, June).
King of Hearts	Male, authority.

Second House	Meaning
King of Spades	Close of life/past, present, future.
2 of Spades	Friends, automobile.
2 of Clubs	Children, new people.
2 of Hearts	Love/affection, second marriage, calendar day.

Third House	Meaning
2 of Diamonds	Money, surprise.
King of Clubs	No sex, wild card, enhancer.
4 of Hearts	News, telephone call.
4 of Diamonds	Society, friends.

ILLUSTRATION 6-4
SAMPLE ASTROLOGY METHOD

Note: (R) indicates a card that is reversed.

Fourth House	Meaning
4 of Clubs	Pleasant news, match.
8 of Spades	Illness, depression, worry, lack card.
8 of Hearts	Friend, marriage, social invitations, furniture, fix-up.
8 of Clubs	Friends, comments of a social nature, business, meetings.

Fifth House	Meaning
8 of Diamonds	Exercise, jewelry.
5 of Spades	Loss of a loved one.
5 of Diamonds	Good fortune, legal settlement.
King of Diamonds	Male, borrowed money or goods.

Sixth House	Meaning
Ace of Diamonds	Present, ring, money.
Ace of Spades (R)	Spiritual or physical death, illness, danger.
Ace of Hearts (R)	Changes, don't own home.
3 of Diamonds	Business, friends.

Seventh House	Meaning
Queen of Spades	Warning card, no sex.
Queen of Hearts	Female, environmental surroundings.
Queen of Diamonds (R)	Female, money, gambler.
9 of Hearts	Wish card, pleasure.

Eighth House	Meaning
9 of Spades	Loss.
Queen of Clubs	Lovers, infidelity, personality traits.
Jack of Spades (R)	Sex, money, depression (October, November, December).
Jack of Diamonds (R)	Male, responsive concepts (January, February, March).

Ninth House	Meaning
3 of Spades	Arguments, tears.
9 of Diamonds	Anger, separation, divorce, money, business.
9 of Clubs (R)	Delays.
3 of Clubs	Caution, letters, news.

Tenth House	Meaning
3 of Hearts	Goals, time (man's time).
4 of Spades	Loneliness.
5 of Hearts (R)	Company coming, home.
5 of Clubs	Dear loved one, talk.

Eleventh House	Meaning
10 of Diamonds	Money.
10 of Clubs	Journey, short trips, good events.
10 of Hearts	Cheerfulness, negates negative cards.
7 of Diamonds (R)	Picture, mail, gift, bored.

Twelfth House	Meaning
7 of Spades (R)	Accidents, uncertainty.
7 of Hearts	Domestic affairs, generally good, supporting wish card.
7 of Clubs (R)	Worry over money, insecurities.
6 of Clubs (R)	Lots of efforts, distractions.

Special Combinations	Meaning
2 Jacks	Losses, scheming.
3 Queens (R)	Friends, visits, caution, gossip.
2 Jacks (R) (R)	Trouble in close proximity.
2 9s (R)	Good money, fairly content in environment, small aggravations and worries.
3 10s	Legal litigation, possible loss of lawsuit, caution.
3 7s (R)	Loss of friends, slight illness approaching.

ILLUSTRATION 6-4 (continued)

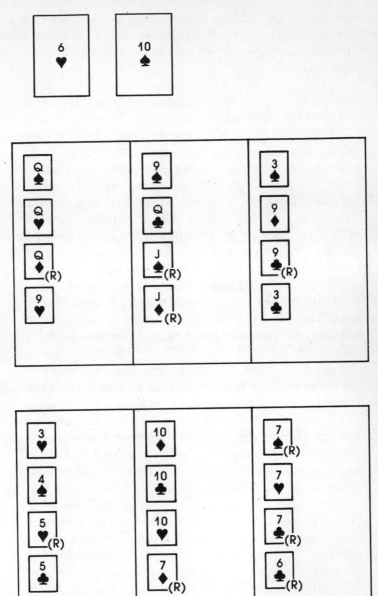

Note: (R) indicates a card that is reversed.

Overall Interpretation

I gave this astrology fifty-two-card layout to my secretary and asked her to interpret the reading from the values I assigned to the layout format and the fifty-two-card deck. What follows are her interpretations.

When I was given the illustration to "read," I had no idea who the client was.

The first set of cards I interpreted was the first four cards on the upper left-hand corner of the board. 1   It told me that the client would travel over or near water. The trip would be pleasant and over a far distance. 2

I immediately moved down to the four cards in the first house, and they told me (along with the first card of the first top four) 3   that the client will receive news that he or she expected from a fair-haired individual regarding the trip. The news will be pleasant. 4   Moving on to the second house, I showed that a dark-haired friend the client has met or will meet through acquaintances could lead to a possible romance. 5   A telephone call from a friend concerning money I interpreted from the third house.6

The fourth house, plus the second card, indicated that the client has been concerned about an illness of a close friend or relative, and that he or she would receive some good news about this person. 8   However, there is a loss of a loved one in connection with jewelry. As regards this loss, the client will come out OK in legal matters, but will have to borrow money, which was indicated by the fifth house.9

The sixth house indicated that there are some unexpected changes in the workplace, and there is a warning card present, which tells me that the client needs to be cautious. 10   A warning is also indicated regarding what the client is trying to accomplish—it is associated with a light-haired female. However, it comes out OK in the end; there are just some obstacles thrown in the way shown in the seventh house, plus the third card. 11

The client's spouse, as well as the client, will be moody and depressed about a loss that will occur some-

time in January, February, or March. This is shown in
the eighth house. **12**   The ninth house shows caution
on the part of the client regarding arguments relating

1. The four cards at the top of the board that relate
   back to the different houses.
2. 10 of Spades (travel, distance) bridged with 6 of
   Diamonds (pleasure) bridged with 6 of Hearts
   (past pleasures) bridged with 6 of Spades (the
   unexpected, travel).
3. 6 of Spades.
4. Ace of Clubs (news) bridged with Jack of Hearts
   (male, news).
5. King of Spades (dark male) bridged with 2 of
   Spades (friends) bridged with 2 of Clubs (new
   people) bridged with 2 of Hearts (affection).
6. 4 of Hearts (phone call) bridged with 4 of
   Diamonds (friends) bridged with 2 of Diamonds
   (money).
7. 6 of Diamonds.
8. 8 of Spades (illness) bridged with 8 of Hearts
   (friends) bridged with 4 of Clubs (pleasant
   news).
9. 5 of Spades (loss of loved one) bridged with 8 of
   Diamonds (jewelry) bridged with 5 of Diamonds
   (good fortune, legal settlement) bridged with
   King of Diamonds (borrowed money).
10. Ace of Hearts (R) (changes) bridged with 3 of
    Diamonds (business) bridged with Ace of Spades
    (R) (warning).
11. 6 of Hearts (pleasure).
12. Queen of Clubs (lovers) bridged with Jack of
    Spades (R) (depression) bridged with 9 of
    Spades (loss) bridged with Jack of Diamonds
    (January, February, March).

13. 3 of Clubs (caution) bridged with 3 of Spades (arguments) bridged with 9 of Diamonds (business) bridged with 9 of Clubs (R) (delays).
14. 6 of Diamonds (optimism, pleasure).
15. 5 of Clubs (talk, loved one) bridged with 5 of Hearts (R) (company, home) bridged with 4 of Spades (loneliness).
16. 10 of Clubs (short trip) bridged with 10 of Diamonds (money) bridged with 7 of Diamonds (R) (bored).
17. 7 of Spades (R) (uncertainty) bridged with 7 of Hearts (domestic affairs) bridged with 7 of Clubs (money) bridged with 6 of Clubs (R) (effort).

---

to business activities that could cause delays. 13

The tenth house plus the fourth card 14 on top tells me that a loved one will come home from a distance and need to talk with this client. He or she is very lonely. 15 The eleventh house shows a short trip that deals with earning money. The trip looks to be OK, but the client could become bored. 16 However, the card combination here negates the negative cards, indicating that money can be made through the trip.

The last house shows that there is a lot of uncertainty in the area of the client's domestic affairs as regards money matters, but the client will give much effort and come out OK. 17

When I finished my interpretation and was told who the client actually was, I spoke with that person and told what my interpretations were. The client helped fill in the gaps, and it started making much more sense to me, since it made sense to the client. Of course, I was not 100 percent accurate—I would say only about 45 percent to 50 percent, but for a "first timer," I feel I did exceptionally well. My accuracy rating jumped to 80–85 percent over time, once things started occurring for the client (it's hard to validate things that haven't happened yet). Getting feedback made a lot of difference and encouraged me to keep trying!

7
THE ANSWER'S IN THE PALM OF YOUR HAND

IT IS NOT a coincidence that palm prints were people's earliest attempts at identity. Early people used their palm prints on cave walls and on cave drawings as their signature, since the palm print was recognized as being distinctive and individual. Today, of course, law enforcement agencies routinely use handprints (specifically, fingerprints, which are the most commonly found parts of handprints—we touch an awful lot with our fingers) as irrefutable proof of identification.

As humans evolved, their curiosity about the Creator and their destiny deepened. In ancient times, of course, people looked to nature as a guide to answering the oldest question in the world: "What is the meaning of life?" Today, we have psychiatrists, organized religion, and racks full of books to help us answer that question, but our ancestors had nowhere to look but to themselves and the world around them. What they found probably did not astound them the way it astounds us today, for they lived in harmony with nature. The interconnectedness of stars, planets, palms, numbers (which, far from being human-made principles, are universal truths), even archetypal symbols, made sense to ancient people, because they were so intensely connected to the earth.

Some insightful soul or souls noticed a strong correlation between shapes and markings of the hand and events that took place in one's life. Most likely, seers, or those with psychic gifts, saw a strong link between hand markings and information that they received psychically. Over the years, markings and other identifying features of palmistry have been codified. This is not to say that these "rules" were set arbitrarily. Rather, those with psychic gifts would, time and again, in receiving psychic flow, make a connection between a certain marking and a certain event. After a while, it became accepted that the line nearest the thumb, say, was a guide to length and quality of life—even without psychic flow. By learning these rules, even a totally nonintuitive type could garner a certain amount of information about an individual through his or her hands.

As this information became more widely disseminated, it became possible for people with little regard for true psychic flow to become adequate "palmists." Of course, they could do quite well, for the markings will tell you a lot. But the real purpose of learning to break the palmistry "code" is to encourage your own psychic flow. Often, a palm will offer contradictory information to the reader. Psychic flow helps the reader to sort this stuff out.

Palmistry, like the other vehicles mentioned in this book, is only a tool for tapping into your psychic flow. If you do nothing but read the section on hand shapes, you will be able to learn a lot about yourself and those around you, but if you use the "science" (memorization, study) of palmistry as a pathway to your own ESP abilities, you'll truly appreciate the "art" of palmistry, as well. Either way, you'll have a lot of fun and amaze yourself (and your friends) with your newfound skills. If you don't believe me, use some of the "parlor tricks" in this chapter next time you're at a party or have a dull moment at the office. You'll be amazed at the results!

THE BLUEPRINTS OF LIFE

The palm has been called a blueprint of life, for when we are born, we enter the world with our personal blueprints etched upon our palms. All markings found upon the palms at birth, and at maturity, are significant to a person's development. The palms and their markings give the earliest clues into a person's traits, talents, health, and oh, so much more.

Since we have two palms, it is important to keep in mind that the subordinate (usually the left) palm is considered to contain the entire genetic blueprint of life given at birth. The dominant (usually right) palm tells the reader how the subject is using his blueprint in day-to-day living.

It works like this: Everyone is born with an affinity for using one hand in preference over the other. In most cases (because most people are right-handed), the left hand is considered the "hand of actuality," which is to say that, in a right-handed person, the left hand shows what is destined, while the right hand reflects free will. Even an inexperienced palmist can identify the hand of destiny (or subdominant hand; the left hand in a right-handed child) of a child at birth and be able to tell whether the child will be right- or left-handed. The hand with the fewest lines on it is the hand of actualization (or active choice), which will of course be obvious once the child is older and starts reaching, drawing, or eating with silverware.

In reading palms, it is important to compare the two hands for differences and similarities. For instance, a person whose hand shapes and markings are very similar is one who has followed his or her destiny, whereas a person whose hands are markedly different will have chosen to exercise free will quite often. Please remember not to judge people for their choices. A person destined to be a secretary who becomes a successful concert pianist certainly should not be criticized. The greatest gift we ever receive is the gift of choice, to do what we please with our lives. (Please note that for a child under seventeen, the hand of free will, the dominant hand will probably not reflect much: the child probably has not had the chance to exercise free will. I'd suggest trying another method if you want to read a child or being careful to read only talent markings.)

Let's look at an example of the choices we are able to make. Consider a child born with a well-developed Mount of Apollo (mount under the ring finger) and significant markings on the mount and finger. This tells the palmist that the child has both the ability and talent for either music or painting (picture painting, not house painting!). The child, not being swayed by parents in either direction, decides to play an instrument, even though he likes to paint, because sound seems to draw him more. What is the difference? The difference is the freedom of choice, not the better of the talents.

READING A BLUEPRINT

We have been schooled, or programmed, through culture and proper etiquette to suppress our natural thought and action patterns. We can rediscover these through the clues in our hands. This chapter will teach you the science of reading the palmistry blueprint, a practice that may be the catalyst for starting your psychic flow. For now, of course, it is important to take in as much information as you are comfortable with. It's admittedly a lot to learn; you might want to do just a section every few days (hand shapes one day, mounts another) until you get it down. Again, if you learn nothing but the information in one section, you will

---

Wording in this and other vehicle chapters has been chosen very carefully; when reading, try to use these words with your subject as much as possible. They are especially good for conveying meaning *to the subject* without imparting the reader's judgment or imagination by mistake.

---

have achieved a means of great insight into others. At all times, try to be open and ready for psychic clips that might come your way. If, as you're giving a reading, you find something coming out of your mouth from Lord knows where (you were going to say, "I see two children in your future," but you say, "You will have twin girls and, three years later, a son"), you'll know your psychic flow has kicked in!

The key to success, as I mentioned, is to look at *both* of the hands. Look at the whole of each hand, front and back. Notice first impressions. Make note of shape, texture, color, lines, fingers, thumbs. They all contain markings (or no markings at all?) that have meaning. You'll learn how to identify each shape or marking, then you'll learn how to interpret it and to compare it and contrast it with other markings.

It is usually easiest to begin with yourself as a "client," since you presumably know yourself well and will be able to gain instant validation for what you see in your hands. I would suggest, however, trying to look at a few hands for comparison when you feel confused. One of my students, for instance, couldn't figure out what shape her palm was until she saw three or four others:

"After I saw a spatulate palm—which I recognized instantly—and a squarer one, it was a lot easier to tell that mine was round. I guess I had a hard time seeing it, because the traits the round palm suggests are *not* traits I think of myself as having. But after *seeing* that my palm is round, I reread what it meant, and I had to admit it made sense."

If you decide to practice only on yourself before going out into the world with your skills, *be sure to identify your markings clearly before interpreting them.* It helps to keep a journal as you do this, so you are not tempted to revise your decisions based on the interpretations they suggest. It is also important to keep an open mind. If you see a trait reflected in a hand that does not seem to correspond with the truth, don't panic. Your basic reading will be the same, or you'll want to look further in the palm for an explanation of this discrepancy. Or you may have to change your assessment of "truth." In palmistry, the hands never lie. The information they hold, however, might be surprising!

While you will best learn ESP bit by bit, your goal will be the integration of these bits to get "the whole picture" of your client. This integration will also facilitate psychic flow. If you feel overwhelmed by the huge amount of information to learn, return to Chapter 4 for a meditation session or visualization for ESP success. It might help to know, too, that a lot of this information has a commonsense aspect (thin-handed people, for example, lack energy) and is thus easy to remember. After a while, all the details of palmistry will fall into place. And this book will walk you through every step of the learning process. Just take a bit at a time, and before you know it, you'll be reading palms!

Begin your study of palmistry in the area where you feel most comfortable. There's no rule that says you have to learn the mounts before you learn the major lines (though it may be easier in the long run). If the order of the sections confuses you, remember that each part of the hand is being presented to you in exactly the order a palmist would read a subject's hand; this is the order you'll be using when you become more adept. Practice and experience will make it easier. Soon you won't need to refer to the book to know what to look for—and how to evaluate what you see. You'll see for yourself—and not just because I've told you—that everything in the hand is *always* backed up by other marks or formations.

ILLUSTRATION 7-1
PARLOR TRICKS

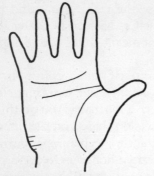

A. Affairs of the Heart

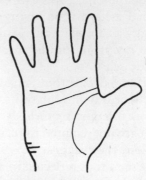

B. Extramarital Affairs

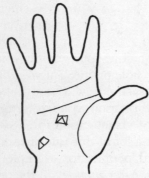

C. Triangles in Squares or
Triangles That Make Squares

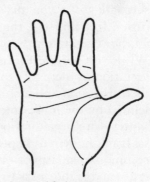

D. Ring of Solomon

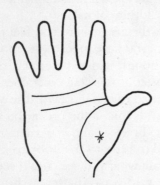

E. Star on Venus

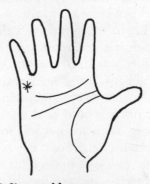

F. Star on Mercury

PARLOR TRICKS

Before you begin a comprehensive study of the complexities of palmistry, you may want to try looking for the following fun clues. You'll be impressed with how true an indication they are of personality, and you'll be a hit at parties!

- A crooked Mercury (pinky) finger indicates a person who likes to gossip and always knows the latest tidbits.
- Little horizontal lines on the side of the palm along the Mount of Luna (see A in Illustration 7-1) indicate a person who likes the opposite sex and affairs of the heart. However, this does not always mean just sexually; this person could just be taken as a flirt. If there are deep lines on the side of the palm at the lower end of the Mount of Luna (see B in Illustration 7-1), this indicates extramarital affairs.
- A well-developed (fleshy) Mount of Venus (see page 205) with good coloring (rosy) indicates an individual who likes an active sex life. If the Mount of Venus is flat and not as fleshy to the touch, this person can take it or leave it when it comes to sex. He could also be a good faker.
- Triangles within squares or triangles that make squares (C in Illustration 7-1) are considered money marks. This indicates the person has or will have money or property.
- Thin, shallow lines on the palm that are hard to see are— no matter what their shape—signs of nervousness.
- The Ring of Solomon is a mark starting at the edge of the palm under the Jupiter finger that curves around the finger to a point between Jupiter and Saturn (see D in Illustration 7-1). This means practical powers in the occult areas.
- A star midway down on the Mount of Venus (E in Illustration 7-1) is a sign of conquering love—women who seduce men, men who seduce women.
- A star on the Mount of Mercury (see F) is a science mark or a mark of acclaim.
- A star on the Upper Mount of Mars (see G) indicates a military honor that will come late in the person's career.
- A triangle on the Mount of Mercury (see page 230) indicates athletic ability.
- Vertical lines on the Mount of Saturn (see H) indicate success late in life.

ILLUSTRATION 7-1 (continued)

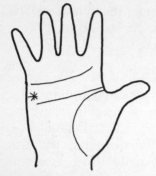

G. Star on Upper Mars

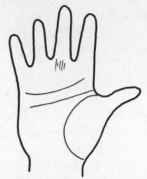

H. Vertical Lines on
Mount of Saturn

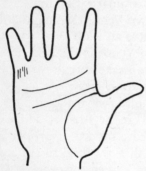

I. Vertical Lines on
Mount of Mercury

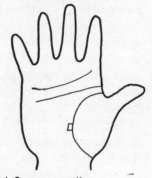

J. Square on the
Life Line

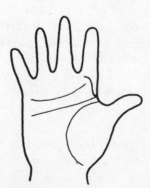

K. Minister's Mark

ILLUSTRATION 7-1 (continued)

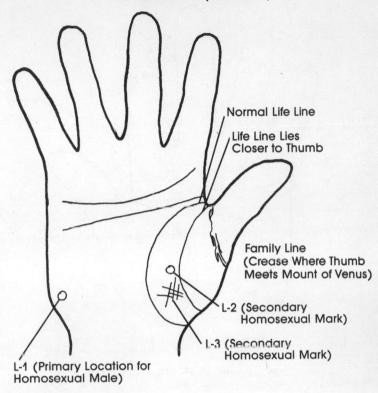

Normal Life Line

Life Line Lies
Closer to Thumb

Family Line
(Crease Where Thumb
Meets Mount of Venus)

L-2 (Secondary
Homosexual Mark)

L-3 (Secondary
Homosexual Mark)

L-1 (Primary Location for
Homosexual Male)

- Vertical lines on the Mount of Mercury (see I) indicate success in business.
- Horizontal lines on the Mount of Venus (see page 229) that do not cross indicate a weakening of the sex drive.
- A grille (see page 217) on the Mount of Jupiter (see page 229) indicates a snobbish person, one with excessive pride.
- A grille on the Mount of Mercury (see page 229) indicates a dishonest person, a cheater.
- A square that touches or is very close to the Life Line (see J) is considered to be a prisoner's mark because it indicates isolation from society.
- A curved line that originates at the Mount of Jupiter and runs down toward the thumb (see K) is a religious mark.
- The homosexual mark can be found in three places (see L): a circle on the bottom corner of the Mount of Luna, a well-

ILLUSTRATION 7-1 (continued)

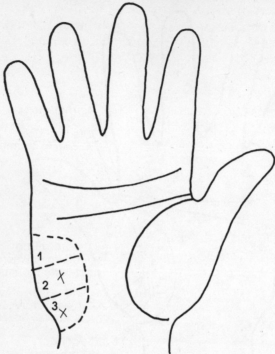

M. Crosses on Mount of Luna

developed grille in the Mount of Venus, or a circle near an extra line next to the thumb crease (this extra line is called the Girdle of Venus). The Luna marking is primary, but the palm always has backup. Any circles and grilles in the Mount of Venus merit a second look.

- A cross on the Mount of Luna, if in section 2 or 3, is the mark of a mental breakdown or emotional disorders (see M).
- A cross on the Mount of Venus that is close to the Life Line or touches the line indicates family trouble.
- A triangle in the Plain of Mars indicates an inheritance of property.
- The St. Andrew's cross (see Illustration 7-30C on page 243) is a distinct cross most commonly found at the bottom of the Life Line, though it can appear anywhere in the

general region of the line. St. Andrew's cross looks more like a crucifix than most crosses and is very well defined. It stands on its own and is very prominent. You will recognize it when you see it. This cross indicates a person who will save the life of someone else—physically, mentally, or emotionally.

- A misshapen little toenail that is thick and yellowish in color indicates kidney and bladder problems.
- If the little toenail is thick, discolored, and has ridges, it means prostate gland problems for a man and female disorders for a woman.
- If the big toenail is discolored and thick, it indicates digestive tract disorders and a tendency toward diabetes.

HAND DIVISIONS

The hand is divided into several sections. Each section is significant and is best looked at within the context of the entire hand; if taken out of context, only partial or biased information may be obtained. The divisions are the palm shapes, mounts, fingers, finger phalanges, thumb, nails, and rascettes, or wrist bracelets (see Illustration 7-2).

As you can see from the illustration, these divisions include nine mounts; four fingers—excluding thumbs, fourteen phalanges, including the thumb's two phalanges, and the rascettes (wrist wrinkles or bracelets). Each of the fingers has a name:

- Index finger—Jupiter
- Middle finger—Saturn
- Ring finger—Apollo
- Little finger—Mercury

Directly under the fingers and thumb begin the mounts. The names of the mounts under the fingers correspond to the names given to the fingers. As you can see from the illustration, there are two mounts of Mars. The upper mount is directly below the Mount of Mercury, and the lower mount is directly above the Mount of Venus. The triangle directly in the center of the palm is called the Plain of Mars. When looking at each mount or plain, you must take into consideration its shape, size, and markings.

ILLUSTRATION 7-2
PALM DIVISIONS

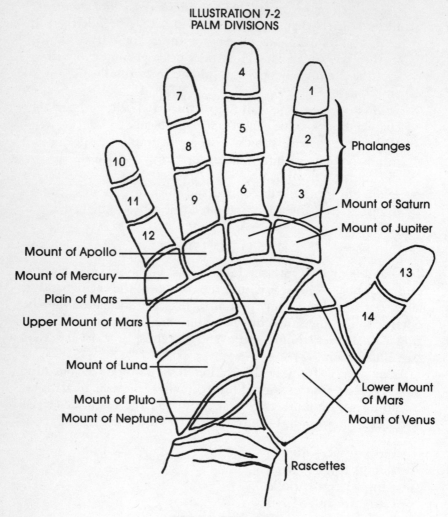

PALM SHAPES

The shape of the palm tells you how a person will react and respond to the physical environment. It is a vital indicator of a person's temperament and personal needs, as well as to the energy of the individual. This energy is the energy in which life flows—this is not only physical energy, but also the energy of the mental processes.

Illustration 7-3 shows four basic hand shapes. For the experienced palmist, there are more diverse hand shapes within the basic

ILLUSTRATION 7-3
PALM SHAPES

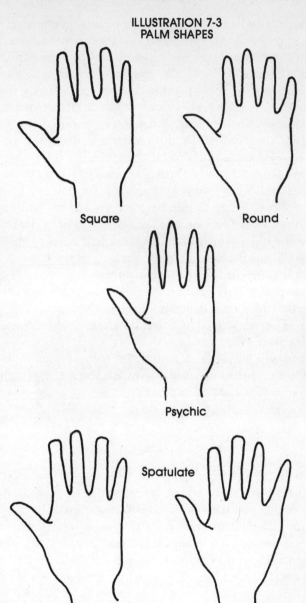

Square

Round

Psychic

Spatulate

Wide at Bottom

Wide at Top

categories, but this will be more than enough to get you started.

Since this is relatively new information, look at the illustration and see if you can pick out the *closest* hand shape to your hand. Oh, no! None of the shapes look like yours? One really does; the shapes just may not be recognizable to you yet. Don't worry— you'll soon see yours. Remember not to look at finger or finger-nail shapes or size—just look at your palm's overall shape.

If you are having trouble deciding what shape a palm is, you might want to try comparing it to other palms. It's really difficult to tell a square from a round or spatulate(except in the most rare circumstances) without looking at ten or so palms—as with anything, experience helps. Remember, you look at the palm itself. Ignore the fingers if it helps. It may help to try to hold the thumb flush against the index finger and imagine a line descending from the crease that forms between them all the way to the base of your palm (as if you were cutting off your thumb).

While most palms will have an overall shape, you may notice that hands tend to contain elements of more than one palm type. Use your common sense to determine how much of each shape's characteristics your client has.

Most hands will be square, round, or some combination of those two. Psychic palms are rare, spatulate less so, especially in this particular era; the world needs doers, and spatulate-handed people are doers.

The Square Palm

The square palm is just what it sounds like: square.

A person who possesses a square palm is neat and tidy in his or her personal habits and lifestyle. This personality will have strong opinions and will tend to classify both people and things into compartments, much as a computer does. People with square palms are generally good listeners, people who absorb and store information until needed later. These people are hard workers and understand that one must keep on going, even in adverse situa-tions. Their best trait is that they are most likely to be able to cope. They are good at implementing ideas as well. They are conserva-tive, materialistic thinkers who make decisions slowly and care-fully, and they don't like to waste their time. In fact, they do not take kindly to those who take too long to speak their minds.

An outstanding trait of the square-hander's personality is his ability to be objective, well organized, and farsighted. His loyalty is rarely questioned, as it is part of the square-handed person's integrity. His values and ideas are usually instilled at an early age, and he will not deviate from those patterns. His I.Q. is usually higher than most people give him credit for, as he may not always express his knowledge. His thinking patterns are concrete.

The energy of a person with a square hand is well balanced, and his health is usually better than most, as square-handed people are determined to enjoy good quality of life and will work at achieving good health. They are usually very generous in sharing their resources, especially with those they love.

In family matters, the square-palmed individual is in tune with family as a group or as individuals. Top priorities for family concerns are the ability to provide support and instruction on how to conduct life.

As an employee, the square-handed person is considered to be a good team worker, one who is congenial and easygoing. This person is adaptable and, if committed to a chosen field, makes an excellent manager.

This sounds just too good to be true! Now for the other side of the square-hander. The square palm indicates no tendency to waste time on the "poor old me," but this person can—through too much self-examination over past errors (or what he considers past errors)—fall into the old trap of chronic depression. While square-handers can easily reproduce anything they can see, touch, or feel, they are not original thinkers, nor do they particularly value originality in others.

The square-hander has the most interest in science of all types, and in philosophy, learning the mechanics of equipment, construction of ideas, concepts, buildings, and all of the practical or teachable areas of living.

In religion, a person with a square palm tends to be more comfortable with a ritualized or orderly method of worship. This person does take his religious faith very seriously, and once committed, does not change.

If a square hand is large, it is known as the broad, practical hand. It is referred to by some as the elementary hand, or the "tightwad." If such a hand appears on a person small in stature, the person will be quite detail-oriented. If, on the other hand, a square hand is small in comparison to the overall body size, its possessor will like to do things on a large scale, or in grandiose style.

The Round Palm

In appearance, the round palm resembles a baseball mitt. At the upper end, toward the fingers, the round hand has a distinctive curve. The end of the palm generally curves in the same way.

The round-palmed person is known as a versatile personality. Such a hand suggests to the reader that the owner has a variety of good qualities without a lot of undesirable traits. For example, people with versatile hands know they have good qualities but don't have overinflated egos or exaggerated images of themselves.

This is the quality that keeps the world ticking; round-handed people are the work force of the world. Hard workers, these people respect method and system, but are not chained to methods or systems unnecessarily. They tend to work best independently, but can be supervised without threat to their egos. They operate best in jobs that have some structure but require self-motivation. They do well at a corporate or supervisory level, or as teachers, farmers, or in any job that requires a love of nature. They also make good actors. The round hand contains the most valuable traits for the foreign service or for spying, because its owners are quick, are agile in verbalization, and have a charm that makes one believe what they say. Also, they usually seem to land on their feet.

Round-handers tend to marry and do best in marriage with the square-handed type, because the round-handed person doesn't mind following the square-hander's directions. Round-palmed people make good parents but tend to be overprotective, not only of their children, but of their spouses or parents as well, and to the detriment of others. But they are also the doers, inspiring their offspring to take part in activities. And yes, they can tend to be pushy. For behind every successful man or woman . . . is a round-handed spouse! (The original quotation was created for round-handed women.)

Round-handers are talented, and things come easily to them. They are usually widely read and can discuss art or world events at length. Females with this type of hand love to entertain, are often good cooks, and can also be arbiters of justice without rancor.

Church is the natural extension of the sociable attitudes expressed by round-palmed people, and they respond to a spiritual cause. They tend to share resources and, if not careful, later in life this will be to their detriment. In general, round-handers can become too trusting and spread themselves too thin in their careers or in pursuing personal interests.

These people also have an ability for seeing into people, things, and conditions. They are most likely to be psychically gifted. They are what I call "keyed in." They act upon their intuitions, and this gift helps them to arrive at their desired goals. *Imagination* is the key word for the round palm; these folks can, and do, use their imaginations. Most often they are also sociable, pleasant, cause-oriented, and have many friends.

On the other side of the coin, the round-hander can be aggressive, strong-willed, and stubborn. Nor are they the pioneers of the universe. Despite their imaginations, they do not always adjust easily to change. They are also capable of becoming vindictive if too involved in a cause. One trait that must be compensated for is their inability to keep to a timetable. Time always seems to be their enemy.

Round-palmed people, in fact, have many of the qualities of the psychic-palmed person without the lack of energy, and with more practicality.

The Psychic Palm

The psychic palm is long and thin—the sort of hand people call an "artist's" hand. (Fingers will tend to be pointed or elliptical, and probably thin or delicate.) The palm will be straighter than the round or spatulate palms, but not as wide as the square. This type of palm is usually thin in comparison to the square palm, which is usually thick. Remember that the true psychic palm is quite rare.

The intuitive hand, dreamer's hand, or psychic hand is the hand of fantasy. People with such hands live in a perpetual fantasy world. They lack energy and motivation to carry through (but they're not sick!). Surprisingly, it does not necessarily indicate true *psychic* abilities the way the round palm does. True to definition, the psychic hand's owner is intuitive and can dream up great ideas. He or she does, however, tend to live in a perpetual dream and cannot implement these ideas. The psychic-handed person does not truly understand the need for people to be overproductive in their work or play. He is not sympathetic toward people who are organizers, or those who seek order and method in their lives. The psychic-hander is witty, intelligent, gifted in several areas—primarily in the creative world of arts. If trained early in life, the psychic-hander can also succeed in the writing field.

The psychic-handed person is known for his or her emotional reactions. These persons have many-faceted personalities, although they may not recognize it. People with psychic hands can be irritable, touchy, even apathetic, and yet express a level-headedness that is often surprising. They can change their moods very quickly. In a short period of time, you may see them exhibit playfulness, enthusiasm, or even shyness in large groups.

This hand indicates a person who can be totally unselfish toward those he loves. The person with a psychic hand sometimes will champion causes but may not actively engage in protest or physical responses. If this type of hand is found in a male, it is usually a signal to the reader that the man may have ambiguous sexual preferences. If found on a female, this hand reflects the epitome of the feminine side of nature. This person can be very wearing but is worth the effort. Psychic-handers are also known as charmers.

The psychic-hander often has low energy and must be careful to pace him- or herself. The overall palm will give more specific health information, but generally a person with this type of hand has a very hard time coping in adverse conditions. This hand can also be known as a chemically dependent hand! Anything not containing "natural" ingredients can cause a number of health-related problems in these people—the teeth, neck, and stomach seem to be most troublesome areas.

Family ties are important to the psychic-handed person, as they have fanatical loyalty, sometimes not seeing these family members as they really are. Like round-handers, psychic-handed people are sometimes overly protective of a spouse, children, or parents, to the detriment of these persons. Education is very important to psychic-handers. They want educational opportunities for their family and will strive hard to provide it—they can be very determined in this area.

As an employee, this type of person will have great insights into what is happening but doesn't do well in most rigid structures. They, more than people with any of the other hand shapes, must have freedom, or they become depressed and consequently will job-hop. Since they have an expressionistic personality, they tend to have a very hard time settling into a work routine, but once there and involved, they do excel. Money is not as important to them as it is to others, so salary is not an effective motivation. Achievement and freedom are the way to motivate these folks.

The psychic-handed person is most interested in the things in life that are not easily defined, such as the occult. They are quick study artists in many areas of life: books, religion (as an intellectual study), sculpture, and art of any kind. They do well in the media as anchorpeople, producers, or directors—any well-defined roles.

In his personal religious concepts, the psychic-hander believes in the universal church more than structured worship services. You can safely state that this person sees all religion as good and as one. Please note again that this hand is *extremely* rare. And while most psychic-palmed people don't cope well, there are always exceptions.

The Spatulate Palm

The spatulate palm is oblong, noticeably wider at *either* the top or bottom than it is at the other end.

The spatulate hand is the adventurer's hand, the hand of the pioneer. Owners of these hands like a challenge and tend to volunteer for most of the different, difficult, or dangerous enterprises in our world. Spatulate-handers need lots of exercise. The spatulate hand is the hand of the test pilot, the race-car driver, the climber of the World Trade Center, the John Wayne types. The person with such a hand will feel that it is his natural right to try all things that interest him, and may even climb Mount Everest because "it's there"! Nothing will surprise this type of person, and he tends to feel that he can overcome all things if he only tries—he usually does. Since he is guided by his emotional impulses, if he thinks of something, he will attempt it.

These people like to build, inspect, and restore things to their original order. Yet they tend to be more scattered with personal or material possessions. They leave their things everywhere. A person with this type of hand (male or female) tends to clutter his room and his life. He never seems to throw away papers or objects that are valuable to him. This is one person who resents and resists cleanup attempts by others yet can seemingly find any needed information or papers.

This type of person doesn't think about his decisions or the consequences. Everything has to be done quickly, for if it takes too long, he feels he is missing out on life. If dissatisfied with conditions in his life, the spatulate-palmed person will start to look for other opportunities. *If* spatulate-palmed people achieve the needed education, they make good attorneys, soldiers of a special type (Green Beret), or writers of short stories.

As a designer, artisan, or explorer, the spatulate-hander serves humanity by getting things done. He is a temperamental person, given to fits of verbalism that border on the ludicrous—threats, but not much action. He loves life to the fullest, enlivens all that is around him, works hard and plays hard till the end of his life.

THE FORMATION OF THE HANDS
Thick or Thin

Now that you have read about the palm shapes, you may be learning already how easy it is to miss clues if you don't look closely. The next clue is simple, quick, and often requires little or no communication with the person you are reading. It is the thickness or thinness of the hand/palm. This thickness or thinness directly relates to energy and its use and dispensation, and has nothing to do with dieting.

You may find yourself confused if you see a hand that looks to be neither thin nor thick, but kind of medium. What now? Well, there is a method of determining what is thick or thin. You can check by asking the owner to stretch out his hand, palm facing you with all fingers extended. If you see distinct tendons from the upper palms to the fingers, then the palms are thin. A thin palm will feel less substantial, more frail and slight. If these tendons don't appear on all fingers but do on the majority, then the palm is considered thin; otherwise the palm is thick.

Determining the thickness or thinness of the palm/hand includes a *sub*clue of firmness or softness. This extra clue is important in deciding whether or not the positive traits are reinforced. A thick hand that feels soft and squishy indicates a distraction for the natural energy flows or physical stamina. If the hand feels firm and hard, then the opposite is true. Energy and physical stamina, along with activity, will be strong.

Here's an example: You shake someone's hand, and as you grasp the hand firmly, you immediately notice the thickness or thinness. You might even be able to tell the hand shape. If you feel as if you have just shaken hands with a ham hock, the person has a thick hand. If on the other hand, you feel as if you have just shaken hands with a limp washcloth—the person has a thin hand.

If someone grasps your hand firmly and you feel a strong sense of power flowing—even though the person has *not* tried to wrench your hand off, these are thick hands. Put another way, you may equate thickness with substance, solidity, or firmness. The thick hand will feel and look meatier to you.

As with palm shapes, there is room for interpretation. There are degrees of thickness and thinness. The more palms you examine, the easier it will be to determine.

The Thick Palm

The most easily spotted palm is the thick one. You can see and estimate the thickness without touching. The first clue to re- member about the thick palm is its owner will possess energy or physical stamina that is average to excellent, depending upon thickness of the hand. If you touch the hand and it feels very thick, then you'll know that the energy is more abundant. Either way, the thick-palmed person is constantly active, on the move, and reacts immediately to what is said, done, or felt.

The Thin Palm

The thin palm is the sensitive or mental hand, the hand of a person who is refined in thoughts. The person with a thin hand is generally known as a thinker, and is not quick to respond in actions. People with thin hands do, however, possess inquiring minds. They are not usually physical in their natures. Be sure you include thin-handed people as dinner guests; they are witty and entertaining.

If you are examining any hand and it feels limp or extra soft and spongy, or like the person has no bones in the center of his palms, it indicates a laziness or lack of ability to adjust to one's life. If, on the other hand, it feels firm and hard, then this person has learned to control energy and stamina, along with a balanced style of physical activity.

Hollows and Depressions

Surely you jest! A palm with hollows or depressions. Where would you find that? Well, look at your palms and see if there is a little scooped-out place in the center of the palm area. A hollow is a slight scoop; a depression is more exaggerated. If you have one, great! If you don't have the hollow or depression, great! It is just another little tidbit of information that is useful in assessing the personality of the palm owner.

Palms that have a pronounced depression indicate that this person will react to all of life's events on a very personal level. These owners have good perceptual ability but have a hard time learning to adjust in the environment.

If the owner of the palm has just a slight hollow, it indicates that this person has learned to adjust more easily and to use his natural perception in relating to his world.

People with a hollow or depression make excellent lecturers, teachers, and researchers, and they are also involved in humanitarian efforts. They need to learn to conserve energy and when to use their energies.

Normally you don't find an extra deep hollow or depression in the firm or hard hand. However, if you do, you are looking at a person who has had a harder time in adjusting to his or her life. If in the firm hand you see a slight depression or hollow, then it indicates one who has tempered his actions and cultivated his perceptual ability. These people make good executives, organizers, corporate leaders, or bosses. Remember that thickness, thinness, softness, and firmness all relate to the energy levels of the real person or the natural person. People must conserve energy in order to achieve goals.

Skin Texture

Skin texture is another one of the *sub*clues that give you insight. This is especially useful at parties or anywhere else you must make instant judgments from a handshake. The skin texture is useful for determining an individual's emotion responses and his or her degree of sensitivity.

There are three types of skin textures: fine, medium, and coarse. If you are not sure of the type, there is a good rule of thumb to determine skin textures; look at and touch the *back* of the palm. It is the best and the easiest location to check for skin textures.

Fine Skin

Fine skin has a delicate appearance, and the pores will not be seen easily on the back of the hand. People with fine skin are sensitive, respond quickly, and remember life's experiences for a long time. Fine-skinned persons are not physically oriented and prefer the indoors to the outdoors.

Medium Skin

Medium skin is the most common skin type. The appearance of medium skin is smooth but less delicate-looking than that of the fine-skinned person, and has many more pores visible. Medium-skinned persons tend to respond to life in a more balanced way. They enjoy both the indoors and the outdoors along with balanced physical activities.

Coarse Skin

The coarse skin type has the appearance of the ruddy, and is sometimes rough to the touch. The coarse-skinned person is energetic and not easily swayed by the opinions of others. The pores are numerous and easily seen. A person with this skin type is not outwardly emotional, nor does he like heavily structured work. He craves more freedom than people with either of the other skin textures.

In checking for health information, skin textures are just another way of gaining information. If the skin feels dry and the owner is only twenty, this person has a poor diet and perhaps a circulatory condition. If the same conditions apply but the owner is obviously much older, then diet is probably all right but fluid intake is questionable. Such a person may need to drink more water daily. If the skin feels supple, neither too dry nor oily, then it indicates a balanced diet in any age group. If the skin feels oily, and you know that lotion has not been applied, it indicates a person with overeating problems and/or glandular conditions.

Remember to judge the skin textures in connection with the subject's age group. Leathery or old-looking skin in young to middle-aged persons is indicative of stress, strains, forced adjustments, and emotional uncertainties.

On the inside palm areas, the skin texture should match the skin texture on the back of the hand. If it does not match, this is a signal for the reader to look further for health information within the palm area.

Skin Color

The color of the skin is important not only as a profile for physical information and psychological insights, but for sexual information as well. These sexual insights can be fun and informative.

The colors on the inside of the hand range from an intense red to a very pale white. Light-skinned people will have a color range that goes from white to pale pink to intense red. In darker-skinned people, you must look at the actual lines within the palm to get the same information.

Dark Red or Intense Rose

A palm that is dark red and intense, with even color coverages on both the back and insides, indicates a person who can be very aggressive in his reactions to life. He is emotional and, under some conditions, tends to be hostile in his reactions. If the palm color ranges from rosy pink to very dark red, and the hand is not sun blistered, then you are seeing an intense amount of unleashed passion. In pure sexual terms, it indicates a profile of high sexual activity or, at least, someone who would like to indulge in frequent sexual activity.

This very red to intense rose color also implies abuse of the body. These people don't take time for good health practices and will continually push their bodies to the limit. Sometimes it seems as if these people get by on sheer energy.

Remember: The more pronounced the palm clue, the more pronounced the characteristic.

Pinkish

If the skin tones are neither overly pink nor death white, then you are looking at a person who has good balance in terms of health. Such a person is outgoing and empathizes with others. The energy seems to be consistent, and while the passion on the sexual level is not extreme, it can be sustained.

Pale

If the skin tones are very pale to death white, then the person has a definite tendency to be introverted or introspective. Health is delicately balanced, and energy is generally low to poor. Sexual expression can be intense, but passion is not sustained well. The sex drive of such a person is low at best.

Spotty

Sometimes you will find a person whose palm color appears to be spotty or mottled. This indicates that energy flows are spasmodic. This person's sexual drive is regular, but he can detach himself during sexual acts and gain pleasure without emotional involvement. This person is not consistent but can maintain a fulfilling emotional attachment.

When the palmist is reading for either a very young or elderly person, some of the color definitions will be changed. The lack of consistent color in the elderly indicates blood-related conditions and heart malfunctions. The sexual expression will be less frequent, but not necessarily less intense. In the young child, loss of color will indicate poor diet and overall poor health practices for which the parents, not the child, are to blame.

Now you need to remember that skin color can and does change depending upon one's life conditions. So keep in mind the age, sex, and personalities involved, along with other information gained in the palm, before making a final assessment.

Flexibility

Why would we care if a person's hands are flexible or not? Because manual flexibility is another clue to the personality's flexibility—openness to changes, new ideas, and viewpoints. Flexibility is considered to be a positive trait, and rigidity is considered a less desired trait. There are, as in every area of life, degrees of the positive or negative traits. Excess in either flexibility or rigidity will imply emotional, mental, and perhaps even physical instability.

There are several ways to check for flexibility, but the most common method is to have the person lay his palm down on a flat surface. Then ask him to lift his palm up from the wrist but not to raise the fingers. Check to make sure there isn't any strain, and judge the flexibility by how high the palm is raised. The higher a person can raise his palm, the more flexible he is. The second most common way of gauging flexibility is to have the subject lay his palm down on a flat surface and for the reader to place his index finger and thumb up against the subject's index finger and thumb. At that point the reader gently pushes to see and feel how far the finger and thumb will stretch apart. If the finger and the thumb give easily and can be moved quite far apart, then this person is flexible; if not, then the person is rigid.

You can check the fingers and fingertips for flexibility as well. Ask your subject to place his or her hands on a flat surface. Then raise his or her fingers one at a time. The farther each finger can be raised, the more flexiblity it indicates. The reader can also feel the fingers for a springlike reaction or feel. If this occurs, it indicates normal or above-average flexibility. If it feels heavy, it is probably more rigid. (There are other areas of flexibility; these will be covered under "Thumbs" later on in the chapter.)

Any finger that is flexible indicates the owner is easily excited, emotional, temperamental (in actions and thoughts), likes to travel, and is people-oriented. Any stiff or rigid fingers indicate the person's need for a secure base from which to function. He will evaluate all action and thoughts before making a decision and tends to be stubborn. He is usually conservative in the financial areas of his life.

Each finger of the palm also carries its own name and definitions, which you will combine with the information described earlier to get a more rounded picture of your subject:

Finger	Definitions
Jupiter (index) finger	Flexible: tactful and intuitive.
	Rigid: lack of sensitivity.
Saturn (middle) finger	Flexible: likes learning and experiments with ideas.
	Rigid: clings to past and thinks archaically.
Apollo (ring) finger	Flexible: art dominates, appreciates colors, and likes to see things done right.
	Rigid: impatient, particularly when things don't go well.
Mercury (little) finger	Flexible: good memory retention for facts, especially in music.
	Rigid: short-term memory only; poor long-term memory.

Spacing

The spacing between your fingers is an unconscious expression of how you feel about yourself. Another way of expressing the trait is "self-esteem." A good general rule to apply is the more space found

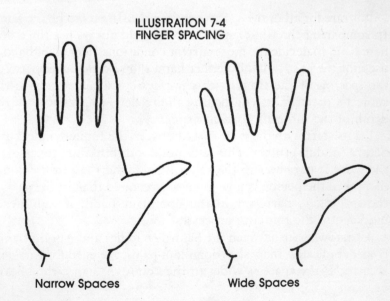

ILLUSTRATION 7-4
FINGER SPACING

Narrow Spaces   Wide Spaces

between the fingers while at rest, the more freedom of thought the person has, along with an abundance of energy. If less space is noted between the fingers, the person will feel more restricted, and generally will tend to keep emotions in check. "At rest" implies that the hand is lying palm down with the whole palm touching the surface (see Illustration 7-4).

Here is a quick guide for space interpretations:

Amount of Space	Definition
Wide spaces	Willingness to do, to go. Likes the unknown. Sure of himself.
Narrow spaces	Contentment with the way things are, cautious in actions, thought, deed. This person is especially defensive in new situations, or when in the presence of strangers. The narrow-space person requires structure to function well, is not spontaneous, but possesses a good ability to finish what has been started. This person is detail-oriented.
Average spaces	Denotes just that, average. A person with average spacing of the fingers likes new or different experiences and is not terribly hung up on security.

It is rare for all of the spaces between the fingers to be the same. In comparing the finger spaces, you should always use the dominant hand to decide the most current conditions. The other hand is used for the past traits. If neither hand shows differences between the spacing of the fingers, this implies consistency only in the subject's patterns, strengthening the reader's impressions of the depth of the subject's characteristics.

Let us start with the wide space between the Jupiter (index) and Saturn (middle) finger. This indicates good thinking processes. If the space is narrower in the subordinate hand than in the dominant, then the person is now more self-centered than in the past. If the spacing is narrower in the dominant hand, it indicates a blockage to the thinking processes.

A narrow space between the Saturn (middle) and Apollo (ring) fingers indicates, in the less dominant palm, the need for financial security. If the space is wider in the dominant hand, this means money is looking up. If the space in the dominant hand becomes narrow, the flow of money will be slowing down.

A wide space between the Apollo (ring) and Mercury (little) fingers on the dominant hand indicates independence in thinking and actions. If the space is wider in the lesser palm than in the dominant, then the person is dependent. Several fingers with narrow spaces between them indicate caution.

Curves

Just as curves help form our alphabet, they are an important indicator in palmistry, because they give us significant clues about people. These curves have been described in the theory of ancient palmistry as the "unconscious traits." This section is designed to give you easy-to-read clips of information on the personality traits revealed by these curves.

The best way to find out if a palm curves is by observing how it arches when it rests (see Illustration 7-5). If the fingers arch, you are looking at a person who is uncertain about his world or environment. If the hand lies flat, this person tends to solve problems well and is more balanced in his thinking processes. However, this person may have more distractions and may not finish projects started.

If the arched fingers turn toward the thumb side of the hand, it indicates that this person likes movement or activities at all times; this person lives at a fast pace, has a restless mind, desires achievement, and has a strong sense of purpose in life.

If the fingers arch more toward the little finger, then you are looking at a person who likes to daydream, someone with an inward-searching mind, someone with a world of curiosity.

Horizontal Finger Curves

Sometimes fingertips will curve toward one another. The fingers that are usually found with distinctive curves are the Jupiter (index), Saturn (middle), and Mercury (little) fingers (see Illustration 7-6). Here are some interesting traits or tidbits that are worth remembering.

When the Jupiter (index) finger curves toward the Saturn (middle) finger, then the person has a serious turn of mind and takes

ILLUSTRATION 7-5
HAND AT REST

Fingers and Palm Arched

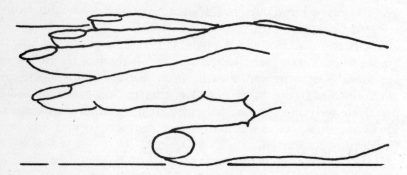

Fingers and Palm Flat

duty seriously. This type of personality will have more trouble in discussing his emotions, which can lead to confused thinking. If the Saturn (middle) finger leans toward the Jupiter finger, it will imply excessive ambitions. On the other hand, if the Saturn (middle) finger leans toward the Mercury (little) finger, the emotional nature is most likely suppressed. Sometimes the Apollo (ring) finger will lean toward the Saturn (middle) finger, which suggests serious conflict between what the subject wants to do and what he feels he should do in important areas of his life. If the finger curve is pronounced, then this person will always carry out his duties in spite of his personal feelings. This person would be the one to risk death in wartime without a second thought, not because he is a martyr or stupid, but because he has a mission. If the Mercury

ILLUSTRATION 7-6
CURVED FINGERTIPS

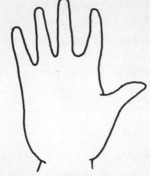

Jupiter Curving Toward Saturn

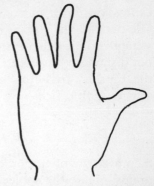

Saturn Curving Toward Jupiter

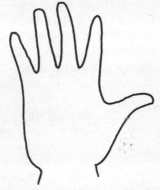

Saturn Curving Toward Apollo

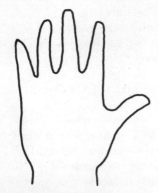

Apollo Curving Toward Saturn

Mercury Curving Toward Apollo

(little) finger should happen to curve toward the Apollo (ring) finger, then you are looking at a person with great powers of expression, great persuasive talents. This is the signature of the salesperson, the overly optimistic person, or one who adheres strongly to his belief system. These abilities, used correctly (without dishonesty), can lead to great oratorical skill—this person has the capacity to be a "great communicator"—and perhaps to achieve high office.

Vertical Finger Curves

Another type of finger leaning is easily seen, one that I call "ski jumps." Have the subject hold his palm out or place it on a flat surface. Any ski jump fingers will curve back toward the owner's face (see Illustration 7-7). If you don't see any ski jumps, have the person hold his hands straight out in the air.

Here are the ski jump finger connotations:

Finger with Ski Jump	Definition
Jupiter (index)	The Jupiter finger represents leadership. A ski jump on the Jupiter finger suggests the owner has uncertainties about his role or ability to lead, especially in the predominant area of his life. If the Jupiter finger is straight and not leaning or tilting, it denotes contentment with oneself and the ability to adapt easily.
Saturn (middle)	The Saturn finger represents values. A Saturn finger with a ski jump shows that the person is trying to clarify his values and how he will relate to the world at large. If the Saturn finger is straight, which is unusual, then you are looking at a person who knows his values are correct. He needs no improvement.
Apollo (ring)	The Apollo finger is the finger of contentment with one's environment or surroundings. A

ILLUSTRATION 7-7
"SKI JUMP" FINGER

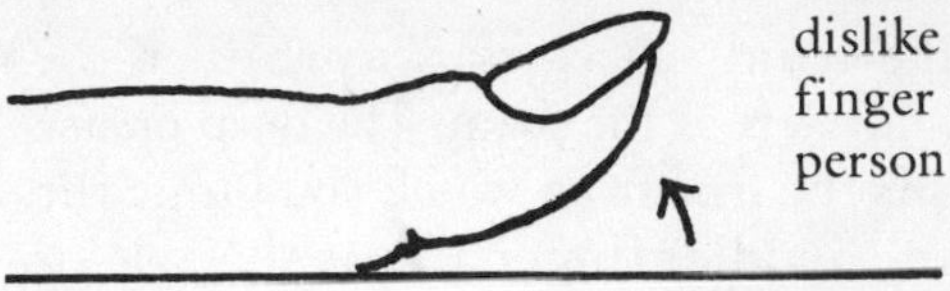

Mercury (little)

ski jump in this finger shows a person who sees his environment as restricting in some way. It also suggests a lack of discipline, a dislike of structure, or an intense dislike for routine. If the Apollo finger is straight, then this is a person who is content in his environment or surroundings. This person is happy, and has achieved a good balance between his world and his emotions. This finger carries several important imprints in the area of human relationships, specifically as regards relationships between the subject and his parents, spouse, and children. If the finger leans forward, then you know that the bonding in one of these areas has been broken or interrupted. The owner is still trying to achieve approval from loved ones by overachieving—this is one of the main reasons that the little finger is known as the "success" finger. This ski jump indicates great amounts of energy are expended to achieve goals. Fortunately, people with this trait usually overcome any obstacles placed in their way, and succeed. If, on the other hand, the Mercury finger is straight, then this person has learned to better balance desire for approval and self-worth. Success can still be achieved, but with less stress.

If all the fingers in the hand have the ski jump, this individual carries anxieties without really understanding why. If all of the fingers are straight, this person has harmony in his life, and the energy flows are good. As a whole, this is a pretty satisfied person.

Finger Set

When you are looking at the hand, check to see whether the fingers are set evenly or unevenly across the palm. The deep crease at the base of the fingers acts as the line from which you judge the set of the fingers. The Saturn (middle) finger acts as the axle or gauge by which you determine whether the other fingers are set below this crease or on line with it (see Illustration 7–8). You will find, as your experience grows, that the Jupiter (index) or Mercury (little) fingers are the ones that are usually set low in the palm. Occasionally the Saturn (middle) finger will be set low; this is considered to be rare.

Unevenly set fingers connote some measure of disharmony in a person's life. The energy flows also can be affected. Unevenly set fingers always mean that more effort is necessary to achieve success in a subject's chosen goals. People with unevenly set fingers also need to learn self-control, as they tend to be abrupt, awkward, and are usually self-conscious and defensive.

If all fingers are set evenly, then this person is balanced, with good common sense. He can usually face facts, and adapts easily to

ILLUSTRATION 7-8
FINGER SET

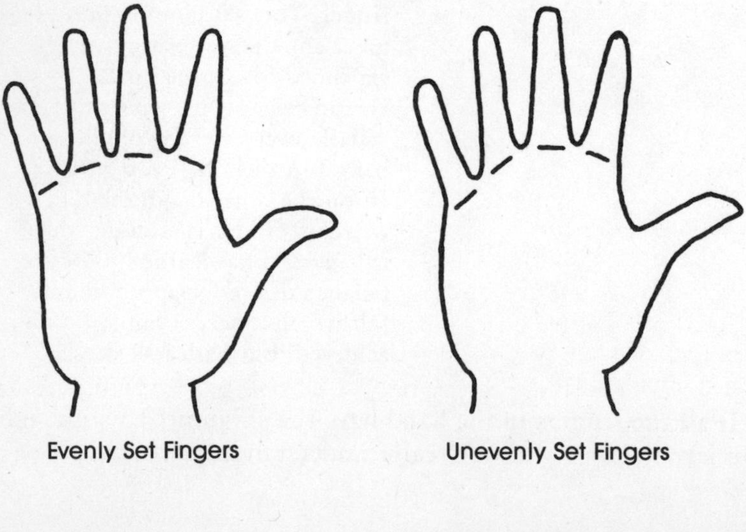

Evenly Set Fingers   Unevenly Set Fingers

changing conditions or circumstances. He radiates a sense of peace with his lifestyle and in his world.

Palms at Rest

The backs of the palms are easy to see, as people tend to use their hands in general conversation. If a person holds his fingers tightly curved while his palms are at rest, you are looking at a person who is insecure with others and who braces himself for protective purposes. If a person's fingers are loosely curled while his hand is at rest, then you are seeing an open personality who tends to communicate easily or can at least make small talk. Hands are a good barometer of feelings in this way—a person who is nervous will probably have tightly curled or clenched fists.

FINGER SHAPES

Let us now review the names of the fingers and deepen your understanding of their connotations. That will make it easier for you to learn about finger shapes, tip shapes, finger thickness, and phalanges.

Finger	Connotations
Jupiter (index)	Leadership, organization, authority.
Saturn (middle)	Teaching, use of time, attitude toward mistakes, determination, values chosen.
Apollo (ring)	Creativity, talents, inspiration, degree of realization of ideas, contentment with surroundings.
Mercury (little)	Potential for success, communications, quickness, alertness, status of relationships with parents, opposite sex, or children.

The most highly developed finger overall will be the predominant finger and its meanings will be emphasized.

Each finger can be one of four shapes: smooth, straight, crooked and twisted, or knotted (see Illustration 7-9). It is conceivable that you can have more than one type of finger shape; when seeing a mixed hand combination, you must remember to look for the predominant shape to see how the person acts in the

ILLUSTRATION 7-9
FINGER SHAPES

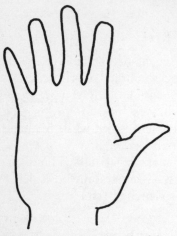

Smooth Fingers (No Knots)

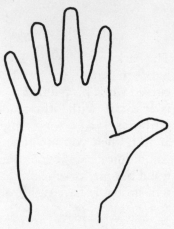

Straight Fingers (No curves)

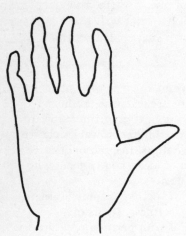

Crooked and Twisted Fingers

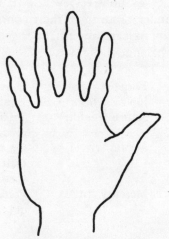

Knotty Fingers

specific area of his life reflected by that finger. Please note that the descriptions apply to the entire finger, not just the tip.

Smooth

A smooth finger seems to have no irregularities, roughness, or indentations. It seems to flow, effortlessly and gracefully, much like a model's walk. These fingers don't exhibit knots or joint distortions.

People who have smooth fingers are alert, have extra energy, and exhibit spontaneity. The instinctive side of their personality takes control and motivates them into action. They have the ability to communicate easily and can create desire in others. Sometimes they are leaders with good directional goals and can control crowds. The downside to smooth-fingered people is that they tend to take on goals and projects without having the necessary experience; they can get in over their heads.

Straight

Straight fingers form an uninterrupted line, of course, without any deviations other than the normal joint formations. These fingers are pure, plain, neat, and straight looking. If you were to feel this finger from base to tip, it would flow in a nice undeviating line.

The straight-fingered person has the aptitude for developing ideas and events in an orderly, balanced manner. He will have a smooth, easy manner of expressing himself, along with the ability to correctly use his energies, and self-confidence. His ideas will flow easily, because he has quick mental processes. On the other hand, straight-fingered people tend to be hasty, which can cause them to have to do things twice before getting them right.

Crooked and Twisted

Crooked or twisted fingers are not uniform or symmetrical. (Discount any medical conditions such as arthritis or improperly healed bones.) Unlike straight fingers, they lack regularity; they twist, bend, turn, and curve distinctively.

People with crooked or twisted fingers show a distinct reluctance to face facts, as well as the inclination to be evasive, suspicious, and unduly cautious—suggesting a lack of inner harmony. If the crooked or twisted finger is either Mercury or Jupiter, it can indicate a tendency toward gross exaggeration. When the crooked appearance is *slight* on the Mercury (little) finger, then it indicates that this person has some medical predilection. If the twisted or crooked finger is located on either Jupiter or Mercury, then it suggests that the person will have a hard time expressing his inner feelings.

Knotty

A knotty finger will have a joint or joints that protrude obviously. This bump, or bulge, is very easy to see. (Arthritis does not count.) Knots can be found on any of the finger joints on any of the fingers.

If knots are found on the first (tip) phalange, it affects the person's intellectualization. If knots are located on the second joint, it is indicative of how that person has adapted to his material world. Knotty fingers imply restrictions of thoughts. A person with knotty fingers has slower than usual reflexes and thinking processes. On the plus side, knotty-fingered people are very practical. They consider details, method, and proof before making a decision or taking action. Sometimes these knots are referred to as the "accountant's knots," as accountants are thought to like everything in its place. These traits often lead these people to success that comes relatively slowly. Material objects are extremely important to them; they use them as a gauge to show if they are on track.

Thickness

Thick fingers will give the appearance that there is little room left between them—they lie near each other and *really* occupy the space. You might even say that these fingers are packed tight. Sometimes they will even look as if they can't be squished together any more than they already are. You will not see finger tendons in these heavy, compactly placed fingers. Thick fingers usually appear rounded, with fleshy roots (at the base of the fingers), and taper toward the tips, which have fleshy pads.

A quick rule of thumb (pun intended) is that thick fingers show

After you become comfortable with the characteristics associated with finger shape and thickness, be sure to look at them in the context of individual finger meanings. A crooked Saturn (middle) finger, for instance, would suggest a person who is too distrustful to relate well to people (a poor teacher) and someone who is cautious with his time. In addition, this subject would probably work hard to avoid making errors and severely criticize others for their mistakes. He would also be likely to have confused values.

---

intuitive perception, quickness, a tendency toward sensual pleasures, and a zest for living. If the finger is very thick at the base, then you are seeing a person who likes food, or as the old saying goes, "lives to eat." This type of thickness also indicates a pressing need to be accepted by peers.

If thick fingers are thicker at the tip, it indicates that particular finger will have an important significance in that person's development. For instance, if the Jupiter (index) finger is thicker at the tip, it suggests that this person likes to be in a position of leadership.

Thin fingers, in contrast, have very little flesh. They are skin and bones, lean as a rake, thin as a rail.

Thin fingers reflect a personality of lofty idealism. People with thin fingers like the rewards of saving for a rainy day. However, you will find that thin-fingered people are hesitant to speak their minds, because they do not want to hurt other people's feelings, or because they feel a strong sense of respect. Thin-fingered people are the ones for whom the mind has dominance over the body or the physical. They have lots of likes and dislikes, food being one of their pet peeves. They insist upon cleanliness, especially with the preparation of food. They are also picky about their freedom.

Don't feel you absolutely must classify your subject's hands as thick or thin—they might be "average"!

Fingertip Shapes

The fingertips offer a means of quick personality assessment. A fast look at a client's fingertips can tell you how to approach a reading and also how to talk with the client. The reading of the fingertips requires a little practice to refine the assessments, especially the mixed hand.

As with palm shapes, there are four basic fingertip shapes: psychic or pointed, conic or rounded, square or blunt, and spatulate or flared (see Illustration 7-10). All of these tips have been assigned definite personality traits, and you will be amazed at how on target they are. Tips are to observe, so you may study them very unobtrusively. (Sneaky, aren't I?) I have gone so far as to check out news anchors while watching their telecasts. This was very interesting. It is also one of the few legal forms of voyeurism! Remember now, these descriptions only apply to the fingertips, not the nails. (Sneaky tips on nails will be covered later.) You'll notice many parallels between palm shapes and tip shapes that will make them easier to remember.

Psychic or Pointed

The psychic, or pointed, tips are associated with quickness of mind. A person with psychic tips prefers ideas to action, and usually has a tendency to choose leisure pursuits that reflect an appreciation of the aesthetically beautiful things in life. These fingertips also convey an idealistic mind set; their owners are generally guided by their first impressions in any activity, whether it be love, job, or atmosphere. They do not like structure or restrictions of freedom, either for themselves or others. Their energy tends to dissipate quickly.

Conic or Round

The person with conic, or round, fingertips uses energy quickly, but not as quickly as one with psychic tips; energy here is more consistent. People with conic tips don't like friction, yet they are more versatile than the psychic-tipped people; they are usually very capable of adapting to their environments. They, like those with psychic tips, have a good ability to perceive people's character, but they are more likely to have to balance this with physical activity. They can be consistent in their pursuits or in working toward a definite goal. People with round tips like to entertain and like to learn from those who are more knowledgeable than they. They are well motivated and prefer to work on their own without close supervision. People with round tips can also usually be classified as the "bleeding-heart liberals" in our society. They like under-

**ILLUSTRATION 7-10
FINGERTIP SHAPES**

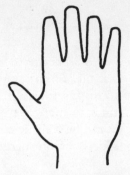

Square or Blunt Tips

Conic or Rounded Tips

Pointed or Psychic Tips

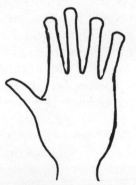

Spatulate or Flared Tips

Mixed Tips

dogs and are champion cause fighters, if they personally identify with a cause.

Square or Blunt

The possessor of square, or blunt, tips has less energy to work with than people with other tip types, and it takes him longer to start his energy flowing. This also applies to mindset; he will tend to be detail-oriented, methodical, and patient in many ways. He may also admire these qualities in others, even if he feels he cannot quite achieve them for himself. The blunt-tipped person surrounds himself with people he admires.

The actual mentality of the person with square fingertips is analytical. The square-tipped person loves math, likes theories, but wants to intellectualize and debate from both sides. Appearance is important to this person, and he likes an orderly image of himself and his lifestyle. If all the fingers are square-tipped, of course this person will consider himself to be balanced and well disciplined. Remember that these folks are realistic, conventional, conservative, and fit into all walks of life. They make excellent but unimaginative employees. They are good bosses where rules are needed or strict management is required. These folks like security and a regular paycheck. These are the *bankers* of America!

Spatulate or Flared

The spatulate, or flared, tips belong to the explorers and the doers of the world. They need physical outlets (the Jane Fonda types). Their energy levels initially are slow but, once in place, tend to be very consistently high. They strive for the unusual, and are extremely restless and impulsive. They have inquiring minds and don't accept trite answers to questions. You find a lot of these type of tips in the field of education, not only on teachers, but also on coaches or researchers. An even better example would be the Indiana Jones type of explorer. These people would rather travel than eat, though they do like to eat. Sometimes this can bring about serious health problems, as they will eat improperly.

In learning to read palms, it is also important to note that a lot of information seems to be repeated. Information in the shapes of the hands is repeated in the shapes of the fingers and in the actual fingertips. The reason for this is that all information in the palms will be reconfirmed throughout. Look for the dominant traits of the personality. In essence, you learn the parts, then you are given the *whole*. Look for reconfirmed information, but also for inconsistencies. Learn to assimilate. Prod your psychic flow!

THE FINGER PHALANGES—
THE COURIERS OF ENERGY

According to the ancient theory of palmistry, the energy or life flow of a person enters through the fingertips and is dispensed through the phalanges and to the rest of the body. This will help you grasp why the phalanges are considered so important to the overall reading of an individual. The phalanges are the "couriers" of energy.

Finger*tip* shapes help determine how life's energy enters the body, and how this energy is dispensed. In ancient palmistry, the theory was that at birth, when a baby drew his first breath, he opened his hands in a stiff way; during that first intake of breath, the energy of life entered his body through his fingertips. In today's readings many palmists tend to discard that theory, but it is helpful in dealing with the tip traits to realize that, while it has no scientific basis, it does in fact reflect psychic reality. I find it easier to understand energy flow when I remember that energy "first" enters the body through the fingers.

The phalanges of all of the fingers are divided into three sections, numbered in consecutive order. Each phalange governs a particular aspect of life.

A reading of the phalanges starts with the subordinate hand, the hand of predisposition (usually the left), beginning with the tip of Jupiter (index) finger and moving down the base. It is then carried forward to the Saturn (middle) finger, and so on (see Illustration 7-11) and on to the dominant hand. Please be aware that there is some crossover—sometimes a trait can be recorded in more than one place.

Left Jupiter

Phalange #1: The touch of the Jupiter fingertip is thought to be the most sensitive of all the fingertips. This tip represents the personal needs, is considered the healing tip (love and eternal love

ILLUSTRATION 7-11
PHALANGES

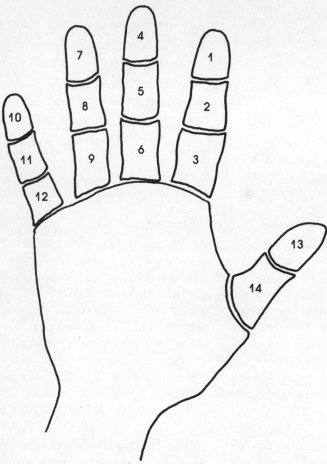

of humanity), and is called the communicator (which is fitting, since the index finger is commonly referred to as the "pointer" finger). It conveys thoughts and sensations to the mind, especially those that relate to the striving for world unity. The Jupiter finger stands for the leadership that all of us strive for, and embedded in this tip is any potential leadership ability endowed in genetic blueprinting. This phalange has many important meanings, and they are thus somewhat difficult to remember. To recap: leadership, ideas, especially lofty ones; what needs for self-understanding the person feels.

Phalange #2: The second phalange governs the social attributes of the individual. This phalange will indicate how he adapts in social situations, as well as how he will be accepted in society.

Phalange #3: The third phalange, located at the base that touches the hand, reflects the person's basic needs for love, affection, warmth, and communication (whether or not these needs have been met). It also suggests a person's sense of obligation in life.

In assimilation of information, do not forget to take into consideration the type of tip shape each finger has. Is this Jupiter fingertip a psychic, round, square, or spatulate? The shape, combined with what we have just discussed, will give you the inside scoop on how this person's thinking processes work and how he or she will react to the environment in which he or she lives.

Reading Second and Third Phalanges

In reading second and third phalanges, you must take the fingertip, as well as the finger as a whole—thickness, firmness, shape, feel, color—into account. Is the second phalange short in comparison to its tip, or is the tip the longest when compared with the other two? *Length determines predominance.* An example: the tip of the Jupiter finger is conic or round, but short by comparison to the second phalange. In this case, the second phalange is the ruler, which tells us that this person is very adaptable, especially in social circumstances. If this person is a leader, it will be more because he is popular than because of his ideas. If the reverse were true, then the mind or ideas would dominate, and you are looking at a person who has more than average leadership qualities. Remember that each section of the finger is to be valued by comparing its length to the overall length of the finger, and its qualities to the overall qualities of the finger.

Here is another example to help you assimilate the information gained thus far: the owner of a palm possesses a round palm shape, which indicates that this is a versatile person. He has primarily conic fingers, which suggest that he has consistent energy flows and is quick of thoughts and actions.

The actual tip of the Jupiter finger represents the person's personal needs, along with conceptual or mental attributes. Since the tip is conic, it enhances the natural abilities of the Jupiter tip.

The second phalange is representative of the person's ability to adapt and of his social acceptance. The overall shape of the finger thus far is smooth, without distortions of any type, so we can say that his thinking processes flow smoothly, and he is sociable, with a great ability to sway or convey information to the world at large. He does this in a style that is both sociable and direct. The color of the two phalanges is pink, suggesting that the balance between emotions and health is good.

The third phalange is thicker at the base than either of the upper two, so it does dominate. This indicates that this person's first active concern, after meeting the basic requirements of life (food, shelter), are to respond to what he feels are his obligations. This person will have a high level of desire for affection and warmth from those around him, and will feel a sense of rejection if he doesn't receive them, but he often doesn't know how to request them. Since the joint is thicker than the upper two, he needs more touching and affection from those around him, or he will feel a sense of rejection.

If the third phalange were thinner, more like the upper two phalanges, then this reading would indicate that the person is well balanced and does not fear that his needs for affection will not be met.

If the entire finger is firm to the touch, this would reinforce what has been said. However, had the overall finger been soft or spongy, this would have indicated a weakness and less control over the areas governed by the phalanges. Had this person's second rather than third phalange been particularly thick and/or long, it would have indicated a natural ability to take a lead in his social world. If smooth as well, it would have suggested good energy and an intelligent person seeking harmony in the environment.

Left Saturn

The Saturn, or middle, finger represents determination, as well as teaching and learning.

Phalange #4: The tip of the Saturn finger denotes control over how quickly this person learns to accept things in his world, and his overall ability to laugh not only at the world but at himself. If the tip is the longest phalange, the positive trait of learning and acceptance is assured, along with proper balance. If this is not the case, then look to see which phalange dominates.

Phalange #5: The second phalange of the Saturn finger governs the moral world and how the person will respond to morality in our world. If the phalange is distorted in any way, the type of distortion will determine how his moral values will dictate his actions. If the joint or phalange is knotty, then money or material possession will have more value than a good book. If the finger joint has only a small bulge, it means that its owner will tend to be practical and will value practicality in all aspects of life. This person *automatically* thinks of alternatives to a situation without any effort at all. (Note: If the second phalange is marked by a box, it is an indicator that this person feels the calling for a specific job or career and thinks of it as destiny.)

Phalange #6: The third phalange of the Saturn finger is sometimes summed up as the "inheritance joint," and it governs how this person has learned to work with what has been given to him. The ability to balance, use humor and laughter, and the degree of possessions acquired can all be found within this joint. This phalange is a good gauge of the inner health of a person, of which even he is unaware. If the phalange is pink to red, then health is balanced.

Left Apollo

The Apollo, or ring, finger as a whole represents creative inspiration, along with the ability to intellectualize, conceive, or carry through with creative impulses. The finger also carries in each of the sections the ability to laugh, to enjoy life, and to find some solitude, preferably in the out-of-doors.

Phalange #7: The tip of the Apollo finger is the mind side of the person, as it relates to art or closeness to his Creator.

Phalange #8: The second phalange represents the adaptability of the person, especially in the area of ego that needs expression. This second phalange also governs whether or not the person has his heart in his profession. Morality and religious concepts will be found here, especially if this joint is thicker than any of the others. If red and thick, then this person will be vocal with his views. Remember that the shape of the tip, color, length, and other characteristics of each phalange have to be considered for a complete summary, and that the longest phalange is the dominant one for that particular finger.

Phalange #9: Markings on the third phalange of the Apollo finger govern the material side of life as regards art and the creative world. For example, a triangle here indicates great wealth and fame brought through the use of these creative skills, whereas well-defined lines indicate a good or better-than-average potential. Other markings indicate whether the person can manage his money. This person cannot function in a nonharmonious environment—he craves peace with his fellow human beings. The outward health of the individual is also seen in this phalange. If the phalange is thin, then diet is poor; if thicker, then the diet is balanced. Remember to look at color indications, too.

Left Mercury

The Mercury (little or "pinky") finger is known as the Maker of Success. In addition to being the finger of business success, it is the finger of verbalization and communication.

Phalange #10: The pinky tip represents the skills that the owner has or will acquire, including the ability to learn and to apply knowledge. It also indicates any need to be united with the environment and the unseen elements in life. If this tip is developed, relationships with parents and spouse are balanced. If the tip is underdeveloped, the opposite applies.

Phalange #11: The second phalange of the Mercury finger governs how this person adapts to his environment and how he will express his need for approval through his social activities. The second phalange of Mercury has its own special meaning in communications: If the phalange is a little thick or has lots of vertical lines, then its owner can use silent communications with loved ones—sometimes known as telepathy. If the middle phalange is longer than either of the other two with the above marking, then you are seeing a well-developed telepathic ability, which may include some visions.

Phalange #12: The third phalange of the Mercury finger shows whether the owner will use his natural resources to the common good of humanity. As always, you must look at the entire finger to see which traits will be most pronounced. In general, if the third phalange is most developed, this person will use his skills for the common good. A well-developed twelfth phalange, as well as a well-developed Mercury finger in general, shows a need for world connection, as well as the need for physical contact—touching, hugging—in the expression of feelings.

The finger phalanges of the right hand are numbered the same way as in the left hand, but the right hand is known as the actualization of the traits and talents found in the left hand. (Reverse this for a left-handed person.) Some phalanges have the same meanings in both hands, in which case you can use the guides for the left hand for the phalanges' meanings. I will point out the ones that are different and give the new meanings so you can assimilate the information in the same way for the right hand.

Right Jupiter

Phalange #1: The Jupiter fingertip still represents the personal needs or, in this case, the actualization of personal needs. Remember to apply the other descriptions—color, shape, length, etc.—to get a more complete reading.

Phalange #2: The second phalange of the Jupiter finger represents socialization, education, and whether or not the person is a status seeker (vertical markings or thickness indicate yes). If this phalange is thicker than the other two, then the person has a practical bent, along with a socially adaptable personality. If the phalange is thinner, then the person will be more concerned with the mental realms of his social and educational goals.

Phalange #3: The third phalange of the Jupiter finger represents the degree of concern over bodily needs and the environment. Of course, if this is not a dominant phalange, it will indicate that this person is not worried about meeting his needs for food, water, and air—he assumes it will be there. If this phalange is dominant and thin, it will indicate a person who cares more about his *personal* needs than the good of the world. A dominant but thick phalange indicates a person whose concerns extend beyond himself to the good of the world—this would be the Ralph Nader type, who wants to protect everyone's resources.

Right Saturn

Phalange #4: The Saturn (middle) fingertip on the right hand has a different meaning than the one on the left: it represents the humanitarian need for world justice. If this tip is square or spatulate, this person will be active in pursuing his beliefs in law and order. If the tip is psychic, then the person is less active and more contemplative as regards justice. When looking at this tip, it is important to note whether the person's hand is balanced in other areas. If so, you could safely assume that this person will most likely be involved in active pursuits of legal causes, perhaps as a police officer or lawyer.

Phalange #5: The second phalange of the Saturn finger shows in which direction the subject has been molded by his social culture. If the phalange is more thin that thick, a traditional background is indicated. If thick rather than thin, this indicates a

---

By now you are probably getting a good idea of the intricate layers of palmistry. In reading a phalange, you must also simultaneously read markings (which will be covered later), color, what the nearby phalanges indicate, what the tip shape means, and so on. Work on getting each layer down pat, then add new ones.

---

more open attitude to new ideas, or the ability to adapt to new roles, such as fatherhood or motherhood. It can also indicate concern with brother or sister roles. The family ties in this phalange, either way, are very strong.

Phalange #6: The third phalange of the Saturn finger is where you find how this person reacts to his material world, especially his possessions. If the phalange is thicker, then the person feels the need for ownership of home, business, stocks and bonds, or savings of some sort. If the phalange is thinner, then the person is more concerned with just home or home environments. Here again, it is important for you to decide which phalange is the dominant one and to apply the other rules discussed previously.

Right Apollo

Phalange #7: The left Apollo fingertip's general definition applies here, but includes the sense of beauty. This tip governs beauty in all lifestyles. If very well developed and thick, it will rule how its

Phalange Cheat Sheet

Phalange	Hand of Destiny and Talent	Hand of Choice
1	Healing love, leadership, lofty ideas, self-understanding.	Same.
2	Social adaptability and acceptance.	Status.
3	Need for love, communication, obligation.	Universal environment.
4	Acceptance of one's life.	World justice.
5	Morality, values.	How molded by social culture.
6	Use of what is given, humor.	Security of money or possessions.
7	Closeness to Creator.	Need for beauty.
8	Egotism, world morality.	Hobbies.
9	Creativity and related material resources.	Need for beauty.
10	Skills.	Truth versus tact.
11	Choice of activities, telepathy.	Class distinctions.
12	Universal consciousness, physical touch.	Know-it-all regarding economics.

owner lives in his world; if an object is not pretty, then the owner of this tip would not have it, regardless of whether it is needed or not.

Phalange #8: The middle phalange of the Apollo finger represents hobbies. The phalange also governs social graces; this phalange is thus indicative of volunteer work. If the phalange is thick, the subject will see these activities as a duty or obligation. If the phalange is thin and longer, then the activity is performed for specific reasons or goals, rather than out of good heart (martyr syndrome).

Phalange #9: The third phalange of the Apollo finger is a reemphasis of the first, in that it governs the material world and how one will use his possessions. If the phalange is thick, then beauty in the home or in personal possessions will dominate. For example, a person with a thick phalange will surround himself with beauty, such as pretty artwork. A person with a thinner phalange, on the other hand, will prefer luxury. This person would value expensive artwork over artwork of generally acknowledged beauty. (If the middle phalange is longer, coupled with a thinner third phalange, then luxury to this person could mean having a maid.)

Right Mercury

The Mercury, or little, finger on the right hand governs the need for expression.

Phalange #10: The tip signifies that the specific need is for truth. If the tip tends toward thickness, then this person values truth at all costs; tact is not important to him. If the phalange tip is thinner, more tact in expression of truth will be present.

Phalange #11: The middle phalange of the Mercury finger is symbolic of how one feels about class distinction and prejudices within society. If the phalange is longer, class will be important to the individual. If the phalange is shorter, class has less importance. This phalange is one of the sections within the hand that tells about marriage. If the phalange is longer and thicker, then you are seeing a person whose feelings on marriage carry strong social conditions regarding class or prejudice, and whose conditions must be met or marriage is forgone. If the phalange is shorter and thinner, then this will not be a concern.

Phalange #12: The third phalange of the Mercury finger is similar to that on the left hand, with the differences being that if this phalange is thick, the owner will be much more likely to tell everyone else how to go about achieving material wealth (even if he himself is not successful!) in business or personal life. If the phalange is thinner, then this person will tend to be smug—he'll think the same things as the thick-phalanged person but not share them.

THE MASTERS OF THE HANDS: THE THUMBS

I like to think of the thumbs as the masters of the hands, because they are reservoirs for the energy of the body. Remember the ancient theory of how energy enters the body at birth (a child is born; it stretches out his hands; life energy enters at the tip and is dispensed downward through the palms). The thumbs become the holding tank, if you will, for the excess energy. The excess energy is then directed toward the mind.

The thumb represents the mental faculties and energy of the body. The type of thumb the individual has determines the kind of energy flows directed to the mind. The more energy stored in the thumb, the more willpower and determination can be carried out by the individual in his life, especially in times of need or in decision making. In terms of the moral or ethical codes of life, the blueprint is determined at the time the energy is transferred at birth. It's thought to be held in storage in the area of the Mount of Venus, which is also the third phalange of the thumb (see Illustration 7-12). The strength of this joint is important, as it indicates the emotional energy that the individual will have for living his life and how well he can detach himself emotionally in order to carry through decisions.

One reason that the thumbs are considered so important in the overall reading of the palm is that they can either reaffirm or negate traits seen elsewhere in the hand. This insight allows the reader to adjust a judgment about an individual based on his or her strength of will. The shapes and length of the thumbs can not only emphasize or deemphasize traits or talents, but are also indicative of how powerful a person's personality can be.

As a reader, you need to look at the thumb to determine your subject's abilities to be consistent and purposeful. The thumbs also indicate how he feels about himself as a person, and how well he can apply himself to goals, desires, beliefs, and convictions and set his ethical codes for living.

Although the thumb appears to have only two phalanges, in fact it has three. The tip is number 1, the joint (from the first knuckle to the end of the second knuckle) is number 2, and the Mount of Venus is number 3. The third section encompasses the Mount of Venus and ends at the wrist. The Mount of Venus is where the energy is stored for use throughout life.

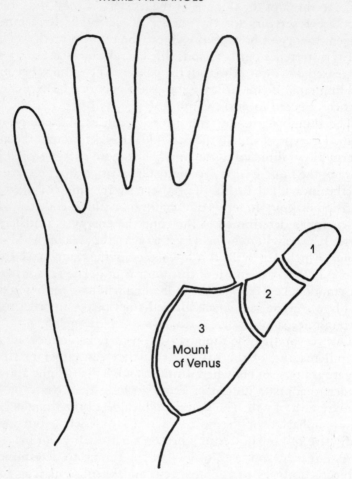

ILLUSTRATION 7-12
THUMB PHALANGES

3
Mount
of Venus

As in the other fingers, the tip, or first joint, is known for will, decision making, and the mental processes involved therein. The second joint is logic, discernment, and reasoning—the ability to relate one type of information to another. The third section refers to the physical sensations and ethical codes. If the first and second phalanges are equal in length, then you have a balance between will, logic, mental energy, and reason.

When looking at the thumb, as with the other fingers, you must remember that the length and shape determine the predominant traits assigned to that section. Don't forget to check for thickness and color as well.

Thumb Set

The thumb set in relationship to the hand is an immediate indicator of how that person will react to his world. We have discussed the even or uneven set for fingers. When first looking at the thumbs, decide whether the thumbs are set near the index (Jupiter) fingers. If this is the case, it will betray desire for independence or movement, a tendency to become selfish, perhaps a wishy-washiness in convictions, as well as likelihood to yield under pressure.

If the thumb set is low (more toward the wrist), it tells the reader that this person loves liberty, hates routines, is probably a champion of the underdogs of the world. Low-set thumbs indicate a crusader. Such a person is liberal in thoughts and actions, and is most often too generous by nature.

Now remember, these are only a few of the first clues you may see when looking at a person's thumbs; these insights will also be verified elsewhere in the palm or in the other fingers. Remember as well that all characteristics apply in varying degrees—based on the strength of that particular marking or trait in the palm, as well as other clues found in the hand.

The Long and Short of It

Thumb length relative to the index finger is probably the second most important thing for the reader to assess in evaluation of the palms. Let the thumb rest beside the hand. If the tip of the thumb reaches halfway up to the bottom joint of the index finger, it is average, which indicates balance. An extra-long thumb will reach all the way up to the crease line that divides the second and third phalanges. Extra-short thumbs just reach the bottom of the index finger itself (see Illustration 7-13).

Long thumbs reflect good energy, as well as the ability to calculate and to reason. They also suggest a person who is organized and can attain goals. They show patience, initiative, and clarity of thought. If the thumb is extra long, these positive traits become negative, because they reflect a person who will go to any length to attain desires or goals without consideration of others,

ILLUSTRATION 7-13
THUMB LENGTH

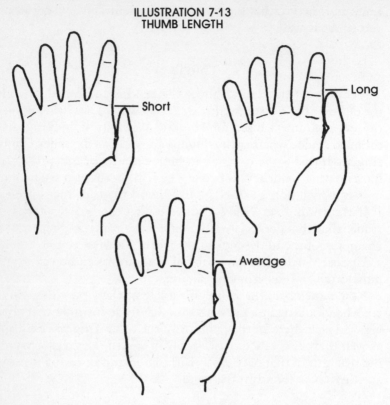

and who may become a tyrant. In either case, in people with long thumbs, self-will is dominant. Most people with long thumbs are found in leadership roles in business, science, or politics. Their greatest desire is to attain distinction.

People with short thumbs follow their hearts. They also tend to take the path of least resistance and to imitate others. Their feelings about things, people, places, and conditions are out of their control. Arguments that employ logic are lost on these compassionate people. A person with a short thumb needs more encouragement to achieve and is always aware that positive thinking is a must. He can, and probably has, achieved, but he must work twice as hard in order to do so. Short-thumbed individuals are good employees—they will easily follow directions—but will not take the initiative.

You can measure the length of each phalange in the thumb visually. The first phalange starts at the tip and goes to the first knuckle. The second starts at the first knuckle and goes to the second knuckle. The third starts at the second knuckle and goes to the wrist (base of the Mount of Venus).

If the first phalange is longer than the second phalange, it indicates a person who wants his way all the time and is determined to get it. The owner may or may not be able or willing to use reason or logic (or both), and will often make decisions based on gut-level feelings, ignoring obvious facts.

If the second phalange is longer than the first, you are looking at a person who wants to achieve perfection. This person likes to reason things out and know the logic behind the reasons.

If the first and second phalange are equal in length, you are looking at a balanced individual who has the will and organizational ability to attain goals by the balanced use of logic, feelings, and energy.

The third phalange, located within the Mount of Venus, is the storehouse of the physical (and mental) energy that will carry us through life. Here are your energy reservoirs—your sex drives, too. Just as the thumb acts as a lever for the palm, it is also your energy level; it balances your mind and body and the energy level required for them to function. If you lose your thumb, you lose more than the ability to grasp objects—you lose your life's energy flows. Energy will always be a problem for you.

To ascertain the amount of energy stored, we use color as a guide. If the color is strong and very pinkish, energy is abundant. If the mount is pale, only slightly pinkish, or blotted, our reserves of energy are not equal to our needs, and care must be taken to conserve energy whenever possible. The color here is also a good indicator of sexual drives. The more even the color, and stronger the pink, the stronger the sexual drive. The lighter the color, the less interest exhibited. If the mount is very fleshy, the more intense that person is in his sexual drives. If the mounts are flat or thin-looking, it is "off again, on again Charlie"—take it or leave it. The passion is just as intense, however; the stamina may just not be there. Bluish coloring may indicate poor circulation, while a yellowish color may indicate jaundice. This may or may not have anything to do with sexual drive, although it may affect performance.

Thumb Thickness

Thick thumbs indicate a person who is forceful and determined to reach goals. A thumb that is thin overall indicates a lively, tactful person who likes to travel and loves people.

Look at both phalanges. If the tip is thick, it just reinforces stubbornness; if the second phalange is also thick, the person does not adapt to changes of mind or opinions. If the thumb tip is thin, this person is naturally tactful but will expend energy quickly. If the second phalange is thin, it indicates a person who has an open mind and one who likes to learn for the sake of learning, a good Trivial Pursuit player. If you decide that a person has a thick tip but not really a thick second phalange, this person embodies a balance of the traits already described.

Thumb Shapes

Thumbs may be straight, curved, or clubbed (see Illustration 7-14). A straight thumb denotes a firm-willed, strong individual, who is not adaptable. This person makes a reliable partner or friend, a good listener, and shows persistence in achieving goals. These thumbs are found on counselors, doctors, and ministers.

A curved thumb that curves to either side or away from the palm denotes impulsiveness, adaptability, a generous nature, and responsiveness to suggestions. This person sounds wonderful, but has a tendency to procrastinate and not finish what is started unless reminded. A person with a curved thumb is very social-minded and loves to entertain.

The clubbed thumb, once seen, is easily remembered. In ancient palmistry, it was thought to be the sign of the assassin or criminal. Today we believe that if the thumb is not passed down through genetics, it is a sign that the owner can be brutal either in word or deed.

The last of the shapes is the waisted thumb. It is also easy to recognize, as it looks like an hourglass figure. It is always curved. This type of shape indicates a person with natural tactfulness, evasiveness, and gentleness, one who is an adaptable mixer in social and business activities. Yet this person has a pronounced trait for caution in all areas of life. In some palmistry circles, the waisted thumb is held in esteem and classified as exceptional. This

ILLUSTRATION 7-14
THUMB SHAPES

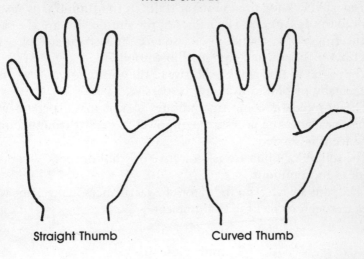

Straight Thumb   Curved Thumb

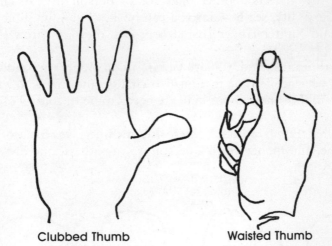

Clubbed Thumb   Waisted Thumb

denotes originality, and the reader seeing this thumb will know to give a reading with all of the potential of the subject magnified. The negative side may manifest itself as difficulty in decision making. Waisted-thumb types have trouble choosing one course in life—to them the choices may seem unlimited.

Thumb Tip Shapes

You must check for predominant traits in the thumb tips just as you did in the fingers. The names of the thumb tips are the same as the fingertips: round, conic, square, and spatulate, plus the addition of the waisted tip (see Illustration 7-15).

The round thumb tip is indicative of the ability to know when to be mentally or physically active or passive.

The pointed or conic tip indicates a diplomatic person who sometimes lacks the necessary willpower to carry through a project once it is started.

The square or blunt tip is indicative of stubbornness, a rigidity in ideas and opinions.

The spatulate tip is an indicator of a tactile personality; one who likes to touch or feel the environment.

Thumb Flexibility

Thumb flexibility is another indicator of personality. To check thumb flexibility, see how far you can push apart your subject's thumb and Jupiter finger (using only one of your hands); see Illustration 7-16.

If the thumb is rigid, you are looking at a conservative individual, one who needs time to adjust to change and one who has a definite stubbornness about him. He needs to be in control of the budget.

A flexible thumb indicates generosity, one who gives freely of his love, time, and money. Such a person is sympathetic and loves to

ILLUSTRATION 7-15
THUMB TIP SHAPES

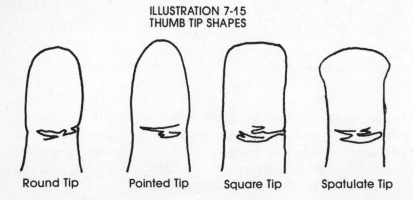

Round Tip   Pointed Tip   Square Tip   Spatulate Tip

ILLUSTRATION 7-16
THUMB FLEXIBILITY

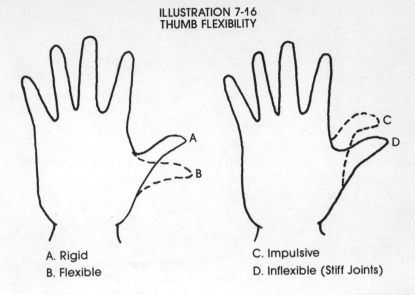

A. Rigid
B. Flexible

C. Impulsive
D. Inflexible (Stiff Joints)

entertain. On the negative side, he can be just plain lazy. People tend to indulge him in his youth. He is always a willing spender of his money.

Rule of Thumb

Excuse me for being indelicate, but if you are interested in a certain portion of the male anatomy, then look at the thumb shape and tip. Believe it or not, the corresponding body part will mirror the thumb shape.

FINGERNAILS: THE DOCTORS OF THE HANDS

Have you ever had a doctor ask you to hold out your hands? Did he or she check your feet? The doctor was checking your nails for color, shape, texture (thick or thin), spots, or ridges. In palmistry, too, the nails have been assigned certain medical correlations. Each finger is related to a part of the body; for example, the thumb, the source of energy, is related to the cerebral faculties. The liver is related to the Jupiter (index) finger. The Saturn (middle) finger is assigned to the skeleton, the Apollo (ring) finger is assigned to the blood and heart systems, and the Mercury (little) finger to the nervous system. The nail on a particular finger tells you how the related body system is doing.

Nails change quickly and are completely transformed about every two and a half months. The thumbnail requires 140 days to renew itself, the index fingernail requires 124 days, the middle fingernail requires 118 (as does the nail of the ring finger), and the nail on Mercury requires only 110. This can be very helpful in assessing the onset and length of illness. When you have a sudden illness, the nails stop growing. Spots, flecks, coloring, fluting, thickness, and thinness can all indicate illness. In the psychological areas, soft or hard nails (or, more obviously, bitten nails) indicate a person's mental state.

Nail Shapes

It is the shape and placement of the nails that give us the clues to mental health, character, and temperament (see Illustration 7-17). If a person's nails are filed, be sure to ask that person about the nails' natural growth. Be sure to look at each nail as it relates to each particular finger, especially if nail shapes differ. A person with mostly oval nails who has a spatulate Mercury nail, for example, would be an energetic, creative communicator.

Oval Nails

The oval nail is the most common nail type, and indicates a balanced person generally. Although he needs conformity in new circumstances or in new environments, this person tends to have the ability to enjoy himself and to adapt. A small oval or conic nail is indicative of one who thinks with clarity and is decisive in taking a stand regarding the issues the particular finger represents. If the oval nail is medium to rather large, it indicates a person who is broad-minded and idealistic.

Square Nails

People with many square nails crave order. These people are the implementors in our world—they need systems for living. They are rational in their environment and make good housekeepers, wood-

ILLUSTRATION 7-17
NAIL SHAPES AND PLACEMENT

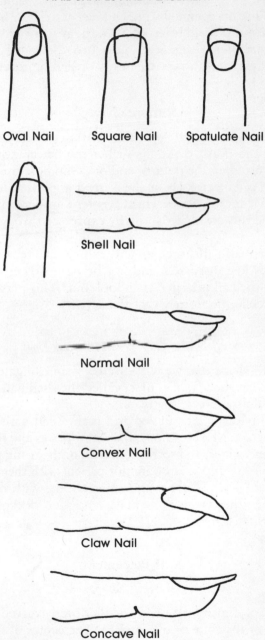

Oval Nail   Square Nail   Spatulate Nail

Shell Nail

Normal Nail

Convex Nail

Claw Nail

Concave Nail

workers, or anything that requires the use of their hands. If the nail is small, then it will lessen the qualities just named, and this person will use his common sense and resort to sheer hard work to achieve goals. If the nail is larger, then the reader can surmise that this is a careful person; neat, tidy, broad-minded, sincere in beliefs, and extremely analytical in his or her approach to life.

Spatulate Nails

A person who has mostly spatulate nails is one who questions everything and nearly drove his or her mother crazy. This is the sign of the explorer, the restless, and one who possesses a depth of insight that can be rare. He or she is great at parties, loves to talk, and is knowledgeable about world events. This person is also very creative, and this creativity is usually expressed through a form of art.

If he has small nails, then he will exhibit quieter tendencies of the qualities just discussed, and not be quite so verbal in social settings. If the nail is larger, then look out! This person's energy will be excessive no matter what the activity.

Shell Nails—The Combination Nail

The last nail shape that we will discuss is an elongated oval that looks like a shell and is, of course, called the shell nail. It can also be described as a reverse spatulate.

This nail is easily recognized and many shell nails on a hand indicate a person who is curious, likes new places and things, likes intellectual activities, and seems to have a high-strung personality. These people are doers. They are not patient with themselves, and they are sometimes irritable and quarrelsome with others. This nail looks neither large nor small, and size doesn't alter the qualities assigned to it.

Nail Placement

Normal Shape

The normal placement of a nail is neither overly curved toward the fleshy part of the finger nor clawlike. The center of the nail lies

Don't forget to look at nail shapes and characteristics in contrast with the specific finger on which it appears.

---

flat on the surface of the finger. This indicates that body health is in balance.

Convex Shape

A convex nail looks like it has cotton under the center part of the nail. The sides curve slightly toward the inside edge of the finger. This denotes a tendency toward upper respiratory conditions.

Claw Shape

Claw-shaped nails are usually exaggerated in appearance—they look like bird claws. In China, this was a symbol of rulers—emperors, for example. This is a sure sign of ego and of one who *likes* to rule. If the nail is extra long and thick, it indicates kidney or bladder problems.

Concave Shape

This nail placement shape is not commonly found. In a concave shape, the sides of the nails tend to turn outward. It indicates poor energy and lack of active interests, and is also associated with poor diet, a metabolism that is out of kilter, and lack of vitamins in the body.

Nail Texture

Nail texture is important in determining your subject's characteristics and health.

- Flat, thin nails on any of the fingers indicates nervous energy; this person should be encouraged to get proper rest and maintain a good diet.
- Nails that are hard to the touch and thick are a good signal that the person lacks true compassion.

- Hard, thin nails are symbols of an irritable personality and someone who is high-strung.
- Brittle and thick nails are symbols of an individual who can absorb stress readily but is very opinionated.
- Brittle and thin nails indicate a person who has very definite opinions that won't stand up under scrutiny. This person has a tendency toward headaches.
- Nails bitten to the quick indicate a person who has very little emotional control but a vivid imagination. These folks are more active mentally than physically.
- Bitten nails with skin covering the nail beds is a signal that the person is more physical in activities but has less skill in imagination.
- Soft and flexible nails (nails that bend but don't break) indicate natural resiliency and adaptability to change. However, environment is important to these people, as they are more easily affected (positively or negatively) by emotional and physical stimuli.
- Uneven nail thickness is an indication of a physical change in a person's body, usually one involving the lungs and/or sexual organs.

Nail Color

Nail color, like texture, can tell you a lot about a person. What follows is a list of characteristics associated with various nail types.

- Pink nails—steadfastness in life, outgoing personality, good general health.
- Dark pink to red nails—quick responses to stimuli, high irritability, resistance to change in ideas, tendency toward high blood pressure or stroke.
- White nails—These people are very aware of themselves and like themselves, yet they have low energy reserves and poor circulation, and blood clots are indicated.
- Blue-tinted nails—Just as you would think, this indicates poor circulation, possible heart malfunction, and one who has very low energy as he matures.
- Yellowish nails (not counting smokers)—These people need

to relax, and yet they feel they can't and have trouble articulating their emotions; possibility of chemical addiction, kidney or bladder problems.
- Nails that are evenly colored (any of the colors named)—If they have dark edges on the sides or top, then you can safely say that this person will have severe kidney problems and renal failure later in life.

Texture and Markings

Nail texture and markings are strong health indicators.

- White spots or dots are indications of the onset of a temporary illness; the illness depends upon which finger the spots are found on.
- A blue spot or dot indicates poor circulation (the more, the worse) or potential circulation problems.
- A black spot or dot is a sign of grieving or worry that also depends on the finger upon which it is found.
- A very white spot or dot is considered to be liver disorder of temporary nature brought on by emotional disturbances. These spots or dots grow or disappear rapidly and should not be considered troublesome. If these spots or dots remain for extremely long periods of time, then of course you would suggest that the client consult a doctor to check his general health.
- White spots or dots that seem to be growing together and covering the nail surface so that it obscures the nail transparency are a signal that this person is hypersensitive and hypertensive.
- Flecks are considered to have the same connotation as spots or dots.
- Fluting or dimpling implies that the client's nail is not receiving enough blood supply, suggesting that nutrients are not being properly distributed throughout the body.
- Horizontal ridges appearing on any nail represents the onset of an illness and usually remain until the illness has left the body or the body's system has overcome the shock. Usually these ridges are associated with upper respiratory infection, flu, walking pneumonia, and the like.

- Vertical ridges appearing on any of the nails represent stomach or other digestive ailments. These types of ridges do not grow out as quickly as the horizontal ridges. If the ridges are only on one finger, then additional medical-condition information is taken from the finger assignment that we discussed at the beginning. Example: The Saturn or middle finger governs the skeleton, and ridges there will imply problems with the skeleton—either an infection or stress on bones or muscles.
- If the subject has a half-moon at the base of the nail, then the central nervous and circulatory systems are well balanced. If there is no half-moon on any of the fingernails, then he has weakened central nervous and circulatory systems. (Don't forget that half-moons on the thumbs don't count, as the thumb is not considered a finger.)

In summary of this section, remember that each finger and the thumb have been assigned a particular part of the body. Markings of any kind found on the fingernails relate to the specific areas that finger governs.

FINGER MARKINGS

This section will deal only with the markings found on the *underside* of the fingers. (See Illustration 7-18 for these markings.) Remember that each finger and each phalange has special markings. Each marking trait must be combined with the meaning of the finger and phalange to produce the summary.

Jupiter (Index) Finger

- Slanting or horizontal line(s)—a desire to please others.
- Vertical line(s)—increase in positive attitude.
- Box(es) or square(s)—concerned with security. This is considered a mark of protection.
- Grille(s)—hyperactive personality, which can either be positive or negative.
- Cross(es)—marriages, companions, or affairs of the heart.
- Triangle(s)—tactful and politically sensitive and astute.
- Circle(s)—notoriety.

ILLUSTRATION 7-18
KEY TO PALMISTRY MARKINGS

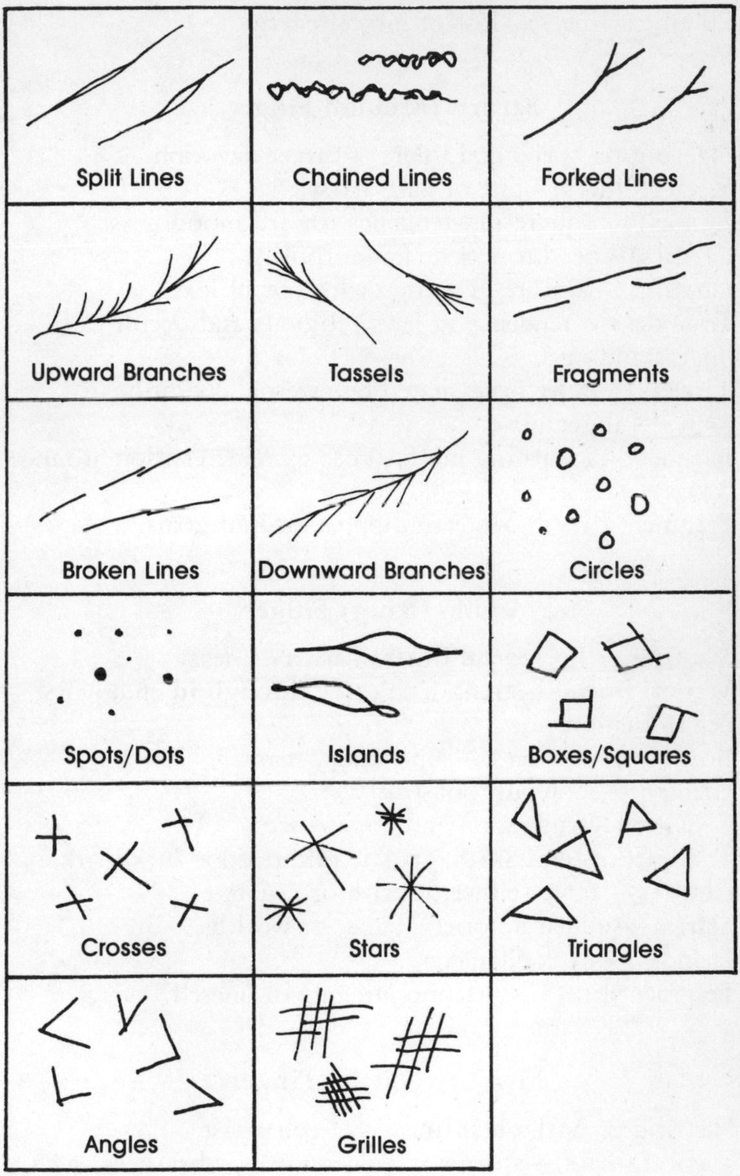

Split Lines	Chained Lines	Forked Lines
Upward Branches	Tassels	Fragments
Broken Lines	Downward Branches	Circles
Spots/Dots	Islands	Boxes/Squares
Crosses	Stars	Triangles
Angles	Grilles	

- Star(s)—accident-prone, achiever, unusual.
- Island(s)—disappointments.
- Fragment line(s)—loss of mental energy.

Saturn (Middle) Finger

- Slanting or horizontal line(s)—career devotion.
- Vertical line(s)—gift of gab, artistic.
- Box(es) or square(s)—tendency toward moodiness.
- Grille(s)—need to feel he has authority.
- Cross(es)—sincere grieving or feeling of loss.
- Triangle(s)—tendency to have religious and occult understanding.
- Circle(s)—move necessitated by external conditions.
- Star(s)—ingenuity.
- Island(s)—a warning mark to use extreme caution around water.
- Fragment line(s)—interruption in desired goals.

Apollo (Ring) Finger

- Slanting or horizontal line(s)—worry lines.
- Vertical line(s)—strength to carry through in endeavors, determination.
- Box(es) or square(s)—supervisory mark.
- Grille(s)—show-off, boastful.
- Cross(es)—frustration and impatience.
- Triangle(s)—craftsman, artistic talent; good-luck mark.
- Circle(s)—fame (either positive or negative).
- Star(s)—sudden notoriety, fame, or wealth.
- Island(s)—weak character.
- Fragment line(s)—disappointments in oneself.

Mercury (Little) Finger

- Slanting or horizontal line(s)—a con artist.
- Vertical line(s)—allergic to environment substances, such as pollen or pollution.
- Box(es) or square(s)—another protection mark.
- Grille(s)—shrewd and clever.

- Cross(es)—ability in writing.
- Triangle(s)—loves jokes and is fun to be around.
- Circle(s)—a minor mark of prophecy.
- Star(s)—hyperactive and easily agitated.
- Fragment line(s)—unclear thinking; hindered in endeavors.

MOUNTS

The mounts located under each of the fingers assume the same astrological names as were assigned to the fingers. Further down in the palm location are the mounts of Luna, Mars, Neptune, and Pluto (see Illustration 7-19). There are two mounts of Mars, one located between the thumb and index finger and one on the upper part of the outside of the palm near the little finger.

The finger mounts are called the social mounts. Normal development assures good social adjustment.

If the mounts are pronounced or overly developed, it indicates excessive amounts of energy or talent in this area, which is most likely becoming a negative trait. This energy and these traits have to be harnessed and guided for them to be used in a positive manner.

There are two palm zones—passive and active. The active zone, which indicates conscious involvement, incorporates Jupiter, the Lower Mount of Mars, half of Saturn, and parts of Venus (middle and lower), Neptune, and the Plain of Mars. The passive zone, also called the unconscious area, incorporates Apollo, Mercury, Luna, the Upper Mount of Mars, Pluto, and parts of Venus and the Plain of Mars. Please note that the Saturn finger is usually the dividing line.

Let's take each of the Mounts and discuss its meanings and markings.

Mount of Jupiter

The Mount of Jupiter represents how the individual thinks of himself and his environment. If the mount is off center and leans toward the thumb or edge of the palm, then the strength of the personality is slightly weakened. If the mount is off center and toward Saturn, then the person will have to make more conscious choices in his life. If the mount is directly centered, then it intensifies leadership qualities and shows a balance in the person's conscious thinking. If the mount is well developed, this indicates the potential for leadership and communication, a feel for authority, a good teacher, as well as an animal champion. Professions indicated by a good development of Jupiter are politician, diplomat, teacher, fighter for children's or human rights. This person is well able to project himself and his ideas.

If the mount is flat-looking, it connotes lack of enthusiasm for projects undertaken, and it can be read as an inferiority complex. It also indicates a procrastinator. If the mount is *excessively* developed, then the person will need to learn how to contain his overenthusiasm for projects and to realize he is not always the answer to the world's problems.

Mount of Saturn

The Mount of Saturn represents the subject's work and social environment. If the Saturn mount is off center toward the Jupiter mount, then he will feel the need to have more influence at his job and will have to work hard to achieve the recognition that he feels is his due. If the mount is off center but toward Apollo, then the social world is more important to him, and his social contacts, he feels, will be the making of him.

The Saturn mount is important, as it enables a person to keep on trying until he learns correctly how to work and socialize in his environment. If the Saturn mount is centered, it indicates a person who is at one with the universe, or "centered." It will serve especially to promote harmony and unity in his work and social life.

Saturn mounts that are well developed indicate a person who is interested in the occult. (Remember that the Saturn mount incorporates the dividing line between the conscious and unconscious. The occult belongs here, and is the driving force behind the search for the wisdom and knowledge of the unseen world.) It also indicates slow but sure progress in the search for understanding life. If the mount is overly developed, it does not mean that the personality is unbalanced, but that the person is more personally concerned with his own self-development, with being at one with the universe and evolving into the higher self. These folks are deeply attracted to music, as music represents harmony in the universe.

ILLUSTRATION 7-19
MOUNTS OF THE PALM

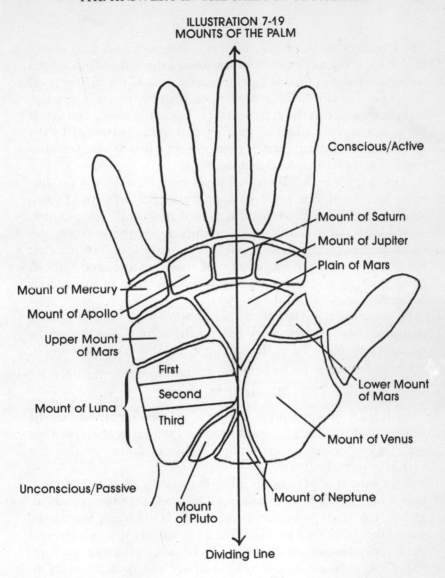

A flat Mount of Saturn indicates a person who goes through life without being forced through struggle to make choices; his decisions occur in a haphazard way instead. Such people are procrastinators. Decision by default is a good way to describe the person with a flat Mount of Saturn.

Mount of Apollo

The Mount of Apollo represents a person's emotional and creative responses. If the mount is off center toward the Saturn finger, then the emotional nature will be more easily seen. If the mount is off center but toward the Mercury finger, then the person's development is stronger in the creative areas, especially music and art. If the mount is centered under the finger, then the person will show an even emotional and creative development. He will have performing ability and a balanced temperament.

If the Mount of Apollo is well developed, then there is productivity and a genuine sense of joy in that person's life. It also signifies a concern about justice, as well as warmth, love, caring, and sharing with others their feelings about the universe. An overly developed mount says that this person has a dramatic flair for living and, in art, has a sense of color, texture, and lines. A good profession for this person would be that of an interior designer.

If the mount is flat, then the person won't exhibit such a dramatic flair but will work behind the scenes even though he harbors a desire to be in the spotlight. He doesn't push himself.

Mount of Mercury

The Mercury mount represents the technique or method that the subject uses in what he considers to be the practical areas of his life. This is especially important in that it shows whether the person is verbally gifted.

If the mount of Mercury is off center toward the Apollo finger, then it implies one who is creative in business yet values practicality and who tends to lecture. If the mount is off center toward the side of the palm, then you will find a personality that is interested in science, and/or medicine, and one who asks the question "why?" This is the mount that indicates the natural ability to become a doctor or scientist. If the mount is centered directly under the Mercury finger, then the personality embodies all of the traits into an equal blend of interests, which are especially appropriate for the business person or entrepreneur. In today's world, it also implies an interest and skill in media. The mount of Mercury is also considered to be the mount of (transmission of) communications. The secondary association is that of the secrets of life, which include knowledge of healing and the occult.

A well-developed mount indicates a quick mind, good comprehension, and the knack of being a "quick study" for any chosen interest areas, including being a good judge of character. This person also has the gift of gab. The professional areas associated with a well-developed Mercury mount are teachers, reporters, news anchors, professional travelers, mediums in the occult, and any self-employment.

If the mount is overly developed, then ambition takes over and may cause undue problems because of impatience. If the mount is flat, then the talent is for thought, but the person needs lots of time to realize his goals.

Mount of Venus

The Mount of Venus is located at and incorporates the root of the thumbs, and the thumb meanings are associated with the mount. The mount itself represents the love of children and spouse, sexual desires, and physical vitality. As discussed in the thumb section, in sexual terms, the color of the mount and its firmness reflect the intensity and activity of sexual drives. In the male hand, the mount is significant because an overly developed mount indicates that a marriage must have a firm sexual base for it to last.

The Mount of Venus is also the mount that subtly expresses a person's ability for love. If the mount is developed on the inward side of the palm, it reflects a great capacity to love, maybe even to the detriment of the individual.

If the Mount of Venus is overly developed in the area where it meets the thumb, then health, diet, and exercise are important to this individual. This person will be sexually expressive and intense within the norm, but will always feel just a little insecure about it. If this mount development is present, this person will tend to show love for spouse and family by taking care of their physical well-being. He'll worry whether he can provide adequately for them.

If the mount is overly developed in general, then a strong emotional energy and an emotional response to life are indicated. If the mount is well developed, then a balance between emotional and intellectual energy is indicated. If the mount is high, the person is fun loving and enjoys activities of a physical nature.

If the mount is flat, then the person is of the intellectual bent. The person also needs to be taught how to have fun.

Mount of Luna

The Mount of Luna can control one's life in subtle ways..Located in the passive, unconscious half of the hand, it is very responsive to moon cycles. This is where childhood memories are stored, as well as information about one's family ties and one's past in general. This mount also indicates how a person will react instinctively to his environment.

The mount is divided into three sections (see Illustration 7-19). The first carries the strongest memory of childhood. It also influences how a person will treat his children. Section 2, if fleshy, indicates a person who likes history and loves stories of the past, especially stories about family. He or she has a natural understanding of people and has very few prejudices. Section 3 represents long voyages and love of travel.

If any of the sections of the Mount of Luna is developed, it indicates a person who has an active understanding of the unconscious life that surrounds him. If the mount in general is highly developed toward the outside of the hand, then you will find an intensely emotional person, a person whose emotions rule almost totally; logic is not found here. If the mount is well developed toward the center of the hand, then you are seeing a person who understands and will follow his intuition or emotions, but who tries to use logic as well. If the mount is more developed toward the upper side of the hand, then art and creativity will guide this person's life. If the mount seems to be underdeveloped in most regions but more developed toward the entire bottom of the hand, it implies a certain reliance on intuitive feelings but a tendency to keep emotions in control, even suppressed. If the mount looks *overly* developed toward the bottom of the mount, toward the wrist, then you are looking at a very secretive person and one who can have mental disorders if he is not careful to keep a balance in his perspective. It is in this area that certain marks are found that imply insanity or criminal acts of violence.

If the entire mount is highly developed, you are looking at a writer, generally of fiction. The highly developed Mount of Luna is also associated with restlessness; this person needs to learn self-discipline. If the mount curves outward, it indicates a love of water, suggesting this person should live on or close by water (sailors usually have this configuration).

Mount of Mars

The Mount of Mars is located at the side of the hand near the Mercury finger (the upper, or passive side, of Mars) and between the index finger and thumb (the lower, or passive side, of Mars). The passive side of Mars represents the willingness to take action. If neither of the mounts is particularly developed, you are looking at a person who has neither strong beliefs nor a desire to change his world. This person is logical and can carry out instructions, but he is probably, frankly, boring. If the mounts are *highly* developed, you're looking at the consummate soldier, someone with deep seated convictions *and* the desire to actively promote these convictions. If both mounts are about equal, it indicates a balance between conviction and activity.

In most people, you'll notice a disparity between the mounts. As you become more experienced, you'll be able to more clearly see which is dominant. Remember, if the upper (passive) Mars is well developed, it indicates the ability to be consistent with goals and ambitions; this person doesn't waver much. It also implies that this person can handle crises and stress well. He is able to face adverse situations without losing face. He has strong morals and convictions. If the upper Mars is flat, then it means that this person has many fears in life and may not be able to fulfill his dreams or goals. If the lower (active) mount is well developed, it indicates someone who can initiate new projects and ideas, and someone with ambition. Few people have a truly well-developed Mars here. If the area is flat, then ambition is not the controlling influence; this person should not be a salesperson, as he will be too low-keyed.

If the upper Mars is well developed and the lower Mars is flat, this person is too set in his ways for much growth and expansion to occur. If lower Mars is developed and upper Mars is flat, this indicates a person who is constantly starting a project but never seems to finish. The person needs early training in his childhood to offset this trait.

The Plain of Mars

The Plain of Mars is located in the center of the palm and forms a triangle. It signifies to the reader the childhood activities of the subject and, since all of the major and minor lines intersect it, it is a symbol of how aggressive a person is with his or her environment. A deep hollow with deep and significant line markup indicates an aggressive individual; less deep means less aggressive. If lines that cross the Plain of Mars are clear and relatively unmarked, this person will be able to handle conflict and resolve it. The opposite is indicated if lots of markings are present.

Mount of Neptune

The Neptune mount is found in the unconscious section of the palm and represents the natural instincts. If the mount is well developed, you are looking at a person with an extra amount of presence—a "ham." Role playing is easy for people who have a well-developed Neptune. It also indicates a good public speaker. If the mount is flat, less energy is present. These people are not comfortable with public appearances.

Mount of Pluto

The Mount of Pluto is symbolic of interest in the unseen and in regeneration. If the mount is well developed, then you will find a person who likes to self-teach and self-heal, and one who has an ability for the occult. If it's well developed at an early age, it suggests a real interest in medicine. Check Mercury to be sure! If the mount is flat, then little interest is shown in active pursuit of this type of knowledge.

Markings Found on the Mounts

Vertical Lines

Vertical lines found on the mounts (see Illustration 7-20) are usually considered a positive sign. If vertical lines are found on Jupiter, Apollo, or Saturn, this emphasizes the positive traits associated with these mount meanings. Three vertical lines on Mercury indicate healing or the healing arts. If on Venus you see

7-20
SLANTING/VERTICAL LINES ON THE MOUNTS

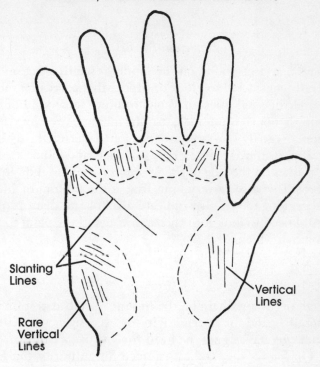

several vertical lines, the person feels good about himself and will show a tendency toward the arts as a means of self-expression. It is rare to see vertical lines on the Mount of Luna, which indicates a person whose destiny is unusual and one who will achieve his destiny in spite of obstacles placed in his way from childhood.

Slanting Lines

Slanting lines on the Mount of Luna (see Illustration 7-20) are considered influence lines; they represent people who have been counselors or mentors to that individual. Slanting lines on Jupiter indicate a desire to please others first. If the lines slant noticeably toward Saturn, then the career is very important to this person and is an outward expression of how he feels about himself. A long, slanting line that extends from the Mount of Venus all the way up to the Mount of Mercury indicates a separation or divorce from a loved one.

Horizontal Lines

Horizontal markings found on the mounts (see Illustration 7-21) are generally considered to block or hinder that particular mount's meaning. Horizontal lines on Venus indicate some kind of irritation, though not a hindrance, to the person in achieving his expression or goal. Horizontal lines on Luna relate to health (specifically to stomach, intestines, bladder, and kidneys). If you see lots of lines on the side of the Mount of Luna, it indicates real restlessness. If you see a very long line at the bottom of Luna, it means allergies and can also indicate alcohol and drug problems (you would need to look for other markings in the palm to verify or distinguish which).

Grilles

Grilles can occur anywhere on the mounts (see Illustration 7-21) and generally stand for hyperactivity or excessiveness. Grilles on the Mount of Venus signal the need for lots of love or expression thereof. On Jupiter they indicate a need for authority. On Saturn they show a definite tendency toward worrying. Grilles on Apollo indicate a boastful attitude and tendency toward showing off. Grilles on Mercury indicate a tendency toward shrewdness or cleverness. Grilles found on the Mount of Luna reaffirm illnesses of the stomach area. A grille on the Upper Mount of Mars is a mark for arthritis. A grille on the Lower Mount of Mars indicates a tendency for the person to argue a lot.

Circles and Stars

A circle or circles (see Illustration 7-21) found on the Mount of Apollo mean fame and fortune. Remember, you need to look at the rest of the markings in the palm to verify and elaborate. A star on the Mount of Jupiter indicates not only a happy marriage but one of wealth. If there is a star on the Mount of Apollo, it indicates sudden fame and fortune. If you find circles and stars on any of the other mounts, it increases the energy associated with the mounts and indicates extra amounts of ability.

7-21
HORIZONTAL LINES, GRILLES, CIRCLES, AND STARS ON THE MOUNTS

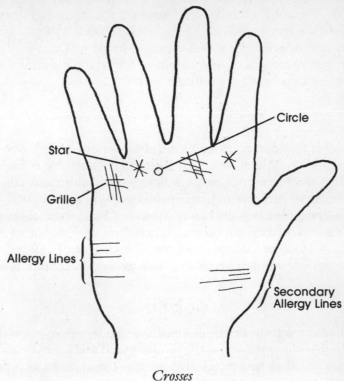

Crosses

A cross on the Mount of Venus indicates a troublesome love union. A cross on the Mount of Saturn indicates grief and sorrow. A cross on the Mount of Apollo indicates frustration in achieving one's goals. A cross on the Mount of Jupiter indicates a good and happy marriage. A cross on the Mount of Luna indicates good imagination.

Squares

Squares are always taken as positive signs and reinforce the qualities of that particular mount.

Triangles

Triangles found on the Mount of Saturn show a gift for the occult. Triangles found on the Mount of Jupiter indicate diplomatic tendencies. Triangles found on the Mount of Apollo indicate this person is a genius in the area of art or music, but is not disciplined. A triangle or triangles found on the Mount of Mercury (close to the crease) indicate a person who loves to talk and gossip. A triangle or triangles found on the Mount of Luna indicate a great gift of prophecy and intuition. A triangle found on the Mount of Luna indicates military activity.

Tassels

A tassel is found in or around lines, but can extend to the mount. A tassel on the Mount of Saturn indicates back and leg ailments. A tassel on the Mount of Apollo indicates eye problems. A tassel on the Mount of Mercury indicates problems with the digestive tract and ulcers. A tassel on the Lower Mount of Mars indicates respiratory and circulation problems. A tassel on the Mount of Luna indicates kidney problems, gallstones, and general infections. A tassel on the Mount of Venus indicates general infectious diseases.

MAJOR LINES

The lines loosely divide the mounts and the deviations upon them, and in their formation give the reader specific information about the area of life to which each line relates. The clarity and depth of the line are important, as they give further clues as to how an individual will react.

The major lines found in the palm are the Life Line, the Head Line, and the Heart Line (see Illustration 7-22). These will remain with us throughout our lives with the markings that were found upon them at birth. The Heart or Head lines can be missing in the palm, but never the Life Line. I might add, at this point, that if you see a palm that is missing both the Head and the Heart lines, then you are seeing a person who has mental deficiencies. The other lines found in the palm are referred to as moving or changing lines, because they can change as our lives move and change courses. Remember, it is important to look at both hands.

There are some general rules for reading the major lines. Deep lines provide stamina and give the reader definite insights about the vitality and endurance of the person. If any of the major lines are deep, then the person has good physical stamina. If the Head Line is deep, then the person has the ability to concentrate. If the

ILLUSTRATION 7-22
THE LINES OF THE PALM

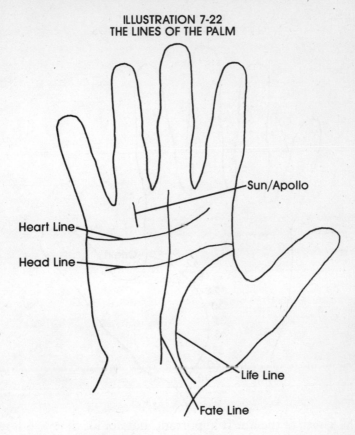

Heart Line is deep, then the person feels emotions very deeply; this is an intense individual.

If any of the major lines is lighter looking, it will weaken the meanings associated with it. Light lines are also indicative of a worrier. If all of the lines are light, then you can be sure that the individual is sensitive to his surroundings, has strong physical needs, and will require more sleep, rest, or quiet time.

The width of the lines is another clue that the reader needs to be aware of, as the width is an indication of quantity and expenditure of energy as regards that line. If the line is narrow, then the person needs to conserve energy.

Color is also an indication of energy. A wide, red-looking line indicates a person who stores energy and can sustain energy flows; a light pink, pale-looking line indicates rapid loss of energy and the need for learning how to increase stamina.

ILLUSTRATION 7-23
LIFE LINE WITH TIME MARKINGS

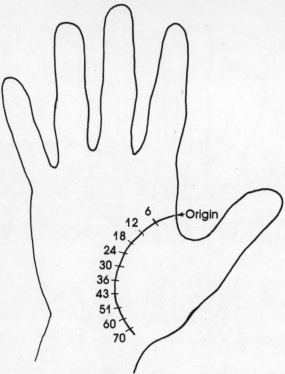

The length of the line is important, but not for the reasons many novices think (and no, a short life line does not necessarily mean early death): Look for faint repair lines (see Illustration 7-32 to see what a repair line looks like) or protection marks, such as squares or boxes, or the Mark of Mars. What is important is where the line begins and ends. The length of the line is important because it contains age correlations (see Illustration 7-23, for example), which can tell the reader when significant events in the subject's life will occur or have occurred. As with all of palmistry, line length is just one clue in the complex map of the palm.

Some beginners have a difficult time understanding how to tell from the palm markings when a given event will occur. For determining the timing of events, as well as development of traits and abilities, it is important to look at *both* hands. If a mark that indicates wealth is on the right hand but not the left, it tells me that this is a person who will work hard to *get* rich. If it's not on the right but on the left, I'll see that the money will be coming to the individual in the future. If it's on both, he's already rich.

Lines themselves have a definite character, as shown in Illustration 7-24. Here are some quick reference points for you to learn so that you can quickly summarize the line character:

- A simple line with very little change in course or with few markings indicates balance in the personality.
- Doubling of a line or a line that runs parallel to a major line indicates protection of the basic line (as if it were wearing a seat belt) and consolidates the character found in that line.
- Double-divergent lines, which whirl, indicate conflict. If the secondary line is short by comparison to the lead or major line, it signifies a lessening of the strength of overall characteristics of the line. However, if the line is longer than the lead or major line, then it will increase the positive line meanings.

ILLUSTRATION 7-24
LINES ON THE PALMS

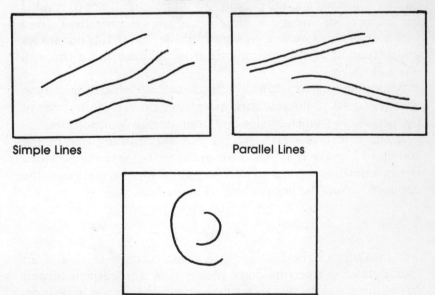

Simple Lines   Parallel Lines

Double-Divergent Lines

At first it may be difficult to tell the difference between significant markings and worry lines, branchy-type lines that seem to go nowhere. Generally, if the mark isn't clear, it is a worry line; meaningful palmic markings are not hard to see in the hand. Worry lines indicate a person who wastes energy worrying. Many worry lines indicate a person who dissipates so much energy through his nerves that it may affect his health.

Life Line

The Life Line is considered the most important line in the palm. It carries many pieces of information and indicates how the person will fare in life in general. It also gives the reader a sense of the person's longevity, events that have had special impact on the person and how the person will use his ability for free will. Be sure to check both hands. The course and qualities of life should be the same in both hands.

Length

A short Life Line is not uncommon; it simply means that energy or vitality is limited and the person should be careful not to run his life on nervous energy. A long Life Line is generally a good indicator of an above-average length of life, but that is not always guaranteed. It is also an indication of an inheritance through unusual sources.

A long and narrow Life Line indicates a high-strung person, with very quick responses. This can exhaust the nervous reserves of the person. In women, such a line indicates early menopause.

If the Life Line's arch swings out significantly toward the Mount of Luna, it indicates travel and an extroverted personality. If the Life Line swings in and hugs the Mount of Venus, the opposite is true: the personality is introverted.

Breaks

Any breaking of the Life Line or fragmentation thereof is an indication of an interruption of energy flow. If the line is broken or fragmented at the very beginning, it indicates illness in infancy, more than likely from food allergies. All breaks on the Life Line indicate serious illnesses and, without a repair line, can indicate death at the location on the time line. If the line deepens after the break, it is an indication of a major change and, if located midsection of the line, one that the person chose to implement. If the lines from the break seem to overlap, then the change or transition went smoothly. If not, the adjustment came or will come more slowly. If the line is fragmented, and the fragment occurs farther down but stops before midway, it indicates inherited circulation problems, fragile health, and a moody disposition until the fragmentation ends.

If both ends of the break are confined by a box or rectangle, this shows great stress in that person's life, stress that will remain with him until death. Understand that this mark does not endanger the person physically.

Depth

A deep Life Line indicates a strong and steady personality. A shallow or light Life Line indicates a person who needs peace and quiet. Energy is low; rest is a must to maintain good health physically, mentally, and emotionally.

If the depth of the line varies in either one or both hands, it indicates a person who has to expend extra effort and will need more rest in his life. An indistinct Life Line in one hand not only shows lots of change but a tendency to cling to the past. An indistinct Life Line that has shallowness then depth, off and on, indicates a change in life or a clean start.

The Beginning of the Life Line

The location of the Life Line gives the reader one of the first clues into the person's personality. Each line in the palm has an origin point and termination point. Generally, the Life Line rises between the Mount of Venus and the Mount of Jupiter and will run in an arch around the thumb area toward the wrist and around the end of the Mount of Venus. If the line is centered almost exactly between the index finger and thumb, it indicates a person of even temperament despite constant changes in his circumstances.

If the Life Line rises closer to the Mount of Jupiter (see A in Illustration 7-25), it is an indication that the person is opinionated, with a tendency toward impulsiveness. Healthwise, it reflects a potential for high blood pressure or hypertension. In addition, this person holds himself in high esteem. Women with a Life Line rising near Jupiter tend to believe their own PR; flattering them will get you everywhere. This is not a negative trait in itself, and it tells the reader this person has good leadership ability, which, if used properly, can be the hallmark of a good politician.

If the Life Line rises closer to the Mount of Venus (see B in Illustration 7-25), it indicates a personality with good general health and a person who likes his quiet time and space. While this person does like people, he needs time for thinking. If this person does not receive the space or time he needs, he will lose energy, which can affect his overall health, causing perhaps lower resistance to colds or flu.

The End of the Life Line

If the Life Line terminates at the wrist area and encircles the Mount of Venus (see C in Illustration 7-25), it indicates a person who is a homebody. In women this indicates a person to whom domestic harmony is important. If lots of little lines are found on the Life Line near the base of the Mount of Venus, you can safely tell the person he has a definite desire to travel, but only close to home. He prefers short trips rather than extended visits, or wants to travel to or with friends or family. If these lines appear only on the left hand, then you have a dreamer and, depending upon the education of this person, possibly an inventor. If this line appears on both hands, the individual leads a busy life centered around family.

If the Life Line terminates toward the Mount of Luna (see D in Illustration 7-25), it indicates a person who likes to travel on his own, without crowds. Among these people are sailors, jocks, and fighter pilots. These people also exhibit optimism in adverse situations, the stuff heroes are made of. If the line is the same in both hands, then you have the explorer or soldier of fortune.

If the Life Line terminates or splits into two branches (see E in Illustration 7-25), it indicates travel over water or extended length of travel, and an active life centered around unusual people or events.

ILLUSTRATION 7-25
LIFE LINE ORIGINS AND TERMINATIONS

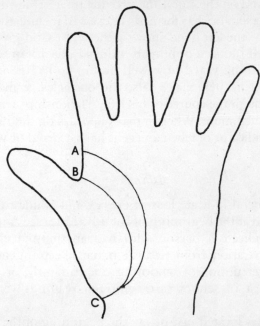

A. Life Line begins close to the Mount of Jupiter.

B. Life Line begins close to the Mount of Venus.

C. Life Line encircles the Mount of Venus.

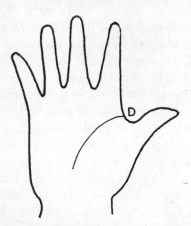

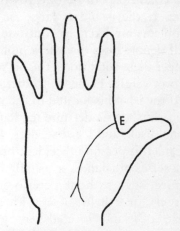

D. Life Line terminates near the Mount of Luna.

E. Life Line splits into two branches.

Markings on the Life Line

Markings found on the Life Line provide interesting information on how the personality has formed. These will include the person's natural health (the left hand shows genetic, or God-given health; right-hand, self-induced or human-induced), health in early years, health in declining years, how well he can do in financial areas, business, meeting personal goals, the obstacles he may have to overcome through the course of his life, relationships with people, and, oh, so much more. Where a mark appears on the Life Line is an excellent indicator of when an event has occurred or will occur.

Islands

Islands in general indicate loss of energy and allude to illnesses. Islands located at the beginning of the Life Line (see A in Illustration 7-26) indicate a person who had an unusual childhood, including separation from natural parents, estrangement from family, an interruption of schooling due to family, or a definite lack of interest in school (after enough readings you'll know which).

If an island is located just below the beginning of the Life Line (see B in Illustration 7-26), it indicates eating, smoking, and possibly digestive tract disorders. If the island is small, it indicates the condition can be outgrown or overcome with proper health care. If the island is large or there is a series of islands, the problems are likely to continue until the end of life. This island will denote lung disorders, not necessarily cancer, in later years. Under these conditions, the person, if a heavy smoker, should stop. If overweight, he needs to diet, for his stomach is weak.

If the island is located in the region of Saturn (C in the illustration), it shows a definite tendency toward nervousness, as well as bone, back, and leg disorders. If the island is small, this usually means this person is accident-prone. If the island is large, or there is a series of islands, it usually means problems of a more serious nature, such as bone deterioration as one matures in age, disk surgery, or arthritis of legs, knees, ankles, hips, back. If you have a series of islands located here, give up football or gymnastics for dancing at a club; it's less risky.

If islands are found in the region of Apollo (at D), it is a definite indication of eye problems, usually corrected by prescription

ILLUSTRATION 7-26
ISLANDS ON THE LIFE LINE

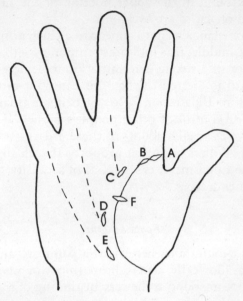

glasses. A small island here also indicates fevers. A large island or series of islands suggest a predisposition toward certain contagious infections, such as flu, colds, yeast infections, and the like—nothing of a serious nature.

If islands are found in the region of Mercury (at E), it denotes a definite predisposition to ulcers of all types. If the island is small, this will bring very little trouble if the individual maintains good eating habits and does not eat spicy foods regularly. If the island is large or there is a series of islands, this could indicate serious stomach problems and is indicative of stomach surgery, especially if the person is self-employed and under heavy stress.

If islands are found anywhere inside the Venus area, it is an indication of general infections, especially in the early years. If there is a series of islands, it indicates rare types of infections, such as Legionnaires' disease. If a series is found close to the bottom of the Mount of Venus, it indicates dual infections, such as those with malaria or hepatitis. If no islands are found in the Venus region, then this person enjoys basic good health. This person shouldn't call in sick to work; they won't believe him.

If the Life Line seems to be full of islands located on the line, it is an indication of problems and/or obstacles over a long time span. If only found in the upper portion of the Life Line, then problems and obstacles are overcome.

If a series of islands seem to appear in a cluster but there are no islands in the middle, this indicates temporary setbacks. This is a good indicator of a strong determination to achieve.

If the island is located in the Life Line but crosses the line lengthwise (F in Illustration 7-26), it denotes financial success, inheritance, or control of other people's money. If the island is small, it indicates small amounts of these, if large or in a series, it indicates more dollars or greater property. If such an island is near the end of the Life Line, it is a symbol of acquisition through the person's own endeavors.

Spots or Dots

Spots or dots found anywhere in the palm are an indicator of health, yet paradoxically, also indicate injury or a type of sorrow. If spots or dots are found at the very beginning of the Life Line, it is an indicator that there are health, injury, or sorrow problems in early childhood (see A in Illustration 7-27). If the spots or dots continue down the line and dissipate, the point at which they stop shows the age at which the subject had his or her tonsils removed.

If the dots or spots start around the middle of the Life Line (B in Illustration 7-27), this indicates problems with the upper respiratory tract; the most common are pneumonia and related disorders. If dots or spots are close to a line or island (C in the illustration), this indicates injury. If the dots or spots appear to have a bluish color, it denotes inherited lung disorders. If the dots or spots are truly blue, it indicates strangulation, water injury, or coughing. If the dots or spots appear reddish, it is indicative of inherited heart problems. If the color is a true red, it relates to breathing, as in a hard thump to the chest.

The age at which problems occur is determined by where the dot or spot is found. If the dots or spots are spaced consistently along the Life Line to its termination point (as shown by D), the person will have to be careful with throat, lungs, colds, and so on.

ILLUSTRATION 7-27
DOTS OR SPOTS ON
THE LIFE LINE

ILLUSTRATION 7-28
SQUARES OR BARS AND LINES
ON THE LIFE LINE

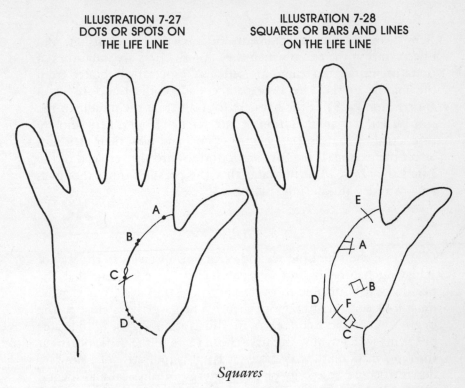

Squares

Squares denote protection for the personality and serve to repair
the Life Line if illness is indicated. This is generally a good mark
to have on the Life Line and is considered to be lucky. You could
say that a person with a square on his Life Line is like a cat with
nine lives.

If the square is located inside the Mount of Venus but close to
the Life Line (just touching it, as shown by A in Illustration 7-
28), it is still considered as a repair line. A square inside the
Mount of Venus isolated (B in the illustration) indicates protection against trouble brought about through sexual involvement.
Squares located toward the end of the Life Line (at C) indicate
transition of personality and subsequent energy redirection. If
there is a series of little squares, this means changes in lifestyle or
location. If the square is large or in a series, however, the client
will feel as if he is in a box, "in jail," or has some form of heavy
restriction. When these squares are located at the end of the Life
Line, this indicates the feeling can be overcome.

Bars

Bars generally indicate moments of anxiety, apprehension, and uncertainty at the age at which they appear. Bars are indicators of irritating minor and temporary setbacks, especially if located from the middle of the Life Line to the end of the line (see D in Illustration 7-28). If the bars are found before the middle of the line (at E), it is an indication of interference from others who are in control of the subject's environment, and how their attitudes affect the person. If the bars are found toward the very end of the Life Line (as at F), it indicates that the person's inner thoughts and attitudes are causing frustration.

Grilles

Grilles on the Life Line are indicators of obstacles in the way of achieving natural desires or goals. They do not mean that the person will be unable to overcome these obstacles, but that he must look for ways to remove them. When a grille is close to the beginning of the line (see A in Illustration 7-29), it indicates problems with learning in early school years. If the grille begins at the third mark on the Life Line (at B), it is indicative of a slowing down to conserve energy or poor energy in physical and mental activity. If the grille is located approximately halfway down the line (at C), it is indicative of changes in finance or business. If the grille is located near the wrist (at D), it tells the reader that this person is introspective and likes privacy above all else.

Stars or Crosses

Stars on the Life Line usually indicate confinement due to injury. Crosses on the Life Line indicate mental conditions. Stars or crosses along either side of the Life Line indicate major setbacks in a person's life that are only in the mind of that person.

If these markings are found midway down the line (see A in Illustration 7-30), it is an indicator that these setbacks will occur in the future. If they are at the very beginning of the Life Line but not actually touching it (at B), it means this person moved early in his life, and his family had few resources.

A cross located at the very bottom of the line (at C) is known as the St. Andrew's Cross and predicts that this person will save

ILLUSTRATION 7-29   ILLUSTRATION 7-30
GRILLES ON THE LIFE LINE   STARS AND CROSSES ON THE LIFE LINE

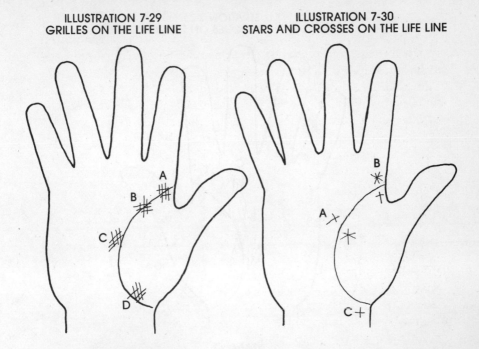

another person's life either in the physical, mental, or emotional sense. This cross often denotes a medical career.

If any of the stars or crosses found on the Life Line are deep red, it indicates heart conditions later in life; if they are bluish, lung problems. If stars or crosses are located to the right of the Life Line, it means accidents.

Chaining

All chaining found on the Life Line carries a general meaning of delicate energy flows with slow recuperation after illnesses. Rest is essential to the person who has consistent chaining on the Life Line. If the chaining is found at the beginning of the line (as at A in Illustration 7-31), it indicates that one of the person's parents also had delicate health. If the chaining starts in the middle of the line (B in the illustration), it indicates problems involving the areas encompassing internal medicine (blood pressure, for example). If the chaining starts and continues for most of the line's length, it is an indication of an emotional personality. For this person to have good health, he must learn to be calm.

ILLUSTRATION 7-31
CHAINS AND BRANCHES ON THE LIFE LINE

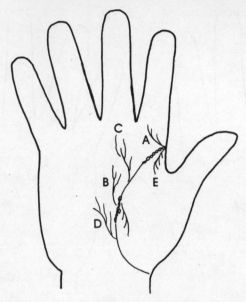

Branches

The meaning of branches found on the Life Line depends on whether they swing up or down. Branches that sweep toward Jupiter at the beginning of the Life Line (see A in Illustration 7-31) denotes many small achievements through the person's life. A deep branch here denotes a religious interest, and some ministers have this clearly marked on the Life Line. Any upward-sweeping branches that are located on the first twenty years denote ambition and a desire for self-improvement. A branch midway down the line that sweeps toward Jupiter (see B) indicates a person searching for self-identity and making self-affirmations.

· If the *branches* sweep toward Saturn but do not touch the Life Line (as at C), the person could achieve great wealth. At the same time, this marking also indicates having to overcome family difficulties. If a branch seems to form a star or cross at the end of the Life Line, this indicates a death of a family member, probably a parent. If the branches lean toward Apollo (D), this indicates potential for success in the artistic world or someone who could be outstanding in his field of endeavor in business, science, or politics. If the branches point toward the Head Line but do not cross it, it is an indication of successful projects, higher than average earnings, or work in a government-related career. As you become experienced, it will be easier to tell which. Branches toward the end of the Life Line also indicate a lessening of vitality, a condition that can be controlled by proper diet, rest, and exercise.

Branches that are located at the beginning of the Life Line (E) and sweep downward indicate loss of ambition and desires. If the branches are located in the middle of the line (B), it indicates problems in business and/or poor earnings. If the branches do not take on too much of a chainlike effect, this person will overcome negative conditions through hard work. If they are located toward the end of the Life Line, it is an indication of a great desire for change and/or travel, as well as difficulty in making decisions quickly. When the branches are located in the area of the Mount of Venus (as seen in the examples at B and E), it is an indication that the person is troubled by anxiety and negative thinking.

Triangles

If a triangle is seen on the Life Line, it must be clearly defined for it to have any significance. If it is located toward the latter section of the Life Line (see A in Illustration 7-32), it indicates an ability in drama or the arts. If the triangle is large, it suggests the person is very gifted. If it is small, then this person has above average interest and ability but does not usually make his talent a career choice.

Forks and Tassels

A forked ending on the Life Line (B in Illustration 7-32) indicates dissipation of life energy, which is to be expected at the close of one's life. If one fork extends toward Luna, there is a desire to travel that remains constant throughout life.

A fork located at the beginning of the Life Line (at C) indicates an interest in spiritual things that is also pursued throughout life. If the mark is deep then becomes shallow, it indicates that the person will turn from organized religion early in life. If the line begins to deepen again toward the ends of the forks, however, it

ILLUSTRATION 7-32
MARKINGS ON THE LIFE LINE

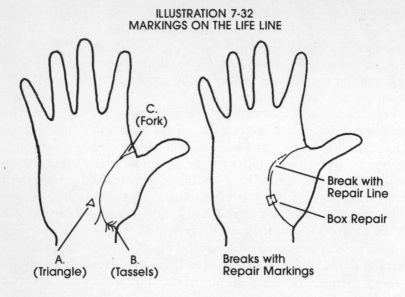

C.
(Fork)

Break with
Repair Line

Box Repair

A.   B.   Breaks with
(Triangle)   (Tassels)   Repair Markings

indicates a change of heart toward organized religion and a person who will be a staunch supporter of the church and church activities.

Tassels located at either end of the Life Line (see B, for example) indicate affairs of the heart and one who loves being in love.

Head Line

Of the major lines, the Head Line (see Illustration 7-33) ranks second in importance and stands for the brain, intelligence, and memory. The length and depth of the line tell the reader just how much interest the personality will exhibit in the mental area. The course of the line is an indication of how much imagination the person has and how independent he is. The location of the Head Line is generally found to start between the thumb and the Jupiter finger and terminates on the percussion side of the palm under the Mount of Apollo or Mercury. The Head Line can be found to dip in its course and to end in the Mount of Luna. The illustrations will show you the starting points for the Head Line, and the termination points.

**ILLUSTRATION 7-33
HEAD LINE**

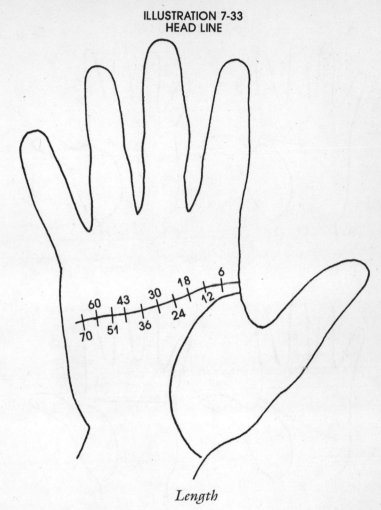

Length

A Head Line that ends under the Mount of Saturn is considered short (A in Illustration 7-34); a Head Line that terminates just slightly past the Apollo mount is considered long (B in Illustration 7-34).

A long Head Line indicates a person who has wide and varied interest in all areas of life. The line is also considered to be a sign of probing intellect; the longer the line, the more curiosity exhibited. This person would be good at any type of research work.

A short Head Line signifies a good memory and good concentration. These people also like to apply what they have learned.

ILLUSTRATION 7-34
LENGTH OF HEAD LINE

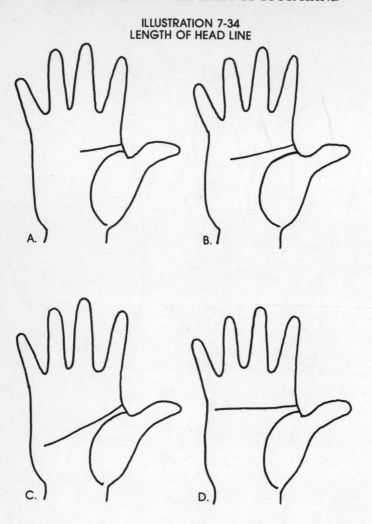

They are not as interested in theory as the person with a long Head Line, but care instead whether the theory will work. A short Head Line is also indicative of a person who specializes in one field of endeavor, an activity that becomes a lifelong pursuit.

Where the line ends is also important. If the Head Line ends directly under the Mount of Saturn, it tells us that this person is ruled by his instincts and doesn't like to plan ahead for events or actions. He will have a definite selfish bent to his personality. If the Head Line ends just past the Mount of Saturn, but not quite to the Mount of Apollo, then these specific traits are weakened and the Apollo traits are strengthened. If the Head Line ends at the beginning of the Mount of Saturn, this is an early-death mark.

If the Head Line ends at the Apollo mount, this person will have traits of universal understanding and an inquiring, problem-solving mind. He will continue his education indefinitely, either formally or through self-teaching.

Some people think that IQ can be read on the Head Line. Well, it can and it can't. An inexperienced palmist will be able to tell many things from the Head Line, including what educators would call a working IQ. But most psychics, as well as enlightened educators, realize that there are different kinds of "smarts." For that reason, good palmistry teachers encourage students to examine the Head Line and, in fact, the palm in general in its entirety. The course and depth of the Head Line will tell you more about a person's intelligence, imagination, and abilities than any IQ number ever will.

If the Head Line ends at or just in the Mount of Luna (see C in Illustration 7-34), this denotes a personality who is a dreamer, and one who is drawn toward two things at one time. This person will have a hard time making decisions and will be prone to daydreaming. This person has a strong imagination.

If the Head Line ends on the Upper Mount of Mars (see D in Illustration 7-34), business and money will be important to this individual. This can be taken as a sign of "tightness" with money and finances.

If the Head Line extends all the way to the side of the palm, this person will be more involved than most with pursuing business ideas and the achievement of his own goals.

Depth

The deeper the line, the greater the owner's ability to complete projects undertaken. If the line is shallow, then the person will have more problems in completion of projects started, and his energy will be poor. If the line changes in depth, then that is an indication of mental development or an effort to learn that has been hard on the person. It also means that the person is not consistent in his efforts. If parents check a child's Head Line before the child enters school, they can, if needed, encourage the child to complete what he starts and see to it that he has the proper rest. In this way, the tendencies can be rechanneled.

Curve

The curve, or course, of the line is important, as it can tell the reader how this person thinks. If the line is straight, then the person is a concrete thinker; it shows a practical bent of the mind. This person uses common sense in every area of his life and gets right to the point. This person is a fast thinker.

A line that curves deep into the Mount of Luna (see A in Illustration 7-35) indicates a person who is intrigued by the symbols of human connection to universal concepts (crosses, astrological symbols, and the like). This denotes a special desire to create new or better understandings of the world.

If the Head Line is wavy or has an uneven curve (see B), this is a signal that this person is easily distracted. If the curve is not too pronounced, it is a mark of creativity. The creativity will be expressed in areas that don't fit conventional society's rules.

The Head Line that has a definite slant (as in C), indicates a practical person who is at the same time creative. Remember, if the line ends at Luna, the person will have dreamy qualities, too. There is a secondary indicator for the owner of this line: this person wants or likes to be self-employed or to be in a work situation where he has lots of autonomy.

If the Head Line has a nice slope (D), it is indicative of the creative person who invents, has artistic ability, and enjoys adventures.

Beginning of the Head Line

The Head Line generally starts between the thumb and Jupiter finger and terminates under the Mount of Apollo or Mercury. Exactly where the Head Line begins is a clue into that person's dependence or independence and his tendency to be cautious or impulsive. A Head Line that is widely separated from the Life Line (see A in Illustration 7-36) indicates a tendency toward impulsiveness, someone who likes to act quickly, has a creative nature, and

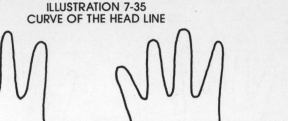

ILLUSTRATION 7-35
CURVE OF THE HEAD LINE

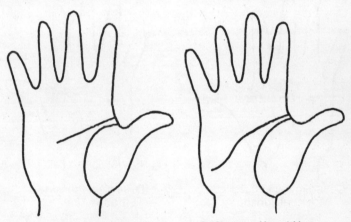

A. Curve Deep into Luna   B. Wavy Head Line

C. Slanting Head Line   D. Sloping Head Line

tends to be overly optimistic, even joyous, in response to his environment. It also connotes separation from loved ones (not only parents) early in childhood and/or adoption. This person is very independent.

If the Head Line just touches but doesn't cross the Life Line (see B in Illustration 7-36), this person's impulsive side and cautious side are better balanced than they are in most people. If this Head Line is long, this person is generally timid and has a fear of meeting new people and going to new places.

ILLUSTRATION 7-36
BEGINNING OF THE HEAD LINE

A. Widely Separated
   from Life Line

B. Just Touching Life Line

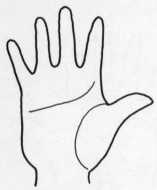

C. Beginning in the
   Mount of Jupiter

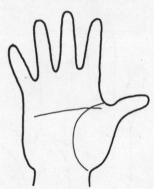

D. Beginning Inside
   the Life Line

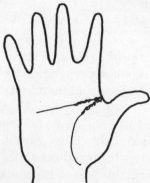

E. Chaining

If the Head Line begins on the Mount of Jupiter and the line doesn't touch the Life Line (see C in the illustration), this is one of the best possible beginnings. It indicates brilliance, as the owner is almost perfectly balanced between caution and risk taking. Such a person knows intuitively how far to go. It is also the mark of the manager of people, places, or things. If the Head Line is long, it is possible for this person to achieve worldwide recognition in his or her area of expertise.

If the Head Line begins inside the Life Line (D), this tells the reader that the subject is defensive. It also indicates a personality who doesn't like to deal with reality. This person has a great many inner fears or insecurities, even a mistrust of others. If this mark is found on a child, it means that he feels that he is having too much responsibility placed upon him and doesn't feel he can cope. In the adult palm, it is a secondary mark for this traumatic event.

The Head Line that starts out being chained and touches the Life Line (E) is an indicator of shyness, especially in early childhood. Where the Head Line shifts marks the age at which the child overcame or will overcome some of his shyness.

Markings on the Head Line

If a person has branches that lead off the Head Line (see A and B in Illustration 7-37) and curve toward Jupiter, this indicates ambition and pride. Branches toward the Mount of Mercury or Upper Mount of Mars indicate business, money, and mechanical abilities. Branches toward the Mount of Saturn indicate depression or a tendency to brood. Branches toward Apollo indicate the desire for fame, and, if the person is exhibiting overall weak hand traits (fine lines, weak phalanges, indistinct markings), then it is known as a criminal mark. A branch toward the Mount of Luna indicates the professional student; please don't confuse this mark for the writer's mark. The student's mark will not be as long or as clear.

A sloping Head Line that branches or forks toward the lower (third) section of Luna (C) denotes a fiction writer and is called the writer's fork. If the fork is short, then the writer is more apt to write instructional books. This mark has very little deviation.

The lawyer's mark (see D) points toward Upper Mars and denotes a person who can see all sides of an issue or question. This

ILLUSTRATION 7-37
MARKS ON THE HEAD LINE

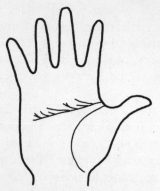

A. Upward Branches

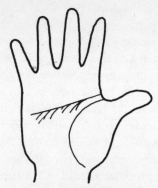

B. Downward Branches

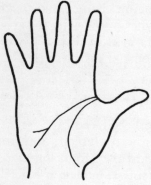

C. Writer's Fork

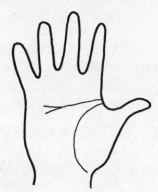

D. Lawyer's Mark

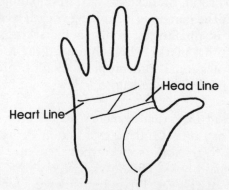

E. Accident Mark Between the Head Line and Heart Line

ILLUSTRATION 7-38
MARKS ON THE HEAD LINE

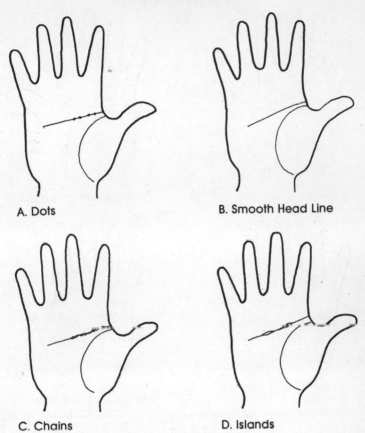

A. Dots

B. Smooth Head Line

C. Chains

D. Islands

mark may deviate. It also carries the ability to be practical, even to too great a degree.

If a branch from the Head Line runs into the Heart Line (see E in Illustration 7-37), this indicates physical harm or danger for the owner. It is referred to as the accident mark.

Dots and spots found at the beginning of the Head Line (see A in Illustration 7-38) indicate the tendency toward headaches and eyesight that needs the correction of glasses.

A smooth, unbroken Head Line (see B) is an indicator of good health without accidents unless the Life Line contains markings that indicate differently.

A chained Head Line (C) indicates inconsistency of thought.

ILLUSTRATION 7-38 (continued)

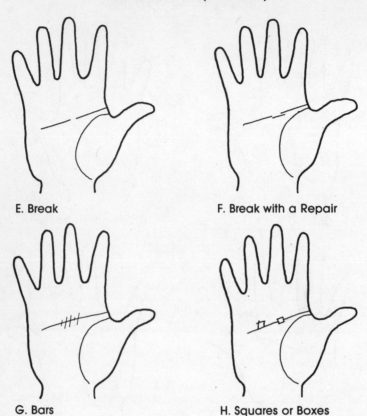

E. Break   F. Break with a Repair

G. Bars   H. Squares or Boxes

Islands found on the Head Line (D) indicate injuries to the head, maybe in childhood. They can also be indicative of brain disease. Broken-bone marks are located by an island under the Mount of Saturn on the Head Line. If breaks occur anywhere on the Head Line (E), it is indicative of early death unless sister repair lines are found (F).

If you see a Head Line that has many fine lines crossing the line but not going anywhere, then you are looking at a person with a tendency toward migraine headaches, especially if coupled with islands on the line.

Bars found on the Head Line (G) are indicative of interruption in educational activities or a change in careers.

Squares or boxes found on the Head Line (H) indicate protection from injuries or a lessening of mental strains.

ILLUSTRATION 7-39
ABNORMALITIES OF THE HEAD LINE

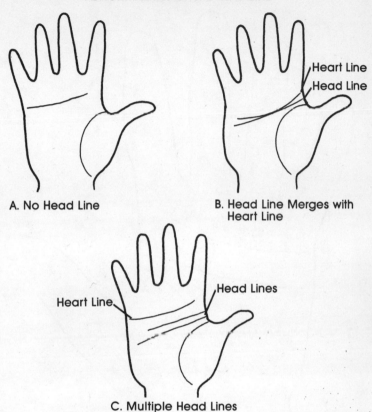

A. No Head Line

B. Head Line Merges with
Heart Line

C. Multiple Head Lines

Abnormalities of the Head Line

A missing Head Line in one or both of the hands (see A in Illustration 7-39) or Head and Heart lines that merge into one (B) indicate mental retardation. Multiple Head Lines (C) indicate a schizophrenic personality. If they are found in both the palms, however, the person exhibits a dual personality but is able to balance them and can manage well. If these lines are abnormal and the Head Line is straight, then you will see an autistic personality with a tendency toward violence. If the Head Line slopes, then the autistic person will be passive.

Some palms are more positive than others, but all contain good traits that need to be emphasized (and the negative played down) for the person to learn and grow. Also be careful to avoid making

ILLUSTRATION 7-40
HEART LINE

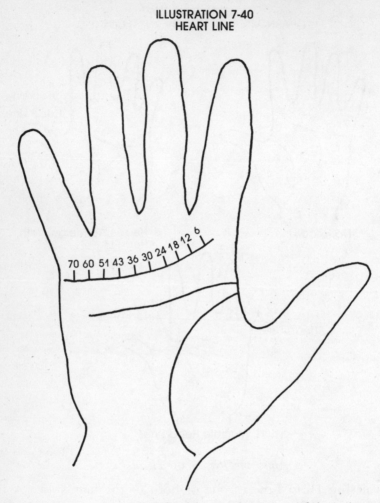

radical statements regarding health, as other parts of the palm will either affirm or reconfirm medical information. You would not want to scare an individual unnecessarily. At the same time, you must share negative medical information if you are sure. Be tactful and suggest the subject see a doctor.

Heart Line

The Heart Line indicates our ability to express love and also shows how the heart, as an organ, is functioning.

The Heart Line generally starts under the Jupiter or Saturn

ILLUSTRATION 7-41
BEGINNING AND COURSE OF THE HEART LINE

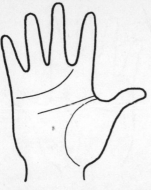

A. Between Saturn and Jupiter

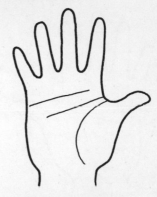

B. Crossing the Base

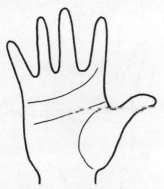

C. High in the Mount of Jupiter
(Almost Touching Jupiter
Finger)

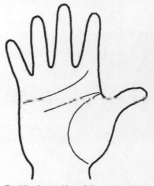

D. High in the Mount of Jupiter

finger and flows toward the edge of the Mount of Mercury. The Heart Line, as with others, can be read for time (see Illustration 7-40). The Heart Line usually doesn't denote events; however, there are three indicators on the Heart Line: how the subject approaches emotional issues, how the heart (the organ) functions, and what will happen in love life.

Beginning and Course of the Heart Line

If the Heart Line originates *between* the index and middle fingers (see A in Illustration 7-41), it denotes a rational and practical

ILLUSTRATION 7-42
BEGINNING AND COURSE OF THE HEART LINE

A. One Side to the Other

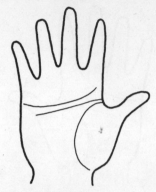

B. Curves Down
Toward Heart Line

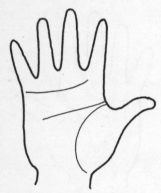

C. High in Palm

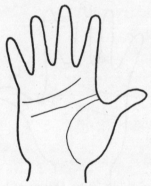

D. Average

approach to the emotions; it signals calmness. Yet this person will have an affectionate nature and a very strong desire for harmony in his emotional life.

If the Heart Line crosses the base of the finger mounts (see B in Illustration 7-41), then this person feels that anyone he loves can do no wrong. Faults just don't exist.

If the line starts *way up* on the Mount of Jupiter toward the finger (C), then the meaning is less positive. This person may tend to be jealous and may expect too much emotional commitment from his or her partner.

If the Heart Line rises high near but not into Jupiter and is longer than normal, extending to the edge of the palm (D), this signals increased strength and enhancement of Jupiter qualities: authority, prestige, enjoyment of living.

If the line goes from one side of the hand to the other side in a straight course (see A in Illustration 7-42), it indicates an intensely loving disposition, but also one who can easily detach his emotions and become unfeeling. It also indicates troubles with the knees or joints in the body.

If the Heart Line curves downward and almost touches the Head Line (see B in Illustration 7-42), it indicates an intensely reserved or formal person who has trouble expressing his feelings.

If the Heart Line is high in the palm and a great distance from the Head Line (C), it is an indication that the person approaches love and other emotions from a logical point of view. The higher the Heart Line is in the palm, the greater the subjectivity the person will have. In contrast, the lower the line is located, then the more objectivity the person will exhibit. This is indicative of critical observation one will have of his loved ones. Yet by the same token, the higher the line, then the more blind loyalty the person exhibits. These placements obviously can carry both positive and negative potential; the person could impose free-will restraints in either direction.

The average beginning and course of the Heart Line (see D in Illustration 7-42) is just under the Mount of Jupiter. It has a natural curve. This line suggest a balanced individual, though line markings, of course, can effect this!

Length and End of Heart Line

The "average" Heart Line extends from the Mount of Jupiter to the Mount of Mercury (see D in Illustration 7-42 again). This indicates a very sensitive person. If there are no branches on the line, it indicates a balance in emotional approaches and expression of love. This person will be steady or consistent. If the Heart Line, as just described, has a very deep and red color, it signifies that the owner has a tendency toward apoplexy. If the line is not so deep and is yellowish in color, then you are seeing a tendency toward liver problems. If the line is wide and pale, then heart disease is indicated and poor circulation is a fact of life, no matter what the line length.

If the Heart Line is very long and thin, then the person has a devastating temper that flares frequently. If the line becomes thin and long-looking at the end of the hand and has branches toward the palm at the edge, it indicates a childless life. The longer the line and the farther the line flows into or near Jupiter, then the more strongly idealistic love will be. If the line is long and distinct, then you are looking at a person with lasting commitments or affections.

The short Heart Line is a signal that the owner will have trouble articulating his feelings. If the line stops abruptly, then this is a person who has intense passion but can be selfish with his spouse or partner. If the Heart Line terminates or fades under the Apollo mount before reaching the Mercury section, it indicates a heart disease. If the line is the same in the minor hand, then that means the parents are weak-hearted and probably had or will have an early death.

If the Heart Line terminates abruptly on Apollo (see A in Illustration 7-43), then it means the person has a love of art that may replace people in the owner's life. If the Heart Line terminates on Mercury and curves toward the base of the finger (see B), it connotes a love of travel and/or business so strong that it may replace people in that person's life. If the Heart Line terminates in the Mount of Luna (C), it indicates very strong jealousy.

A Heart Line with a curving course that ends at Mercury (see D in Illustration 7-43) indicates a person who needs to act out or express what he feels. This is the sign of the hugger and the toucher. The straight Heart Line (E) indicates a person who doesn't need constant signs of affection showered upon him and doesn't open up as to how he feels. A wavy Heart Line (F) suggests a person who acts upon impulse and has inconsistent feelings; he hates routine.

Markings on the Heart Line

Read the Heart Line from the side of the hand toward Jupiter. Branches on the Mount of Jupiter (see A in Illustration 7-44) are great if the branch forms a small V under the index finger. It denotes absolute honesty. A branch toward the Saturn finger (see B in the illustration) indicates a person who is uncertain. A branch to Apollo (C) indicates a person who will be influenced by external things, particularly travel or business. If the Heart Line is branched under Mercury (D), then the owner is a flirt. If this is a

ILLUSTRATION 7-43
LENGTH AND END OF HEART LINE

A. Ends at Mount of Apollo

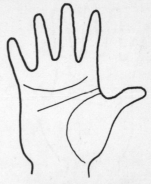

B. Ends in Mount of Mercury and Curves

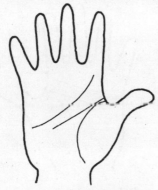

C. Ends in Mount of Luna

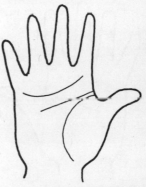

D. Curved Course Line Ending in Mercury

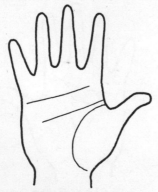

E. Straight Heart Line

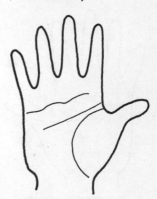

F. Wavy Heart Line

ILLUSTRATION 7-44
MARKS ON HEART LINE

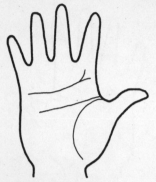

A. Branch on the
Mount of Jupiter

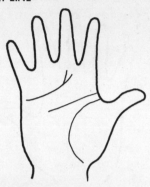

B. Branch on the
Mount of Saturn

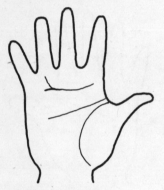

C. Branch on the
Mount of Apollo

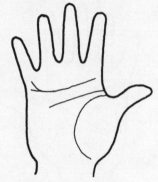

D. Branch on the
Mount of Mercury

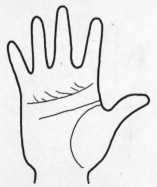

E. Fine Lines Going Up
from the Heart Line

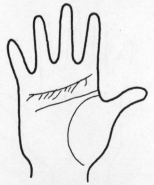

F. Fine Lines Going Down
from the Heart Line

woman, she can conceive (babies) easily. These people act out their emotions more often than people without this mark.

Very fine lines falling on the Heart Line indicate a nervous person. If the fine lines seem to point up toward the fingers (E), they connote a definite interest in the opposite sex. If the majority of the lines point toward the wrist (F), then this is an expression of disappointment in sex life. If the fine lines cross the Heart Line, it indicates inability to express affection. It also indicates wealth.

Chaining on the Heart Line (G) indicates a person who has emotional inconsistency and needs to strive for more calmness in his emotions. A pale but broad and chained Heart Line indicates a calculating individual who doesn't like to place himself in a vulnerable position in love relationships. Chaining only at the beginning of the Heart Line indicates misfortune in love affairs.

A Heart Line that breaks (see H) indicates a loss of a loved one through death.

Islands on the Heart Line (see I in the illustration) indicate emotional attachments; the longer the island, the longer the attachment lasts. If the island is located toward the side of the hand, it means external conditions (war, parental interferences) forced the termination of the affair. If the island is located on the line under the section of Apollo, then it means the lover put too many demands on the subject, and the relationship had to be terminated for the subject's well-being.

If you see dots or spots on the Heart Line (as in J) and the line is deep, then it will indicate stroke potential.

Small bars on the Heart Line (K) indicate obstacles. If the bars are found under the Saturn finger, then it indicates the recurring need for a change in life, such as a move to new geographical location.

Any squares found on the Heart Line (L) signify protection from both physical and emotional shocks to the body.

Forks affect increased ability for expression. A single fork under the Jupiter finger (M) is considered the ideal, as it means that the person and his affections are consistent and balanced. If the Jupiter-Saturn fork is present (N), it indicates a very great desire for domestic harmony; home is the haven to which the subject likes to escape. He must have quiet space. If this is not possible, then the person will exhibit withdrawal. If the fork is located under Saturn (O), it indicates the need for more expression; this person

ILLUSTRATION 7-44 (continued)

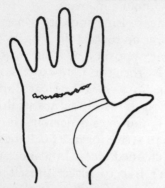

G. Chained Heart line

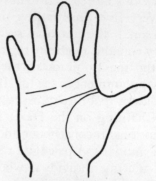

H. Breaks in Heart Line

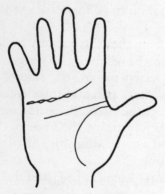

I. Islands on Heart Line

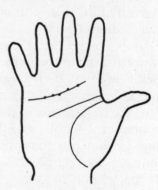

J. Dots on Heart Line

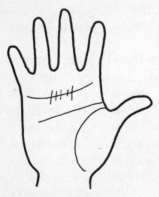

K. Bars on Heart Line

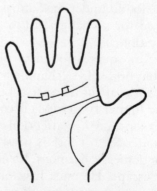

L. Squares on Heart Line

ILLUSTRATION 7-44 (continued)

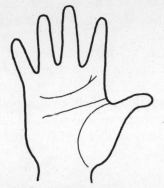

M. Fork Under Jupiter

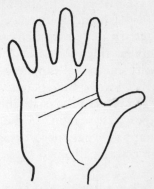

N. Fork to Jupiter and Saturn

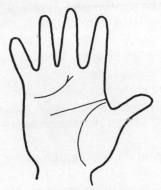

O. Fork under Saturn

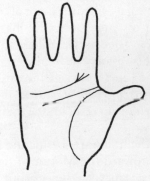

P. Triple-Pronged Fork

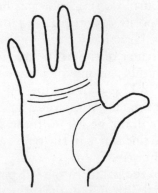

Q. Lines Parallel to Heart Line

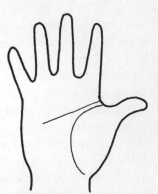

R. No Heart Line

will search for ways of expression. If you see a triple-pronged fork on the Heart Line (P), then you can safely assume that this person can handle home, love, emotions, and career at the same time. He has terrific amounts of emotional energy.

Parallel lines found at the Heart Line (Q) indicate a lot of positive emotional expression. These people are the live wires of spouses, lovers, and friends.

If the Heart Line is absent (R), then it is a signal of a mentally handicapped person. If the line seems to be fading, then the person has experienced disappointments in love and is shutting down emotionally.

Fate (Saturn) Line

This line is commonly referred to as the success line. While most people have fate lines, not all do. If there is any Fate Line at all, this indicates a person who has to overcome obstacles to achieve success as he sees it. Where the line stops and starts gives you clues to when efforts were made.

The Fate (Saturn) Line can originate anywhere on the palm, but no matter where it starts, it terminates either on the Mount of Saturn or directly under the Mount of Saturn (see Illustration 7-45).

If the line starts inside the Life Line on the Mount of Venus and runs toward the Mount of Saturn (see A in Illustration 7-46), it indicates material success but with help from one or more relatives.

If the Fate Line starts from the Mount of Luna and runs toward the Mount of Saturn (see B in the illustration), it indicates help from one or more members of the opposite sex other than family members—by either money, advice, or direction.

If the Fate Line originates in the center of the palm and runs toward the Mount of Saturn (C), then this person will achieve his goals by his own efforts. He will control his own destiny.

If the line starts farther up in the palm (D), it indicates a poor start in life; the influence of the line will not be felt until the age that the line indicates. The higher the line starts in the palm, the later in life the positive activities will begin.

If the line starts low (at the base of the palm) in the left palm but starts high in the right palm, then health and/or the influence of family caused the alteration in the plan of life. If the opposite

ILLUSTRATION 7-45
FATE LINE

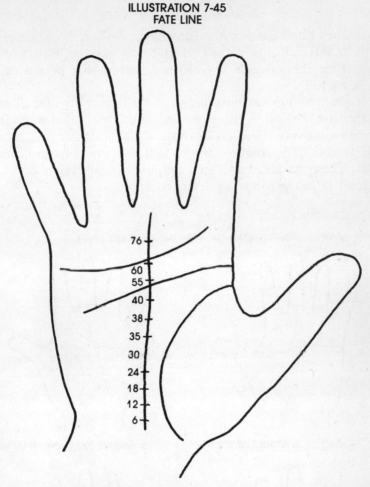

configuration exists, then it was also health or lack of direction that caused the alteration to occur.

If the Fate (Saturn) Line is deep and well cut into the palm, then the person has the endurance and mental capacity to carry out goals. If the line extends to the Mount of Saturn, then these favorable conditions will continue throughout life. However, if the line is short but deep, then the positive influences last only as long as the line is.

If the Fate Line is thin, it says that the person has natural ability, but the person has much to overcome. A broad and shallow line indicates that the person will have continual struggles.

Markings on the Fate Line

A chained Fate Line (see A in Illustration 7-47) tells us that career will be difficult, but if the chaining only occurs on part of the line, then the struggle is contained within that period of the person's life.

If any markings are found either on the beginning of the line or at the base of the line, this person suffers a defect that stems from childhood that usually has its roots in the health or influence of the parents or external conditions that the person has no control over. These markings are often coupled with differing Fate Line placement in the palms, as discussed above.

ILLUSTRATION 7-46
BEGINNING OF FATE LINE (SATURN LINE)

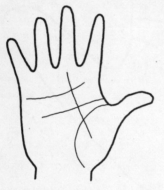

A. Begins in Mount of Venus

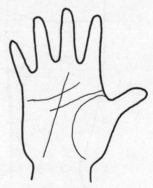

B. Begins in Mount of Luna

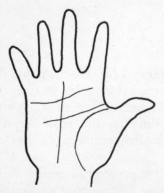

C. Begins in Middle of Palm

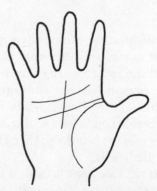

D. Begins High in the Palm

ILLUSTRATION 7-47
MARKINGS ON FATE LINE (SATURN LINE)

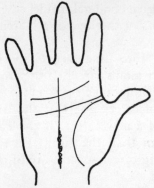

A. Chains on the Fate Line

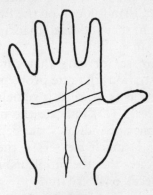

**B. Island at the Base
of the Fate Line**

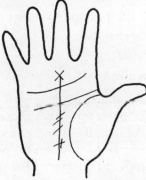

C. Crosses/Bars on the Fate Line

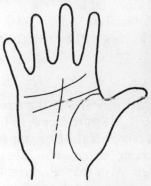

D. Breaks in the Fate Line

E. Uneven Fate Line

If islands are found at the beginning of the Fate Line (see B in Illustration 7-47), it indicates a troubled home life. On a woman's palm, islands found on the Fate Line signal conjugal infidelity. On a man, they indicate financial problems or the love of a married woman.

Crosses or bars that cut into the Fate Line (see C in the illustration) indicate problems in the person's career. If the cross or bar is faint, then it signals a minor annoyance or irritant.

Breaks (D) indicate the blockage of career goals. If the line resumes, it indicates the beginning of a new career. If the Fate Line is much clearer in the left palm than the right, then it indicates that the problems in achieving career success are of the subject's own making.

If the Fate Line is uneven, running deep then shallow or vice versa (E), it means the course of that person's life will be unstable and changeable.

A wavy Fate Line indicates a changing lifestyle and suggests that difficulties will be encountered.

The End of the Fate Line

If the line starts at the base of the hand and runs clearly to the Mount of Saturn (see A in Illustration 7-48), it foretells a prosperous career. If the line stops at the Head Line (B), it indicates his career or business will have serious interruptions through his poor judgment or that of others. If the line stops at the Heart Line (C), it indicates the career is interrupted due to disappointments in the affairs of the heart or possibly to actual problems within the organ of the heart.

If the Fate Line terminates or branches off to Jupiter (D), then the person will attain success through ambition. If the branch ends under Apollo (E), then art or even the stage will be where he will succeed. If a branch ends under the Mount of Mercury (F), it means science is the realm of success.

Apollo Line

The Apollo Line (see Illustration 7-49) is located in or under the general area of the Mount of Apollo. This line will only terminate at the Mount of Apollo, which will make it easier for the beginner

ILLUSTRATION 7-48
FATE LINE (SATURN LINE)

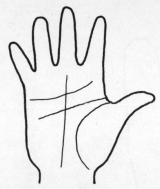

A. Runs from the Base to Mount of Saturn

B. Stops at the Head Line

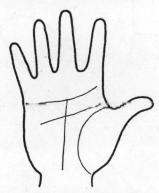

C. Stops at the Heart Line

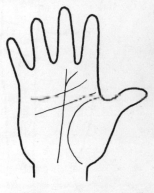

D. With a Branch to Jupiter

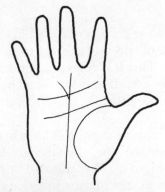

E. With a Branch to Apollo

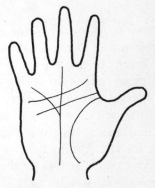

F. With a Branch to Mercury

ILLUSTRATION 7-49
SUN LINE (APOLLO LINE)

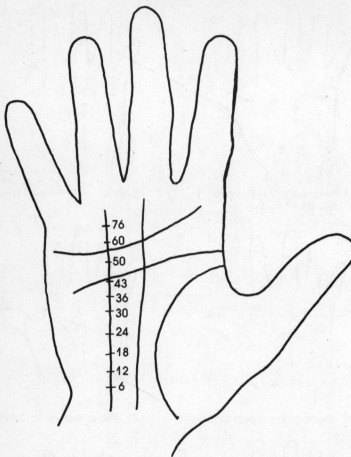

palmist to locate. This line is found in the section of the palm that is referred to as the unconscious area of life, and it helps to carry life energy to that region of the palm. This line represents creative ability, as well as the ability to develop what talents are found here. It forecasts wealth, power, and success either in the physical or spiritual sense.

In all cases, this line is good to have in the palm. The general rule for the Apollo Line is the longer the line, the stronger the inclinations. The shorter the Apollo Line, the harder it will be for that individual to bring to fruition the talents that are found in the personality.

The Beginning and Course of the Apollo Line

The line of Apollo can start from several places within the palm and can end quickly or can weave its way through the palm. If the line starts at the Life Line (see A in Illustration 7-50), within the Mount of Venus (B), or in the Plain of Mars (C), the line characteristics have the same meaning as they do for the other lines found in the hand. See, for example, chains or breaks for any of the lines.

The length of the line is important, as it determines the extent and duration of the Apollo influence over the personality. The shorter the line of Apollo, the less influence it has over the personality.

Sometimes the lines will start and end, then restart again. This

ILLUSTRATION 7-50
BEGINNING OF APOLLO LINE

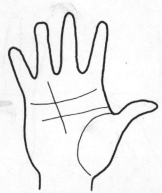

A. Starts on Life Line   B. Starts in Mount of Venus

C. Starts in Plain of Mars

ILLUSTRATION 7-51
BEGINNING AND COURSE OF APOLLO LINE

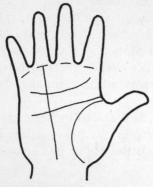

A. High into Mount Finger Base

B. Starts in Luna

C. Starts in the Mount of Saturn

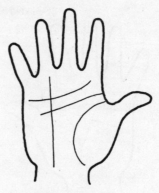

D. Wrist to Apollo

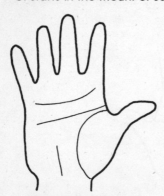

E. Starts Low, but Short

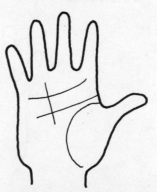

F. High, but Extends Through Head and Heart Lines

doesn't matter; the line still carries the possibilities of accomplishing much and the capacity for carrythrough. If the line is not found in the hand, then don't panic, it just means that the natural abilities have been rechanneled to another line, usually the Fate Line, and the character of that line is applied to the ability to use creative talents to gain success and wealth.

A broad or shallow Apollo Line indicates little ability for completion of the line potential without having to strive and struggle. The person who has this line generally values beauty. If the palm has this type of line and yet the palm appears to be coarse or rough in comparison to other palms, then you are seeing a person who likes flashy or gaudy trinkets or is showy in dress, such as Liberace. If the hand is refined or fine, however, then the person exhibits good taste in appearance or lifestyle. Good examples of this type of personality would be Grace Kelly, Audrey Hepburn, Fred Astaire, and David Niven. These people have a good eye for color and harmony of textures and colors.

If the Apollo Line starts at the Mount of Venus, this person is a nature lover who is very sympathetic to the world at large. This is a caring person who is strongly in the mental plane; he makes a good career or guidance counselor. The line of Apollo that starts *inside* the Mount of Venus indicates an intensifying of these traits, as well as environmental concern. These are the "bleeding-heart liberals."

If the Apollo Line runs into the Mount of Apollo or is found high on the Mount of Apollo running into the finger base (A), the personality will exhibit talent and will gain a good reputation—and may even be considered brilliant—in society at large.

If the Apollo Line starts at the Mount of Luna (B), it shows that the person will have a good imagination combined with excellent abilities for expression. This particular line placement is the first indicator that the personality is a mental type and will find literature the specific talent outlined. If the line from Luna is combined with smooth, conic-tipped fingers, then the specific talent is for poetry. If the line starts in Luna but the individual has knotty fingers with square fingertips being predominant, then you are looking at either the professional or amateur historian. If the Apollo Line starts at Luna but leads up through the Upper Mount of Mars section, then you are looking at a person fond of military strategy based upon historical data.

If the Apollo Line starts on the Mount of Saturn (C) (this is sometimes referred to as the sister line), then you are looking at a person who will have definite scientific leanings.

If the line starts from the wrist area and extends to the Mount of Apollo (see D in Illustration 7-51), it indicates a person who holds great talent and the energy to promote those talents.

If the Apollo Line starts low in the palm and goes only a short distance (see E in Illustration 7-51), the person has talent, but his ability to be productive with that talent is lessened. In some cases, when the line of Apollo starts low and terminates very quickly, it is a signal that the talent is insufficiently developed to enable the person to reach the desired goal.

If the line starts higher in the palm and covers the space between the head and heart line (as in F), it is during that time period that talent will be in evidence, perhaps because success at that time is the primary goal of the individual.

Markings on the Apollo Line

The best of all possibilities of the Apollo Line is that the line be straight, smooth, of medium depth, and clear of any marking. This is unusual and would mean that the individual will *definitely* achieve success in his endeavors.

Chaining on the Apollo Line (see A in Illustration 7-52) is significant; when you see chaining on a line, you immediately recognize that the line has lost some of its energy or power. When you see chaining on the Apollo Line, it is a sure indication that the Apollo traits are weakened and the person will most likely be unable to accomplish goals. This is the type of personality who will keep talking about what he is going to do—he just doesn't ever do it.

The wavy Apollo Line (see B in Illustration 7-52) indicates vacillating career goals. When I see a wavy line in the palm, I immediately realize that this is a person who will consistently get sidetracked. But the person with a wavy line can, through early and consistent discipline, overcome this blockage to the Apollo Line and can achieve recognition in his area of talent. This is also the mark of a clever personality.

The most serious marking found on the Apollo Line is the island (C in the illustration). If the line is medium to deep red and straight, then islands represent a blockage of completion of talents and indicate loss of wealth or fame that can be attributed to the

ILLUSTRATION 7-52
MARKINGS ON THE APOLLO (SUN) LINE

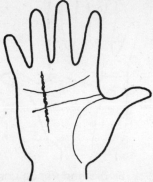

A. Chaining

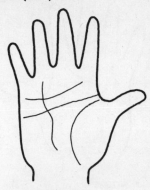

B. Wavy Line

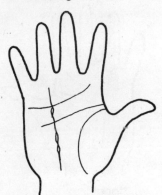

C. Islands

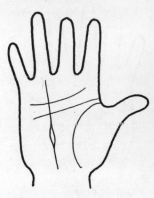

D. Island with Long
Apollo Finger

E. Apollo Finger with a
Long, Thick Phalange,
and Apollo Line with an Island

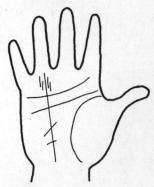

F. Bars

ILLUSTRATION 7-52 (continued)

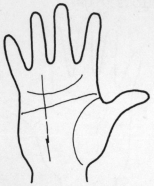

G. Breaks

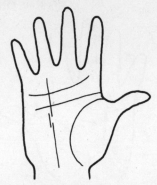

H. Breaks and Repair Line

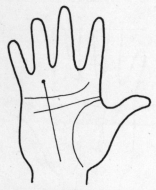

I. Dot at end

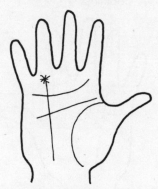

J. Star at End

K. Bar at End

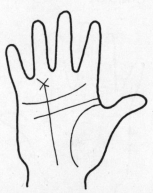

L. Cross at End

mishandling of money or business activities. If the finger of Apollo is long too (as in D), or longer than the Saturn finger, this person will tend to jump in where angels dare not tread. If the third phalange of the Apollo finger is long and thick, and there is an island on the Apollo Line (E), then you are looking at a gambler. A gambling mark indicates that the person is not always able to control his impulses.

Bars on the Apollo Line (F) that don't cut the line are indicators of blockage of the natural talents evidenced there. If the bars actually cut the line, it tells the reader that the career of that person will be affected rather than general talents. If the bars appear to be fine and not deeply etched, this is an indicator of worry that will tend to retard that person's progress due to periods of low self-esteem if not contained through vigorous self-motivation.

Dots or spots of any type or color found on the Apollo Line are definite warnings of loss of reputation due to criminal activities.

Breaks on the line (G) are indications of setbacks to the ambitions. These breaks are usually repaired later on the line (H). If the breaks are not repaired, then it means that the breaks are most likely caused through mistakes that not only involved external stimuli but could be through health. As mentioned earlier, unrepaired breaks do not necessarily mean failure.

If the Apollo Line terminates with a spot or dot (I), this indicates a loss of self-esteem. A star at either end of the line (J) indicates brilliant success in any field of endeavor. If you find a double star, you are looking at a person who has an unusual destiny along with fame and/or wealth. If you find a deep bar at the end of the line (K), it indicates a major obstacle at the close of life that cannot be overcome. This marking usually means health becomes poor and success is achieved more slowly. If there are crosses at the end of the line (L), it shows a definite lack of judgment on the part of the person; this is someone who doesn't learn from his or her mistakes. My children have this mark!

Squares found at the end of the Apollo Line (see A in Illustration 7-53) indicate protection from the negative marking traits we have just mentioned. A square negates health problems and promotes the ability of the person to attain his goals.

If a fork is located at the end of the Apollo Line (see B in Illustration 7-53), then this is a multitalented person; he must decide which of the talents he will develop, or he will attain mastery of none.

ILLUSTRATION 7-53
FURTHER MARKINGS ON THE APOLLO LINE

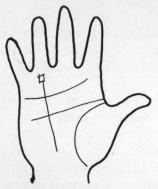

A. Square at End

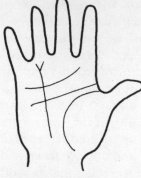

B. Fork at End

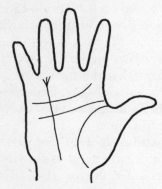

C. Three-Pronged Fork at End

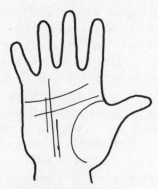

D. Parallel Lines

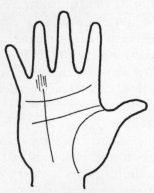

E. Vertical Lines on the
Mount of Apollo

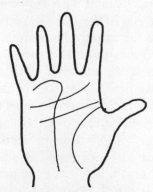

F. Ends in Mercury but
Incorporates Saturn
and Apollo

ILLUSTRATION 7-53 (continued)

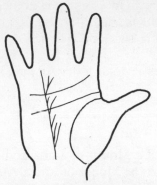

G. Upward Branches

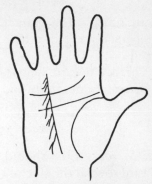

H. Downward Branches

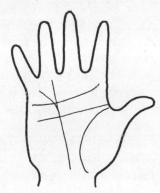

I. Branch Toward Mercury

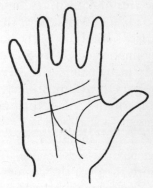

J. Branch Toward Venus

If a three-pronged fork is located at the end of the Apollo Line (C), then you are looking at a true celebrity and one who will amass great wealth without effort. Why, oh, why not me?

Parallel lines on the Apollo Line, one on each side of it (D), provide additional strength to a good line. If you see several vertical lines on the Mount of Apollo (E), it indicates too much varied interest for the line to produce success. The meaning is the same if the Mount of Apollo has tassels instead of lines.

If the Apollo Line terminates in the region of Saturn or Mercury, then the brilliance of the Apollo Line, combined with the wisdom of Saturn, produces a unique personal destiny. If the line terminates under the Mount of Mercury and incorporates both the mounts of Saturn and Apollo (F), then this person will have wealth and reputation. It is unusual to find the marking.

Any branching or fine lines *rising* from the Apollo Line itself

(G) increase the beneficial qualities of the line. All branching that *falls* from the line (H) indicate that much more effort is needed to assure success. If a branched line runs toward Mercury (I), then the person will have had help in his success from family and friends.

A branch toward Venus (J) indicates a person who will have help in success from family and friends.

Mercury Line

The Mercury Line should start on the Mount of Luna and run upward toward the side of the palm to the Mount of Mercury (see Illustration 7-54) but is more often than not found to start from the area of Saturn, region of the Life Line, center of the palm, or the Plain of Mars. Even though this is considered a minor line, it carries indications of the health of the digestive organs. Its secondary importance is its guide to business success.

In many palms, the Mercury Line is absent. If this is the case, the person will most likely be quick in speech and feel that life is worth living. Also, this indicates that liver problems will not be present in that person.

A long Mercury Line will indicate more material possessions can be amassed. It also means good health flows. If the line is short, then health becomes less vigorous, and business events will be determined by the health.

A deep, pink, clear Mercury Line indicates good health flows and good vitality and, probably most important, a clear brain pattern and memory. If the person has the same type of lines in the Life, Head, and Heart, this person will rarely see illness. If any of the other lines are defective (markings upon them) but the person has a good Mercury Line, then you can say that this person will be susceptible to abuse of drugs or alcohol and would resort to criminal activities to support the habits. If the Mercury Line is broad but shallow, this person will have stomach problems, perhaps ulcers.

Beginning of and Breaks in Mercury Line

If the line starts from the Life Line (see A in Illustration 7-55), it definitely indicates weakness of the heart that will interfere with

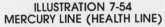

ILLUSTRATION 7-54
MERCURY LINE (HEALTH LINE)

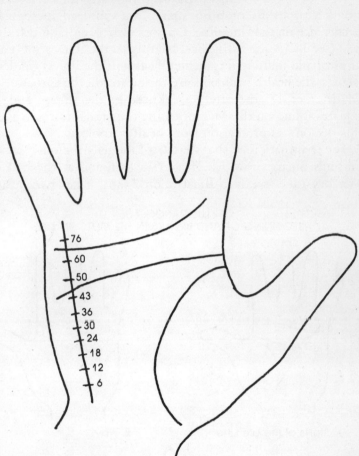

business success. If the line starts from other points in the palm, it will not be a problem. If the line is wavy (see B), the person suffers from biliousness and rheumatism. Breaks (C) are a serious indication of problems with the stomach and digestive tract.

Markings on the Mercury Line

A chained line of Mercury (see A in Illustration 7-56) shows a diseased liver or stomach. The time line can tell when the problem will become or became evident. This type of line marking will also forecast less success in business activities.

Dots or spots found on the line indicate transient attacks of stomach problems or biliousness. You can read the age of the occurrence on the time line. Crosses or bars cutting through the line (see B) indicate illnesses. Islands on the line (see C) are not unusual and indicate fragmented health. If the line is riddled with islands, the health problems are in the area of the throat or lungs. Grilles (see D) indicate a weakness in the throat and lungs. Squares found on the Mercury Line (E) signal to the reader that this person has protection from health problems.

The termination of the Mercury Line tells the outcome of the person's business ability. If a grille is found at the end of the Mercury Line (see F in Illustration 7-56), it has two meanings:

ILLUSTRATION 7-55
BEGINNING OF AND BREAKS IN THE MERCURY LINE

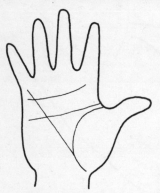

A. Starts at the Life Line

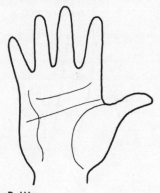

B. Wavy

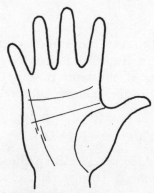

C. Breaks

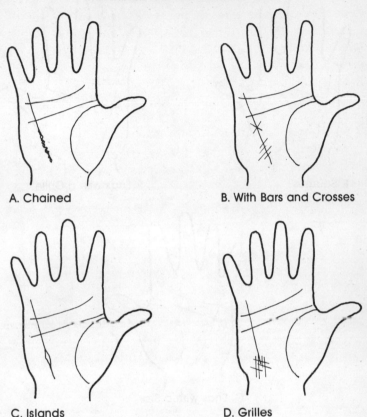

ILLUSTRATION 7-56
MARKINGS ON THE MERCURY LINE

A. Chained

B. With Bars and Crosses

C. Islands

D. Grilles

one of poor health and one of dishonesty in business. A star at the end of the Mercury Line (see G in illustration) means that success will be gained by the talent indicated by the predominant finger.

Marriage Lines

The lines of union or marriage are found on the Mount of Mercury. They run horizontally from the side of the palm toward the center of the Mount of Mercury (see Illustration 7-57). These lines suggest the number of persons who have made a deep romantic impression on the owner's life. Not everyone will have Union Lines; the Heart Line carries the same information.

ILLUSTRATION 7-56 (continued)

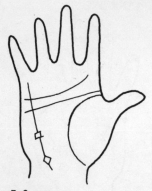

E. Squares

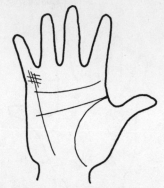

F. Ends with a Grille

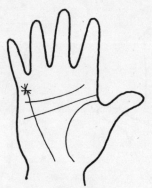

G. Ends with a Star

ILLUSTRATION 7-57
MARRIAGE LINES

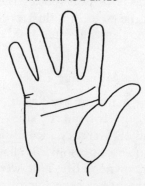

ILLUSTRATION 7-58
MARKS ON MARRIAGE LINES

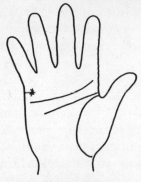

A. Star at End

B. Breaks

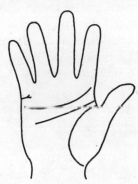

C. Fork

D. Branch Toward the Heart Line

E. Branch Touching the Heart Line

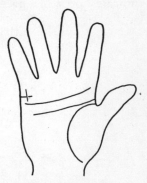

F. Complete Break

If lots of lines are found, then these are companion lines, indicating a natural flirt and an interest in sexual conquest. If the lines are thin in comparison to other lines in the palm, then it means that this person won't have strong emotional ties and won't show affection easily. If the lines are deep, then the emotional ties are strong.

A cross found on the Marriage Line tells of some external interference. A star on the line (see A in Illustration 7-58) tells of a breach and is sometimes called a jilt mark. A break in the marriage line (B) indicates emotional interference in the marriage. A fork at the end of the line (C) indicates emotional separation and/or divorce. A branching or a line turning toward the Heart Line (D) indicates the death of a loved one but only when it completely touches the Heart Line (E). The point at which it connects will also tell you the subject's age at the time; use the Heart Line time line. Branches falling from the Marriage Line foretell disappointments in love and marriage. A total break in the Marriage Line indicates sudden death of a spouse. If a broken Marriage Line is cut at its end by another line (see F), it indicates death of a spouse or the marriage.

Children Lines

Deep vertical lines found directly above the Marriage Line (see Illustration 7-59) are considered children lines. They can also be found on the side of the palm in the crease marks. If straight they indicate a boy, and if slanted indicate a girl. If the lines are faint, this indicates possible pregnancies that have not yet come to fruition.

ILLUSTRATION 7-59
CHILDREN LINES

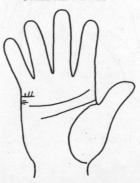

RASCETTES (BRACELETS)

Normally, each of the palms has side-to-side lines at the end of the hand and at the beginning of the wrist known as the rascettes, or bracelets. These lines can even encircle the wrist. You may need to hold a palm forward to see rascettes clearly.

Early in the development of palmistry, rascettes were considered most important in divining the overall health of the person. Today, the rascettes are significant not only for health, but also for personality and longevity. They back up the Life Line as far as the

ILLUSTRATION 7-60
RASCETTES (BRACELETS)

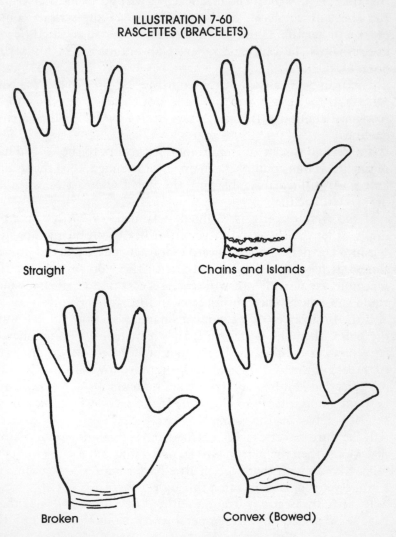

Straight

Chains and Islands

Broken

Convex (Bowed)

number of years the person will live and when health will begin to decline.

The rascettes found on women tell an additional story, relating more to menstrual periods and childbirth information. In men the rascettes are related to longevity and health of the sexual organs.

The first rascette (see Illustration 7-60) on the wrists is considered the most important, as it indicates general health. If the rascette is straight and not chained, islanded, or broken, then the health is good. If on the woman's hand, the line is not chained, islanded, or broken, then childbearing will be easier than usual, and she will not have "female problems" of any serious consequence in her life. If the line is straight and not deviated on the male's palms, he can expect few if any problems in his sexual organs.

Time can be measured by the length of the rascette line (as with others). If the first line is good and not broken, then life will be fine until about age fifty-six, when health will normally start to decline.

The second rascette is important, as it relates to the second half of the life. If it is not broken, chained, or islanded, then the second half of life will remain stable until the age of seventy-five, when the health will decline.

If the first rascette is chained, islanded, or broken, then it implies that the client will have minor health problems throughout life. The person tends toward extravagance in material possessions but has an easygoing nature. In the woman, the specific meaning is that her family will take precedence over all else, which could cause her some concern later in life.

If the first rascette on a woman's hand has a bow curve toward the palm, then she will have hard pregnancies. The number of curved rascettes indicates the number of children she will have (up to three!). If the first rascette curves upward toward a man's hand, it means that children and family are quite important to him, and he wants more than two children. If the second rascette follows suit, it emphasizes the first.

If the third rascette is well defined and is straight with few or no deviations, then the person will achieve fame and fortune. Lots of folks I know with that type of line have acquired some fame or fortune yet squander it, often through divorce.

If the first rascette is straight without deviation, and the others have some deviation, then the personality is one that will take the middle course in life and has a natural resilience. If the first rascette has lots of breaks, islands, or chaining, then this is a person who enjoys life but doesn't always take care of his health.

In ancient palmistry, the rascettes told the reader where the person would live at the close of life. If the first rascette was convex (bowed upward), the subject would end his life south of his birthplace; if the first two rascettes were different, east. To be valid, lines on both hands must reflect this information. As strange as this may sound, I have found it to be accurate.

SAMPLE PALM READINGS

The two palm readings that follow serve two purposes. The first is to let you practice your newfound skills; look at illustrations 7-61, 7-62, 7-63, and 7-64, and see how well you do, then check yourself against the readings provided here. Second, these sample palm readings will give you an idea of the tone a reading should take, helping you learn how to talk to your subject.

Joy, 49

Joy enjoyed her reading, and her comments (included here) gave me lots of validation.

Joy, your palm, the psychic hand, is a rare one. It is the palm of a dreamer and a mentally oriented person. An irritable, moody and apathetic person, you will react emotionally to life. Paradoxically, you can be very level-headed and totally unselfish toward those you love.

Your energy is low, and you need to expend it with care, as you sometimes have trouble coping. Health problems exist with your teeth, neck, and stomach. This hand indicates possible chemical dependency, Joy. You should take notice and regard this as a clear warning.

You do not do well as an employee in a rigid structure. You need freedom, or you will become depressed. Money does not motivate you, achievement is your forte. You would do well in the theater, with books, sculpture, or art in any form.

Your religious concepts and beliefs are rather unorthodox, to say the least. You feel that *all* is universal and good.

We'll begin with your fingers. The smoothness of your fingers denotes alertness with some extra energy flows, which you need,

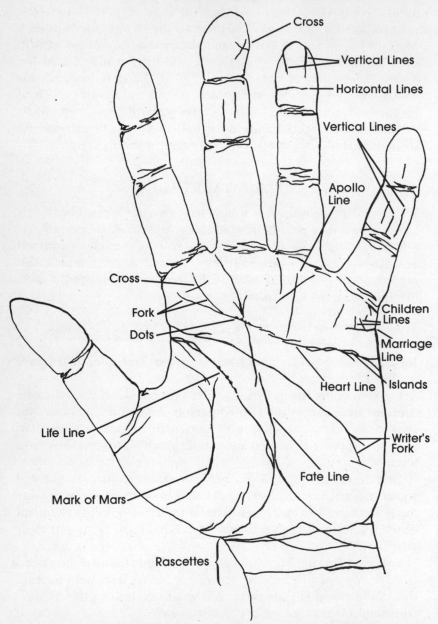

ILLUSTRATION 7-61*
JOY'S LEFT HAND

Cross

Vertical Lines

Horizontal Lines

Vertical Lines

Apollo
Line

Cross

Fork

Dots

Children
Lines

Marriage
Line

Heart Line

Islands

Life Line

Writer's
Fork

Fate Line

Mark of Mars

Rascettes

*Please note that this illustraton and Illustrations 7-62, 7-63, and 7-64 for the sample palm readings are simplified. Some markings have been left off for the sake of clarity; others have been left on because they are prominent and/or they are good examples of that marking (although they may not be particularly significant).

along with spontaneity. You have a combination of straight and crooked fingers. The straight fingers denote an easy flow of ideas and quick mental processes. Shame on you, Joy, your crooked fingers denote a distinct reluctance to face facts, an inclination to be evasive, and also a possible lack of inner harmony. [Joy loudly denies this with a very wide grin.]

The crooked Mercury finger on your right hand tells me that you like gossip and may tend to overexaggerate, as well as have difficulty expressing your inner feelings. Your fingers are thin, which reflects lofty idealism. Your mind dominates your physical side. [Joy admits that yes, she exaggerates, "But only in the interest of good story telling, and by the way—I was not put on this earth to do physical labor!"]

Joy, your fingertips are conic or round (see Illustration 7-10), indicating versatility, good perception into others' personalities, and a preference to work alone without close supervision. You are classified as a bleeding-heart liberal . . . the champion of the underdog. [Joy hoots, "Amen!"]

The tips of your Jupiter fingers have horizontal lines, indicating a desire to please others. The vertical lines on the tip signify a positive attitude.

The narrow spaces between your Saturn and Apollo fingers indicate your need for financial security (see Illustration 7-4). [Joy says, "Heavens yes! Joe *has* to make good money."] The wide space between your Apollo and Mercury fingers denotes independence in thinking and action. The wide space between your Jupiter and Saturn fingers indicates that you have good thinking processes.

Joy, the uneven set of your fingers connotes some measure of disharmony and that your energy flow is affected. More effort than is normal will be needed for you to achieve success in your goals. ["That figures," says Joy.] This also tells me that you tend to be abrupt and awkward, and maybe even a little self-conscious and defensive. Joy, you need to learn control (see Illustration 7-8). ["I deny this totally and resent that highly!" says Joy.] You are people-oriented and like to travel.

Joy, because your hands lie flat when at rest, I can tell that you have the ability to solve problems and that your thinking processes are well balanced. Congratulations!

Your thumbs are of average length (see Illustration 7-13), which connotes a tendency for mental balance.

Flexible thumbs indicate a generous and sympathetic individual. You can be plain old lazy, however. ["Hey, I'm creative even when I'm lazy," says Joy.] This is true, Joy, but you are still lazy. Your flexible thumb, in relation to your Jupiter finger, tells me you are tactful and intuitive (see Illustration 7-16).

Your thumb shape is waisted, which means you are a naturally adaptable mixer. This indicates originality in thought, but also a tendency for trouble with decision making.

The shape of your thumb tip indicates that you are a tactful, lively, active person who likes to travel. You should be a wonderful Trivial Pursuit player. ["I am great," Joy says, "but no one will play with me!"]

Your curved fingertips denote impulsiveness and a social-minded nature. You are, however, a procrastinator. ["I don't believe in doing anything today that I can put off until tomorrow," says Joy.]

Your low-set thumbs tell me that you love liberty, hate routine, and are liberal in thoughts and actions.

Now, moving on to your nails, Joy, I see they are oval with convex tendencies. This means you need conformity in your environment or in new circumstances. You think with clarity, are broad-minded and idealistic in concepts. The convex nails denote tendencies for lung problems. Your nails are thin and brittle and indicate definite opinions and also a predilection toward headaches. Pale and white nails indicate low energy reserves, poor circulation, and a tendency for blood clots.

Your yellow thumb-nail tells me again that you have a predilection for chemical dependency and also kidney and bladder infections. You have difficulty articulating your deep emotions.

That you will be plagued by kidney problems later in life is evidenced by dark edges on the side or top of your nails. Sorry, Joy, but you will probably suffer from renal failure. The fluting on your nails indicates that you have insufficient blood circulation for the proper distribution of nutrients. ["Is this why my hands and feet stay cold?" asks Joy.] Joy, the vertical ridges on your nails represent stomach and/or digestive ailments. On the Saturn nail (which governs the skeleton) the ridges signify stress on bones and muscles.

The numerous vertical lines on your Saturn fingertip (only a few shown here, for clarity) indicate that you have the gift of gab

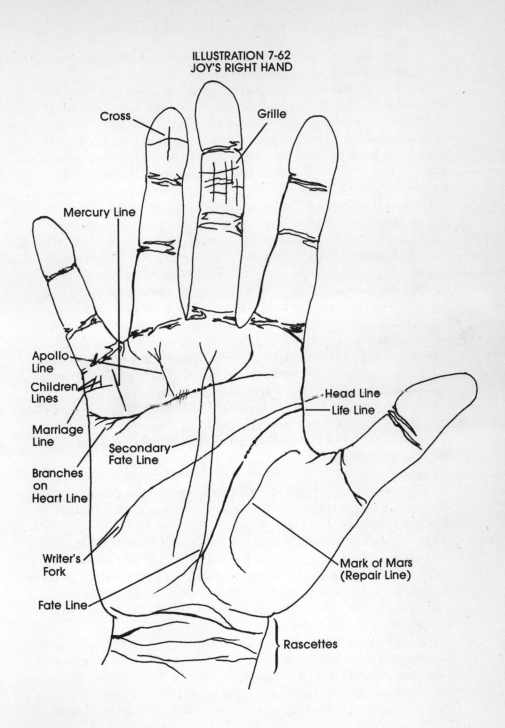

ILLUSTRATION 7-62
JOY'S RIGHT HAND

Cross

Grille

Mercury Line

Apollo
Line

Children
Lines

Marriage
Line

Branches
on
Heart Line

Writer's
Fork

Fate Line

Secondary
Fate Line

Head Line

Life Line

Mark of Mars
(Repair Line)

Rascettes

and artistic ability. The cross on the first phalange means you sometimes experience emotional losses.

The third phalange on the Jupiter finger of your left hand is predominant. This reflects a basic need for love, affection, and communication [which Joy definitely affirms]. The first phalange on Mercury—left hand—is predominant (trust me here), which indicates a need to learn and apply knowledge. You have good relationships with your parents and your spouse. [Joy says, "Yes, I'm spoiled, and I love it."]

The first phalange on the Saturn finger of your left hand is also predominant, and concerns your mental attitude. Joy, you are involved and have a penchant for pursuits and causes, such as justice. [Joy says, "Yeah, just give me a soap box!"]

You have a suppressive and emotional nature, because your Jupiter finger curves toward Mercury on the right hand.

Pinkish and spotty skin color tells me that your energy is low, but sexual expression is intense. [No comment from Joy—she simply grins.] It also indicates an erratic personality.

Joy, you have a pronounced hollow depression in your palm and will react to all of life's environments. You will have good perceptual ability but difficulty adjusting to change. [Joy says, "I wouldn't know about that . . . I *refuse* to change."] You would be an excellent researcher or teacher. [Joy has a degree in education and has taught school in the past.] You have poor energy but are learning to conserve it.

Horizontal lines on the tip of your Apollo finger are worry lines, Joy, but the vertical lines indicate strength of endeavor and determination. The vertical lines on the tip of your Mercury finger denote allergies.

You have well-developed mounts of Apollo and Mercury that are the same in both hands. They are slightly off-center and appear to be between the fingers. This tells me that your social world and contacts are important to you. You search for wisdom and knowledge, and are concerned with one universe and evolving into your higher self.

The rest of your mounts are underdeveloped, Joy, and are almost flat, except for the Mount of Luna. Your Mount of Luna indicates a well-developed imagination and good ability (quality) for writing (fiction). The lower area of Luna (see Illustration 7-19) indicates a love, and abundance, of travel. The fact that the mount is well developed and leans toward the side of your hand indicates that you are ruled by your emotions. Logic is practically nonexistent, Joy. [To which Joy nods and agrees.]

In the Mount of Mars, the developed space between the index finger and the thumb indicates a tendency to voice your opinions, convictions, and strong moral ideas.

Markings on your mounts include a cross on the Mount of Jupiter, which indicates a good and happy marriage. On the right hand, you have a cross on the Mount of Mercury and, shame on you, Joy, this means you love to talk and gossip! [Joy denies this. I call her down as she proceeds to give me the latest lowdown on a local newscaster.] The triangle on your Mount of Luna means you are intuitive. A box, or square, on the Mount of Mercury is a positive sign and reinforces the influences of Mercury.

It is probably becoming clearer to you that there can be two or more identifying marks for specific traits (the writer, the dreamer, business smarts). Remember that the experienced palmist looks at the hand(s) as a whole, searching for reaffirmation and strengthening, of what he sees. A mark can even be negated by other stronger or more adequately supported marks. Also remember that just because a person doesn't have a mark (for poor eyesight, for example) doesn't mean he definitely does not exhibit the trait—it may be seen elsewhere in the palm.

Now, Joy, we'll look at your major lines, beginning with your Life Line. You will live to be between eighty and ninety years old (see Illustration 7-23). Because it rises closer to Venus, it indicates a predilection for quiet time and space. You will also have colds and flu bugs. You have a combination Life Line that starts out resembling Illustration 7–25B but looks like Illustration 7–25E at the end. As you can see, your Life Line terminates in a split. You will have an active life that includes travel and is centered around interesting, unusual people.

The fork at the end of your Life Line also tells me that you will experience a dissipation of life energies toward the end of life. The shallow, light Life Line indicates the need for rest to maintain health. A narrow line indicates that you are a high-strung individual, Joy, with quick responses. You had an early onset of menopause.

Dots and spots on the Life Lines in both hands indicate childhood illnesses, tonsillitis, and upper respiratory problems. [Joy confirms both.] The red and blue dots indicate both genetic heart and lung disorders. Darker blue dots indicate coughing, and you need to be careful of your throat, lungs, and chest.

The island under Saturn (see Illustration 7-26) tells me that you will experience nervousness and bone, back, and leg ailments. As the island is large, it indicates that bone ailments become more apparent as you mature.

Chaining at the beginning of your Life Line is an indication of delicate health in early life, and also that one parent has delicate health. [Joy had whooping cough and severe tonsillitis bouts—and her mother was a "blue baby" at birth.]

Your Head Line is in a normal position between the Jupiter and thumb area, but ends in the Mount of Luna. The length indicates varied interests in all areas of life, probing intellect, and the ability to be a good researcher (see Illustration 7-34E).

On the right hand, the Head Line is separated from the Heart Line (although the separation is not overly wide). This indicates you are optimistic and independent. The chaining at the beginning of the Head Line on your left hand indicates inconsistency of thoughts. ["Yes," Joy says, "My thoughts are very scattered." She says she is "consistently inconsistent."] You also have a writer's mark (see Illustration 7-37C), connoting a good imagination and command of words [Joy speaks like a dictionary]. You only have the mark in your left hand, which tells me you have not actively pursued your natural ability.

Joy, your Heart Line has chaining toward the edge on your right hand, which tells me that you have emotional inconsistency and should strive for calmness in your emotions. You cannot lie or lead a life of crime, as evidenced by the branch to Jupiter. You are absolutely honest (see Illustration 7-44A).

In your left hand, the Heart Line starts under Jupiter and flows past the edge of the Mount of Mercury; this relates to emotions and/or feelings. The Heart Line is long, Joy, and flows upward into Jupiter, which indicates strong love flows. Therefore, you have lasting commitments.

Your Fate Line indicates success and, usually, a self-made person. In your left hand, it starts in the Mount of Luna and runs toward Saturn. This indicates that you receive help from the opposite sex—with money, advice, or direction (see Illustration 7-46B, as it is closest to Joy's configuration).

Joy, your right hand has a sister line running parallel to the Fate Line, which begins in the Mount of Luna and merges under or on the Mount of Saturn. This is indicative of a repair line and tells me that you will change career flows, and success will follow after you reach forty years of age. [Joy states that she has, however, "been *thinking* of success for years!"]

The Apollo Line is located in, or under, the general area of the Mount of Apollo. Your line indicates that you are a talented person in the areas of art, music, writing, and/or the theater. You have the ability to develop those talent markings.

In your right hand, there is a trident on the Apollo line (see Illustration 7-53C). Believe it or not, Joy, this means you have the potential to become a true celebrity and can (through efforts) amass wealth. [The thrill is gone for Joy as she hears the word *efforts*.]

The Apollo Line in your left hand runs into the Mount of Apollo (see Illustration 7-51F) and indicates that you exhibit talent, can obtain a reputation in your world, and may even be considered brilliant by society. This could be lessened to some degree because the line is relatively short.

The Mercury Line on your right hand is short, which indicates less vigorous health. Business events will be a determining factor to your health, especially in relation to energy dissipation.

Your Mercury Line is longer in your left hand, reinforcing your ability to amass material wealth or possessions.

Both hands indicate one marriage. [Joy confirms. "No more— I've been married to the same man for twenty-eight years and have no desire to break in a new one."]

Joy's Children Lines are right above her Marriage Line and indicate that she should have one male and one female child. [Joy also confirms this fact and states proudly that there won't be any more, since her "giblets" have been removed.]

In summation of Joy's overall palm we can safely say that she does exhibit wit, is definitely intelligent, has a natural charm, and can be tactful. She is one who can intuitively relate to people and their circumstances. Yet she must conserve her energy to maintain good health by providing herself with adequate space and time for self-rejuvenation.

Joy is an unusual, interesting person and will surround herself with bohemian types like herself.

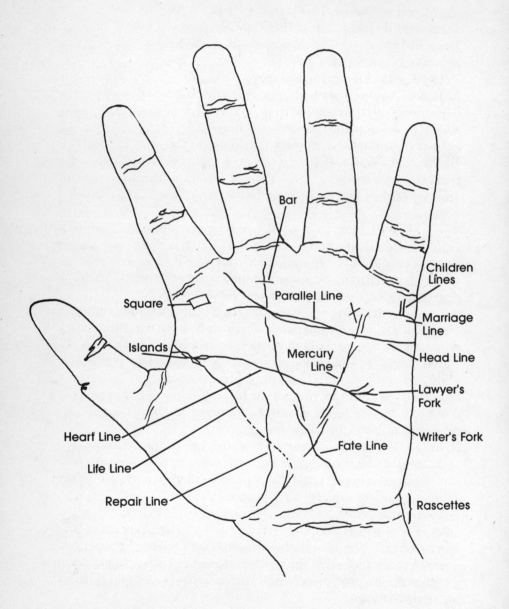

ILLUSTRATION 7-63
LORI'S LEFT HAND

Bar

Children
Lines

Square

Parallel Line

Marriage
Line

Islands

Mercury
Line

Head Line

Lawyer's
Fork

Heart Line

Writer's Fork

Life Line

Fate Line

Repair Line

Rascettes

As a professional palmist, I suggested that she direct her energies toward developing her creative abilities, particularly writing.

Lori, 19

As you will notice, Lori's hands (markings, lines, fingers, and so on) are very different in comparison to Joy's. Lori's hands are very clean; she does not have a great number of lines due to her age. Lori is nineteen, and the lines of her hands were not firmly set until the age of seventeen. This is because children are at the mercy of their environment until they are on their own and able to control their lives. Lori's lines are just beginning to develop.

Lori, your round palms indicate that you have a versatile personality. You know you have good qualities, but you don't have an overinflated ego. You are among the "work force" of the world.

Imagination is your key word, but you can—and do—control your imagination. You tend to work best independently, yet can be supervised without having your ego threatened. You follow instructions well.

Round-handed people are usually talented, and things come fairly easily to them, Lori. Usually, people with round palms are well-read and can discuss art, books, world events, and so on. You will be a good parent but will tend to be overly protective, not only with your children, but also your spouse and parents. You are a doer and will inspire your offspring to take part in activities.

In dealing with your spouse, you are the epitome of "behind every successful man is a round-palmed (designing) woman." This is the sensitive or mental hand, and you, the owner, are refined in your thoughts. You are not too physical in nature. You will also continue to learn as you get older; you view life as a learning experience.

The slight hollow in your palm indicates that you can adjust more easily than most. You use your natural perceptive ability in relating to your world.

Skin texture is helpful in determining an individual's emotional responses and also the degrees of sensitivity expressed. Lori, your medium skin indicates a tendency to respond in a balanced manner to life's experiences. You also enjoy both indoor and outdoor activities in moderation.

The skin color is important as a profile for physical and sexual information, as well as psychological insights. Your pinkish skin color indicates well-balanced health flows. You are outgoing and empathetic. Energy seems consistent, and while sexual passion is not extreme, passion can be sustained.

Lori, your fingers are inflexible, which indicates your need for a secure base of operation. You are conservative when dealing with finances, and some may even consider you to be "tightfisted."

The wide spaces between your fingers denote a willingness to do, to go, and an enjoyment of the unknown. Wide finger spaces also connote that you have, at times, a hard time controlling money; money could just slip right through your fingers, despite the tight-fistedness seen in your inflexible fingers.

At rest, your hands lie flat, Lori. This indicates the ability to solve problems, and tells me that your thinking processes are well balanced. This trait is indicative of the ability to see alternative solutions to most situations (see Illustration 7-5).

You have combination fingertips—some are conic, and some are spatulate (see Illustration 7-10). The conic tips tell me that you convey energy quickly, and the energy is consistent. You do not like friction and have a definite tendency toward excessively liberal concepts. Your spatulate tips are indicative of the doer and explorer (an Indiana Jones type), and they provide you with the determination to carry through with your ideas. The spatulate tips also tell me that you like to travel, maybe even more than you like to eat (this eating can bring about health problems if the diet isn't closely monitored). Take time to eat regularly, but don't eat too much at any one sitting.

Lori, your thumbs are of average length, which indicates a tendency toward mental balance. The waisted shape of the thumb means you are a naturally adaptable mixer, original in thoughts, but could have some trouble with decision making.

The low set of the thumbs tells me that you love liberty, hate consistent routine, and—here again—are liberal in thoughts and actions.

The flat thumbtip indicates that you know when, or when not, to maneuver. Your rigid thumb tells me that you are conservative, need some time to adjust to change, and definitely have a stubborn streak!

Lori, your square nails mean that you need a system for living. You are rational in your environment, a good housekeeper (once organized), and good with your hands.

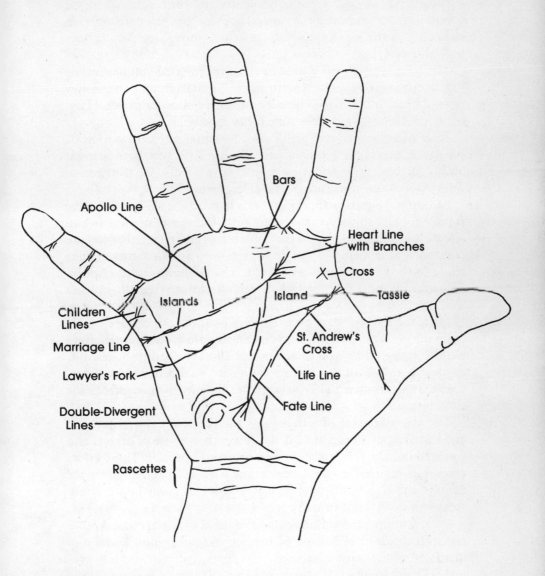

ILLUSTRATION 7-64
LORI'S RIGHT HAND

Bars

Apollo Line

Heart Line
with Branches

Cross

Islands

Island

Tassle

Children
Lines

Marriage Line

St. Andrew's
Cross

Lawyer's Fork

Life Line

Double-Divergent
Lines

Fate Line

Rascettes

Your shell-shaped nails tell me that you like new places and things—and are, in general, curious.

The nail texture is flexible, which indicates that you are resilient in health flows and are adaptable to environmental changes. Environment is important, however, because you react stronger, in either a positive or negative way, to the atmosphere. You cannot hide this reaction.

The pale, whitish color of your nails means that you have some low energy reserves, along with poor circulation and a tendency toward blood clots. This is usually indicative of genetic code. [Lori confirmed that blood clots run in her family.]

Your Mercury fingertips, on both hands, curve toward your Apollo fingers. So I immediately know that you have a great ability for expression and strong persuasive talents (see Illustration 7-6). This is the signature of the salesperson.

Ski jump fingertips appear on both hands. The ski jumps on the Jupiter fingers suggest that you are not always sure of your role in situations. The ski jumps on the Saturn fingers tell me that you are constantly attempting to clarify your values, and how these values relate to the world as you perceive it. The ski jumps of the Apollo fingers indicate a definite lack of self-discipline (see Illustration 7-7).

Lori, the uneven set of your fingers connotes some measure of disharmony. This also affects your energy flows, and more effort will be required for you to achieve goals. You tend to be abrupt, awkward, and at times self-conscious with a tendency to be defensive. This is an area that you will need to learn to control (see Illustration 7-8).

The knotty finger phalanges tell me that your initial reflexes and thinking processes are a little slower than those of others, and you will need to take more time to motivate yourself. These knots are often referred to as "accountant's knots," and this finger configuration indicates practicality (and we all know how accountants like everything in its proper place!).

Lori, you do have well-developed mounts of Jupiter and Apollo on both hands. The Mount of Jupiter indicates good leadership qualities, along with a balance in your conscious thinking processes. The Mount of Apollo means that there is a genuine sense of joy and productivity in your life. You are very concerned with moral issues and values.

Because the Mounts of Luna are well developed in both hands, this immediately tells me that you have the ability to develop the talent for creative writing, or to pursue a law career.

Since the Mounts of Mars are rather flat in both of your hands, it tells me that you have a normal amount of physical courage, as well as the tendency to voice your opinions.

Your mount of Venus indicates that your love is reasonable in its expression, and the trait of jealousy is not excessive. Your sex drive is within the normal range.

There is a box on your Mount of Jupiter in the left hand that enhances your leadership qualities in a very positive way. Of course, boxes are also protection marks, so any mistakes you make can be easily rectified.

The cross on the Mount of Jupiter on your right hand indicates a good and happy marriage. [Lori grins as she says, "All right!"]

Lori, you have what are referred to as "double-divergent lines" on your Mount of Luna, which are again a signal of conflict. Since they are on the lower section of Luna, they refer to inner conflict and emotional stress during your early childhood years [Lori confirms this].

A cross on the Mount of Mercury in the left hand is a definite indicator of the ability to express thoughts well in written form.

On the right hand, your Life Line rises between the thumb and the Mount of Jupiter. The line in this location is an indicator that you have an even temperament, even with constant changes occurring in your circumstances. Because your Life Line begins closer to the Mount of Venus in the left hand, Lori, you need time to yourself and a space of your own to think, or you will lose energy and could become less resistant to illness (see Illustration 7-25A). Lori, your Life Line terminates in the wrist area and encircles the Mount of Venus in both hands. This implies that you are a homebody [Lori agrees].

Your Life Line has many markings. There are chains and tassels at the beginning (see Illustration 7-18). The chaining indicates a delicate energy flow with slow recuperative abilities. It also means that you have problems with tonsillitis, upper respiratory infections, and allergies [Lori confirms that allergies run rampant in her family, and that her tonsils have caused her real problems—especially in her early childhood. She says she is still plagued with seasonal allergies]. The secondary information garnered from the chaining is that one of her parents suffers delicate health. [Lori says, "My mom still has delicate health and has to be careful, or she catches everything!"] The tassels at the beginning of your Life Line are an indication of affairs of the heart. Your love-to-be-in-love attitude is expressed through your actions.

Your Life Line is also fragmented at the halfway mark. This is indicative of a serious medical problem that is potentially fatal. Because there is a repair mark (the line is overlapped and continues), you will probably have a near-death experience when you are about thirty years old, but will be saved.

Lori, your Head Line is long, indicating that you have wide and varied interests in all areas of life. You have a probing intellect and a great deal of curiosity. The long line also indicates that you would excel at work involving research.

Your Head Line ends in the Upper Mount of Mars, which means you understand business, and money will be important to you. This can also be a sign of "tightness" with money and finances (remember what we saw earlier?). [Lori says that she can be tight, but not if she *really* wants something.] Your Head Line is also slightly wavy, so you have a tendency to be easily distracted. This also indicates a certain amount of creativity.

Because your Head Line just touches your Life Line, this shows that you have a check on the impulsive side of your nature and tend to be cautious.

At the end of your Head Line on both hands you have a lawyer's mark, (Illustration 7-37D), which reinforces your well-developed Mounts of Luna. This denotes that you can see all sides of an issue. On your left hand only, you have a writer's fork (Illustration 7-37C), along with the lawyer's mark. As stated before, you are good at research and understand business. Combine this with the lawyer's and writer's forks, and you would make a great paralegal or lawyer.

The island at the beginning of your Head Line indicates a probable trauma to your head at an early age [Lori says yes, she fell out of a car in her preschool years].

Lori, you also have an unusual mark connecting your Head Line and your Life Line. It is St. Andrew's cross, and is found at the beginning of the two lines in your hand. This is a sign that you will save somebody's life—either physically or spiritually. This cross can be found anywhere on the Life Line, but is usually found somewhere in the midsection.

Your Heart Line begins between the Jupiter and Saturn fingers, indicating a rational, practical approach to the emotions, and signaling calmness. You are affectionate and have a strong desire for harmony in your emotional life. There are branches at the beginning of your Heart Line, which denote total honesty (Illustration 7-44A). Lori, you have islands on your Heart Line on the edge of your left hand. This tells me that you terminated an affair because of external forces. [Lori asks, "How did you know that?" In her case, her grandparents were the "external forces."]

On your right hand Heart Line there is a small break, indicating

---

The Heart Line can be difficult to read; it will be easier if you remember that the course of the line is only important insofar as it relates to the beginning and ending of the line.

---

an event. In your case, Lori, it was the breakup of a romance. The line overlaps, indicating repair. You also have a parallel line to your Heart Line on the left hand, which also indicates repair and positive emotional expression.

Lori, your Fate Line begins in the center of your palm, showing that you will achieve goals through your own efforts. You are in control of your own destiny (Illustration 7-46C). The line is broad and shallow, Lori, so you will have to struggle to attain goals—sorry.

Your Fate Line is wavy and fragmented, which denotes blockage of career goals and changes in lifestyle (Illustration 7-47D). You also have faint bars crossing your Fate Line, which are a sign of annoyances and worry (Illustration 7-47C). Your Fate Line does, however, run clearly to the Mount of Saturn. Therefore, given your personality and determination, you will overcome difficulties and have a prosperous career. (Whew!)

Lori, your Apollo Line starts above the Head Line. It is a good, strong line that shows a certain amount of creativity and potential. Because you are so young, the line has not developed enough to determine the area where your talents lie, but you do have a strong base.

The Fate Line on your hand is wavy and fragmented, indicating potential arthritis and gout problems later in life. Your health will come in cycles. For example, you will exhibit robust health for a while and then have periods where you are troubled by minor ills. Lori, your Marriage Line is good and strong, so married life should be untroubled. Remember, you are very home-oriented and strive for domestic harmony, so your family life will be a priority [Lori confirms this].

Your Children Lines show a conflict, Lori. On your left hand are two straight lines, indicating boys. On your right hand there are two slanted lines, indicating girls. This tells me that there is a great possibility that you will have twins [possibility confirmed—twins run in her family]. You could either have twin boys, twin girls, or . . . bless your heart . . . a set of each! (It's a good thing that family is so important to you!)

In summation, this young client has a terrific amount of potential to be successful in the material or economic world. She has good determination about achievement. Though, due to her age, she does not have numerous lines or markings, those she has are clear and relatively strong, with few apparent weaknesses at this point.

The Head Line in her right hand isn't as varied with talent as the left, but neither has she made any concrete decisions about career direction. Before the lines show the strength of character indicated, she must make some choices involving career—and several choices are available to her.

Since this woman has married young in life, she will need to balance her domestic and emotional needs with her desire for career choices.

Lori's health is strong, but she tends to take on too much and use her energy inappropriately by not being focused (see the dissipation on the Life Line and note the repair line). She needs to give herself time to eat, rest, and recharge.

As an employee, Lori comprehends easily and quickly, and once comfortable in an environment, can initiate action easily. This will promote self-discipline through consistent structure and routine. Lack of self-discipline is one of her weakest character traits.

I suspect, based on her lines, that Lori will eventually be self-employed. She is self-motivated and likes the finer things in life.

8
NUMEROLOGY

NUMBERS PROVIDE THE foundation for our orderly society, as evidenced by the use of our social security numbers, driver's license numbers, and phone numbers. As our use of numbers developed, so too did our attachment to numbers and how they seemed to influence our daily lives.

Our modern numerical and mathematical systems actually have their roots in the Hindu and Arabic number systems. The man most responsible for furthering our knowledge about numbers was Pythagoras, a teacher and religious philosopher. He formulated theories that still stand today. His Pythagorean theorem, which every high schooler memorizes among other mathematical equations, was taught along with his doctrines of religious philosophy. He believed in the transmigration of souls and incorporated this and other religious beliefs into his teachings, termed "Pythagoreanism." These teachings included the symbology of numbers and their relationship to the Supreme Being and humanity. Pythagoras used a single digit, arrived at through simple addition and reduction, to symbolize basic truths. He suggested that a single-digit number vibrated to a definite life cycle on the date of one's birth, producing a life number that describes the life we are to assume. These number vibrations occur in accordance with Pythagoras's theory of reincarnation and karmic laws, and each contains certain information by symbolic association.

Numerology is the study of numbers—their cycles, patterns, vibrations, and influence. With the use of numbers, we can better

311

prepare ourselves for our lives. Instead of resisting our natural life flow, we can actually flow to our rhythms and produce a more balanced personality.

Numerology is growing in popularity as an easy and fun alternative to astrology. At least one popular women's magazine includes a numerology page in addition to astrological forecasts. Like astrology, numerology is an exacting science. Unlike astrology, however, numerology can be done without precise charts of planetary positions (as seen in an ephemeris).

In numerology, the birth number is considered the major number, as it indicates the base personality, talents, and traits. The secondary numbering association is derived from the names we are given at birth, and helps determine the outward expression of our personality. To some extent, it determines how we conduct our lives.

Numbers can convey both traits and talents, and positive and negative sides of our personalities. Of course, we strive to emphasize our good points, minimize our weaknesses, or strive to achieve a balance and fulfillment. The combination of both our birth/life and name numbers gives us not only the expression of our potential, but also how we perceive our "universal destiny."

BIRTH/LIFE NUMBERS

Your date of birth is the most important number in your life, reflecting not only your base personality but also home, friendships, lovers, parents, and business. As I mentioned, positive and negative traits are found within each number. Each individual must choose which traits to develop.

Arriving at Your Birth/Life Number

Your birth/life number is obtained by taking the month, day, and year of your birth and reducing them to a single digit. Example: If your birthday is August 25, 1964, you would add $8 + 2 + 5 + 1 + 9 + 6 + 4 = 35$. You then reduce 35 $(3 + 5 = 8)$ to a single digit, which in this case is 8.

Note: There are three exceptions to the rule of reducing a number to a single digit. If the sum of your birthdate is 11, 22, or 33, you do not reduce any further. These three numbers are considered the "master numbers" and have special meanings all their own. Let's take the example March 30, 1976: You would add $3 + 3 + 0 + 1 + 9 + 7 + 6 = 29$. You then reduce 29 ($2 + 9 = 11$), which gives you the birth number 11. Another example of this exception is September 6, 1953: You add $9 + 6 + 1 + 9 + 5 + 3 = 33$. The birth/life number is 33.

Once you have figured your birth/life number or that of your subject, look at the definitions below. Be sure to keep an open mind. Some characteristics that don't seem to fit do. Others are mitigated by name or talent numbers. Think of your birth number as a "sun" sign and the others as rising signs of descending importance. As with other vehicles, remember that numerology is a tool for stimulating psychic flow. Bridge various numbers. Be open to psychic clips.

Profile of the Number 1

Personality Profile

Ones are doers and natural trendsetters. They are leaders, and can be headstrong, impulsive, ambitious, and full of enterprise and "new ideas." They aren't normally found at the bottom of the totem pole. They are known to be original thinkers and personify the term *individualistic*. Ones are quick-tempered and resent abuse or imposition. Their saving grace is that they forgive quickly and do not hold grudges.

Ones love freedom and justice, sometimes jump before they look, but can carry through on a decision once made. Ones exhibit hasty speech and action at times, but will correct their mistakes if given time. Ones are philosophical, admire scientific thought, and are at their best when at the head of things (directors, instructors, superintendents, managers, or self-employed).

Usually born to domineering, interfering, and restrictive parents, ones begin to experience tension and conflict at an early age, which often erupts by the teenage years, precipitating their early departure from home. This, in itself, doesn't provide independence or self-direction. By thirty years of age, they begin to rid themselves of resentment and overcome conflicts with a true form of independence and a greater awareness of self-reliance and strength.

If ones are not allowed to express themselves, over the years this suppression becomes evident in their lack of ability to make decisions. They may become submissive and tend to procrastinate. Disharmony in their surroundings and emotional life produces headaches, asthma, and chest constrictions (which, if the ones are heavy smokers, can lead to heart problems). These people have to work hard to reestablish their natural exuberance and self-confidence. This lack of self-confidence retards their rightful ascension within the universe.

Sex/Love/Marriage Profiles

Ones are extreme in sex, love, or marriage. They begin their sexual awakening in early teenhood and make many conquests because of their striking good looks, fashion trendsetting, and natural charm. Well groomed, poised, and unruffled, they capture attention.

Underneath their detachment, ones are romantics. Although they exhibit a tough exterior, they are sensitive and easily hurt. Once a relationship ceases to fulfill their expectations, they become jealous, demanding, and question their mate's loyalty. Ones need lots of attention. If it is not given, then the relationship's days are numbered (no pun intended). Ones mourn ended relationships as if their previous mate has expired.

Ones start their mating process early and are likely to marry more than once. Their first mate is usually strong-willed and domineering and restricts their freedom. Ones respond to giving and generous mates and can be very generous with gifts, thoughtful in actions, and supportive of their mate's achievements.

Children of ones have free run of the house but are taught respect for furnishings and equipment. Ones are gentle with children and patient when teaching children. They take great pride in helping them learn to build, use tools, and work with animals.

Home Profile

Ones express their individuality in their homes and choose locations that face east. The prefer corner lots, dry climates, hills, and barren landscape. They like fireplaces and lots of interior space and/or many rooms. Furnishings can be traditional or mixed in earth tones with vivid accent colors. Because ones are trendsetters, they use unusual combinations of colors, textures, and styles to produce functional but eye-pleasing decors. They are picky about cleanliness and demand neatness.

They like to entertain in small intimate groups and shine in the kitchen as specialty cooks. They keep a well-stocked pantry or wet bar, wanting visitors to have all the comforts of home. Ones enjoy puttering, fixing little things, and minor/major landscaping.

Health Profile

Ones are robust and vigorous, and use determination to accomplish health goals. If they decide they are overweight, then watch out—it is diet time, and they will succeed. Ones go from one extreme to the other, and need to learn balance. They usually have a defined routine for health maintenance and may overdo exercise or deprive themselves of sleep and relaxation. Anger, anxiety, worry, or too much excitement will drain their energy levels and cause poor general health. Disharmony can cause emotions to be intensified, so they need peaceful surroundings to retreat to in times of stress.

A one's diet is important, as they are physically motivated. They need fresh vegetables, and they should avoid all stimulants and limit intake of red meats and spices.

In childhood, ones experienced frequent accidents leading to injuries around or on the face, neck, and head. In their youth, they are susceptible to pimples, ringworms, headaches, and head congestion. In infancy, they had runny noses at any given time. As they matured, and resistance increased, they lost patience with themselves and others who experienced illnesses, as it interfered with what they wanted to do.

Money and Career Profile

Money is a motivator that drives ones to be successful. Ones don't want the money for itself, but rather as a symbol or measure of how others will perceive them. Ones tend to save money in more than one place, either in financial institutions or their homes. As ones grow and mature, they learn to correctly use money as a tool, and can become successful financially by applying their considerable talents to investment fields.

Ones are most successful in the areas of weapons, aerospace, defense, iron, steel, fire-fighting equipment, mining (gas and oil), general entertainment ventures, and in stocks and bonds.

Ones prefer to pay cash or use layaway programs. They take their financial responsibilities seriously, and are generous in providing their children with gifts and needed funds for education. They always have a little "stash" hidden away, as they don't like to be caught by surprise financially.

Profile of the Number 2

Personality Profile

Number twos express and strive for cooperation and peace in their lives through their speech, careers, and daily actions.

Twos' talents are many, but they have difficulty deciding what they want to pursue. These diversified talents give twos natural charm to fit in any walk of life, yet can cause problems with decision making, picking courses of action, or getting so hung up on details that they become lost in their own thinking processes. This indecisive trait stems from their childhood, as they were usually involved in family pettiness, constraint, and criticism. They were seldom complimented or sincerely encouraged, and as a result, rarely develop healthy self-esteem or confidence. This environment enhances, throughout the formative years, sensitivity to all forms of criticism.

Twos, therefore, are hesitant to make decisions lest they make the wrong ones. They invariably need help in decision making, so if a mistake does result, they will not stand alone with egg on their face. Twos must strive to release hostile feelings in a positive fashion.

Well-balanced twos become natural diplomats, as they are adaptable, can flow with the natural rhythm of things, and have the ability to see the overall picture before taking a stand or giving a point of view. Their ability to use words and evoke emotions can "soothe the fevered brow" and enhances their natural ability to be arbitrators. In their career or jobs, they do their best work behind the scenes and are efficient organizers.

Twos work very hard to provide a different family life from that in which they grew up, and they promote team effort. They tend to use art or art forms as a tool for teaching these concepts. Twos generally have two children and are known as the neighborhood parents, keeping "open houses." Most twos are talented in art, music, decorating, building, heavy detail work, gardening, the mechanical, technology, and education.

Sex/Love/Marriage Profiles

Twos don't start their sexual awakening until they are fourteen or fifteen and they are also clinically well informed. Twos understand their magnetlike ability to draw the opposite sex toward them, and they secretly enjoy flirting. They develop sexual role models early. Several years of dating experience are needed for them to become more liberal, however, as twos have a deep sense of morality. Conflicts about sex must recede before they feel free of guilt and can express their feelings of love through sex.

The twos' charm is their ability to talk and their expressive use of body language, including the "come hither" look. They dress neatly and wear what looks good on them, not what is in fashion. Their eyes are soft and doelike (on females) or bright with a hypnotic quality (on males). If disappointed in romance, they become detached as if the affair never occurred. They try very hard in marriages, feeling that divorce is a moral issue. If disenchanted and unable to resolve conflicts, they become sullen, faultfinding, and hateful toward their mate.

Love is the primary requisite for twos to bloom and develop. When they feel truly loved, they actually seem to glow. This expression of love bleeds over into their family life, especially in regards to children, and can engender forgiveness for family slights that occurred early in their lives.

Twos are patient with children and enjoy their accomplishments. They stress incidental learning and art as a form of education. They encourage their children to try different types of experiences, yet if they become uneasy, twos can be very restrictive and protective.

Home Profile

Twos' homes can be in the city or country, on hilly or flat terrain, but will reflect nature's beauty. They need flowers, trees, and flowering shrubs to satisfy their sense of order and color.

They prefer two-story houses, and like wood structures, windows, and natural wood accents. The decor reflects unusual accessories, musical instruments (especially a piano), unusual wall hangings and modern art, copper, and crystal. A study is a must, as they collect books and papers.

They are efficient in the kitchen and like to entertain. They like company to just drop by and visit. They like functional, easy-to-maintain homes, with little clutter.

Health Profile

Twos have inherent health weaknesses that, if not protected, can become major problems in later life. Since they have fragile health, they are sometimes unfairly referred to as hypochondriacs. All twos share disorders of the stomach, nervous hypertension, kidney diseases, lower-back dysfunctions, and possible ruptures of numerous veins, disks, and the like. In their childhood they exhibited allergies, and allergic headaches, as well as throat and related infections.

Nutrition for twos should include lots of cereals and a mostly vegetarian diet. Strong drinks or condiments should be avoided. Twos need a balance between acidic and starchy foods, lots of water, and a mild exercise program. Rest is especially important, as they push their physical energy until depleted.

Money and Career Profile

Twos have many attributes necessary for good business sense. Guided by reason rather than emotion, they aren't always confident of their business policy and need backup research.

Twos are cautious with purchases and talk themselves out of buying through a type of guilt system. The one exception is spending for family needs. They feel that if they can justify it, then they may spend it.

Twos work best in mutually respectful partnerships. They can make money in radio, television, computers, electronics, small tool manufacturing, diamonds, editorial services, manufacturing of instruments, antipollution devices, surgical goods and instruments, art supplies, and land development. Twos should avoid catering businesses, the food industry, the costume or fashion design industries, art activities, and technical book publishing.

Even though twos need partnerships in business, they should not share marital funds, as it promotes disharmony. Twos either do very, very well, or must learn through mistakes. They may have to lose money before learning the correct use of their intuitive nature to secure their financial lives.

Profile of the Number 3

Personality Profile

Number threes are expressive, verbal, and naturally empathetic. They are great conversationalists with knowledge of many topics. Well-balanced threes are articulate, artistic, happy individuals with good clothing taste and social decorum. They can become writers or entertainers, and do well in any of the communicative arts and/or sales areas. Threes are particularly interested in God, the order of the universe, and universal laws. Threes have religious experiences very early in life, and understand and apply universal laws. They try to fulfill what they see as their life's "path."

As threes grow and mature, they inadvertently become hosts or hostesses and social trendsetters. Since words are their first friends, they use them effectively. Threes enjoy some of life's luxuries, but usually choose a backward route to achieve them.

Number threes are usually born into families with few (or hoarded) resources. Creativity is not understood and therefore ridiculed. Threes are very sensitive, and their natural creativity can be stifled as a result. If not overcome, this produces mental and emotional confusion, with loss of self-expression. This can cause subconscious guilt, shame, and/or fear of new ventures, fear of success, and indecisiveness in choosing career goals. It is important for parents of threes to exercise moderation in discipline and to encourage completion of projects. Parents should focus on artistic endeavors—music, art, writing, and acting.

Threes are well balanced, and people respond to them easily. Threes handle responsibility with ease, make good parents, and make excellent partners in business.

Sex/Love/Marriage Profiles

Threes enter the arena of sexuality in the early teenage years by watching and observing others. Their role models are many, but threes will retreat from their first encounter unless all of the romantic trappings are in place. Early on they radiate alluring signals without being consciously aware of them. This provocative and mysterious air attracts the opposite sex. As threes mature, sexual encounters become deep expressions of love and commitment. If hurt and disillusioned early, threes become distrustful and cynical.

Threes are usually well dressed but not fashion plates per se. They like clothing to fit and be comfortable. Threes figures are well proportioned, and they don't normally gain weight until later in life.

Threes usually marry early and are strongly opposed to divorce. Broken marriages can make them vindictive and reluctant to share possessions with their ex-mate. When threes find their lifelong mate, and if they can erase their previous negative experiences, they become very family-oriented and generous with their resources. Family is always first!

Threes remain sexually active throughout their lives, although becoming more dictatorial in their concepts of right and wrong. If not careful, they become "preachers" and can alienate their friends, relatives, and children.

Threes are outwardly affectionate to those they care about, and they don't exhibit any type of prejudices. They truly believe in the idea of humanity as one family.

Three parents handle children more easily, that is, with less structure, than their parents did and are more generous with their resources. Discipline is not usually dictated by social mores but rather by how the child responds and feels about herself. Three parents assume a great deal of responsibility for children and can carry it to extremes. Threes' children always know that they can come home and would be welcomed back with open arms. Sometimes three parents need to be more detached from their children, so the children can mature properly.

Although demanding of their children, threes can also be very forgiving. They like their children in respected roles or careers. Education is important, and they place great emphasis on the type of education and skills that will help their children be self-supporting. Children are always encouraged to try different fields of endeavor in order to achieve stability. Three parents try to teach their children to be self-motivated, as they are, and can become frustrated if their children don't learn this trait. They can, however, go overboard in providing for older children, which can be detrimental to all. Children of threes have many friends, and their friends enjoy the family life that threes provide.

Home Profile

Number threes choose homes with space—places in which to retreat. They like hills and the country but want the convenience of metropolitan areas, so they don't mind commuting. Their home needs fairly large rooms, many windows, and a sense of homeyness.

Threes like the lived-in look. Their decor will have many pointed objects (such as pyramids), smooth clean lines, and lots of tables. Family members are indoctrinated early to do their share of keeping the home in shape. Threes can be very picky about cleanliness and don't like clutter, but are unconscious collectors. Threes like outbuildings and generally have them full.

Threes like landscaping to be unusual but maintenance-free. They are home putterers and usually have more than one project going at once. If not careful, they don't always finish them.

Number threes' homes are like Grand Central Station; visitors are welcomed and fed. Their spouses feel they can invite business associates at any time and that they will be made to feel comfortable and at home.

Health Profile

The health profile of threes relates to the nervous system, bloodstream, and liver. Threes are given to overextension, which produces stress and depletion of energy reserves. Threes need to pace their activities in order to conserve and correctly direct their energy reserves.

Number threes' overall health is generally excellent in their early lives. Once they reach the age of 50, if they didn't pace themselves, they can expect health ailments. They will have a tendency for colds or chest congestion. Throughout their adult lives, they have a definite tendency to develop rheumatism, gout, dislocations of hip joints, lung and blood disorders. In later years, diet and control of liquids should prevent serious kidney disease. Threes should follow moderate eating and exercise plans in order to promote stable health.

Constant rushing puts undue stress and strain on threes' physical and emotional bodies. They need quiet time for reflection and planning for future activities.

Money and Career Profile

Positive, intuitive threes need diversification in their financial dealings in order to achieve good foundations.

The types of investments or career choices they should make are as follows: publishing business, toys and games that promote mind expansion, educational audiovisual aids, manufacturing of religious objects, travel industries, sporting goods, art supplies, and small manufacturing companies that produce instruments for the health field or aerospace industries. They can also become financially secure through lecturing or teaching arenas, and in writing or publishing.

When well balanced, threes are thorough in business and work very hard to achieve goals. Threes, due to their natural curiosity, deal with people who can teach them best. They are practical, realistic, and progressive. Number threes rarely put their family property at risk, nor do they risk their job or career. They are charity-oriented, choosing two or three charities and working tirelessly for them.

Threes tend to be overly generous with funds for their family, children, and friends. This is a trait they must curb. They need to learn to budget properly. They instinctively plan for the future and invest in large tracts of land, usually because they think it will help the family.

Profile of the Number Four

Personality Profile

Number fours stress discipline. Their assertive traits (traits they demonstrate when they are motivated to action) are stubbornness, rigidity, intolerance, lack of emotional sensitivity, and tendency to overwork. Their passive traits (if they take the path of least resistance) are laziness, resistance to new ideas or change, and intellectualism. When these traits are balanced, fours are loyal, consistent, patient, well organized, and honest. They are known as the champion of the underdog, often to their personal detriment.

Fours are the movers, shakers, and doers of the working class. They are able to overcome obstacles in order to attain their goals.

The family of a four has very little influence on a four's approach to life. Fours are known as shortcutters, dislike normal routines, and enjoy the unconventional. Stubbornness is their major method for proving a point.

Fours limit their friendships; but when loyalty, love, and friendship are firm, they seldom change their opinions. If they feel pushed or dealt with unfairly, they can ignore one right out of existence, and they must learn to be more tolerant and light-hearted.

Sex/Love/Marriage Profiles

Number fours are experts in sexual pleasure. Both the male and female please their partners and work very hard to do so. Their sexual urges begin early in childhood and last their entire life. Male fours approach a conquest through the use of their considerable charms, and know how to introduce sexual activities as a spiritual experience. Females approach sex with an attitude of experimentation and are always ready to receive sexual gratification.

Fours are capable of deep love and affection and make good marriage partners. Most fours will have problems in their first marriages, as they expect their spouse to play a preconceived role. If the marriage doesn't end in divorce, the latent sexual energy is converted to other areas of the four's life—business, job, school, children, and so on. If the first marriage does end, the former marriage partners still speak, share some of the same interests, and are considered to be on friendly terms. When fours decide to remarry, they are selective in choosing the next partner.

Number fours are great role players, fashion inventors, and know how to draw attention and yet retain the image of the boy or girl next door. They are of average height and weight. Their facial structures are not outstanding, yet their eyes are usually large and doelike. Fours use their hands expressively. They are at their best when directing or managing someone else's life. Fours gravitate to the well known, experts, people who are financially well off, or those who create excitement.

In family life, fours are loyal, loving, caring, and genuinely concerned about their friends, associates, and business contacts. They are good providers and conscientious parents. Number fours are just plain nice people. If their home life (which, to a four, includes an active sex life) gets out of balance, look out!—they become restless, worried, nervous, depressed, and quite vocal about how they feel.

Fours will go to great lengths to teach their family the correct use of money, and to purchase the best brand-name products. These people spend a lot of time with immediate family and become actively involved in the children's education, particularly in the creative arts. If not careful, four parents will have children so overly involved that they lose interest before becoming proficient.

Fours love all family members (but see them in realistic terms) and understand how to work with them, but don't necessarily like them. They support those they feel are deserving and who listen to advice, and detach themselves from those persons who don't.

Fours need stable friends who accept them as they are and let them blow off steam as needed. Friends are the substitutes for early problems (lack of acceptance and affection) fours encountered in their childhood.

Home Profile

Number fours tend to choose homes located in the middle of the block, street, or subdivision. They like the security of having home and people close, yet at a distance.

Fours like homes and objects built to last, massive structures, and things that represent bygone eras. They look for shady places to retreat to, such as parks, back lawns, or old cemeteries.

Fours are neat and tend to have neat homes with the lived-in look. They like orderly activities and respond best to a routine. They want large spaces, as they need to move frequently to help rid themselves of restless, or excess, energy.

Furniture is usually sleek with wood and natural fibers noticeable. They enjoy bay windows, stone walls, the local color of their neighborhood (historic area, haunted houses, antiques) and two-story homes.

Fours like to cook, as it is an expression of their creative skills. They like sweets and are very good dessert cooks.

Health Profile

Fours have good to excellent energy reserves and can offset most physical maladies of their youth. They are prone to throat infections, glandular swelling in the neck, croup, mumps, abscesses, polyps, and bladder problems. Fours have sensitive skin and can experience eczema, impetigo, and bruises to their limbs. Later in life, they tend to contract rheumatism.

They need to surround themselves with positive, optimistic people, as they can suffer from long-term "blues," discontent, worry, and nervousness, which could lead to serious emotional disturbances.

Fours start out with good health and average weight, which last until around thirty-five, then they begin a slow decline, especially if they have not adhered to strict health controls. If they balance their health, they can expect to remain active until the end.

Fours need proper diet and exercise to provide long-term health and longevity. Fattening foods should be avoided to decrease the likelihood of obesity. Hot foods or liquids are recommended. Water intake is usually less than needed. Alcohol of any form is not recommended. If fours don't stay active, they will gain weight and suffer from earlier onset of rheumatism.

Money and Career Profile

Fours crave and desire luxuries and luxurious lifestyles, and they draw people with money into business relationships. They usually employ some form of strategy in financial matters and have the persistence to carry it out.

Primary businesses for fours are building and construction, restoration, art supplies, business machines, and stock brokering. They should avoid a hands-on job in publishing, as well as careers in airlines, all fad industries (clothes, records, jewelry), and business involvements requiring quick action or decision making.

Fours can be very successful in financial areas if they don't get too comfortable in their present lifestyle, use money as a power tool, or fail to follow sound advice. Fours need to be cautious in spending without assured returns, as well as less stubborn and unwilling to flow with current business trends. Most of all, they need to take their nervous systems into account, as they cannot think or function correctly if overly worried or depressed. Fours' finances are tied to their emotional makeup. They need to practice good budgeting and avoid status games.

Profile of the Number 5

Personality Profile

Number fives usually love their freedom and thrive on change. Their assertive traits (when they are motivated) are restlessness (physical or mental or both), disregard for established values, irresponsibility, nervousness, and overindulgence in too many interests. Their passive traits (when they're taking things easier) are fear of change, requirement of a rule for every behavioral pattern, sexual confusion, and failure to learn from experience. When balanced, they are progressive, with diverse talents, have many friends, are curious, and seek personal freedom. They are quick, flexible, adventurous, energetic, and love to travel. They need lots of stimulation. Fives are known for their bottom-line attitude. They like to mingle with all sorts of people and have a proclivity for ethnic groups and foreign cultures.

Usually fives are born into families that travel in conjunction with parental careers, and they learned to adjust to constant changes of environment. They see themselves as intellectuals and probably are far above average. They must, however, learn to be less rigid in their concepts and more tolerant of people. All fives deal with powerful, wealthy people, as well as the less fortunate.

Experience is the best teacher for fives. They seek balance between intellectual, emotional, and practical matters. They will otherwise have definite tendencies to turn to drugs, alcohol, and sensual activities, ultimately creating a depressive personality.

Fives do not like to acknowledge that family ties play an important role in their self-expression. They feel they must have freedom at all costs. If well balanced, they respect all laws governing humanity. Fives may do well as priests, nuns, parents, lawyers, writers, painters, and in nurturing roles or as authority figures.

Sex/Love/Marriage Profiles

Male fives are usually fair and light-eyed with good body builds. Females fives are willowy individuals with striking good looks and figures that other women envy.

Both male and female fives are sexual experimenters. They need a lot of physical and emotional attention. They are intensely loyal to their lovers or mates—for life.

As fives develop into adulthood, they begin to exhibit gentle charm. In marriage they take their chosen roles seriously and have a good sense of humor along with healthy doses of ego. They do know how to please their mates!

All fives are sentimental and carry a sense of the dramatic into their love lives. They like romantic interludes. They are usually experienced before marriage and have a good idea of how they want their marriage to be. They expect and demand fidelity, and I pity their mates if their views on fidelity are not the same.

Five parents are understanding (to a fault) with their offspring and show great patience and dedication to the rearing of their children. Education, either formal or by experience, is important to the five parent, as he or she sees children as definite extensions of him or herself. Fives are usually not strict disciplinarians, using reasoning with children instead.

Children within the five's home have a reserved space. Their developmental well-being is important to fives. Fives like books and encourage their children to read. They allow their children free run of the home and encourage them to strike out early and explore the world.

Home Profile

Fives like a variety of scenic views around their homes. They like the outdoors, plenty of trees and wildlife, yet prefer to be close to a cosmopolitan area. As fives are restless, they need lots of space to roam. Number fives generally build on high ground, close to a rocky and barren area, yet within view of vibrantly green hills. Very high places will be their final home. Fives like to travel, but once rooted, stay in place.

They prefer large rooms with glass to let in the sun and promote the feeling of outdoors. Fives' furnishings are simple but in good taste. The style is usually contemporary. They like wood and metal combined with glass and use yellow in varying shades.

Number fives are not too concerned that the home be spotlessly clean but want it well organized and uncluttered. They like to see flowers in bloom year-round and are interested in landscaping. They like to putter with mechanical apparatus and are very patient mechanical instructors.

They like to entertain, are very social, like to cook and play games. They have many complex and different gadgets.

Health Profile

Fives are energetic and exhibit a hypertension and restlessness that, if not controlled, could lead to poor health early in their lives. To reduce the likelihood of heart conditions, fives need to learn control of emotions and proper release of excessive energy.

As fives mature, their parents need to watch for unspecified fevers, heat exhaustion, and other types of inflammation. As they reach adolescence, they may endanger their health by lack of rest, causing fevers and infections that are hard to trace (such as spinal meningitis). In later years the history of minor and major illnesses can lead to rather severe heart-related problems.

Fives should establish a routine, a balanced home environment, emotional harmony, and order and moderation in their lifestyle. Haste leads to clumsiness, accidents (broken bones in most cases), bruises, and other injuries. Their physiological balance is important, as self-image is directly tied to their emotional understanding of who they are. A depressed five is hard to reprogram into the previously energetic, outgoing individual.

A five's diet should have plenty of blood builders, not calories. Stimulating drinks and hot foods should be used sparingly, as fives have trouble digesting them. Overheating is definitely a problem, both in exercise and in food and liquid consumption.

Money and Career Profile

Number fives are usually found at the head of powerful and influential organizations. They are not opposed to starting at the bottom and working up, as long as their efforts are recognized. Their employers can place complete faith in fives' integrity. Some of their best abilities lie within the advertising industry and in public relations. Usually, however, work does not appeal to them. If it's fun, though, they'll work until they drop. They want to keep flexibility.

The one negative trait is gambling, or in making moves and decisions without checking all details. This can bring them financial problems. If fives invest in the stock market or new developing companies, this gambling streak becomes more evident. They exhibit good insight into oil and related products and usually don't lose money. Fives do not like tight cash flow, and if cash becomes tight, depression sets in, and they have to work very hard to overcome it. Fives believe that bills and other debts must be paid. If they can't pay on time, they become very testy indeed. They are hard and consistent workers but take time to reward themselves regularly.

With careful management, fives can accumulate not only cash, but property, which over a period of several years can make them comfortably wealthy. The following list gives the investments best for fives: utility companies, gas, oil, and their related products, drug companies, the entertainment world, advertising and public relations. If fives are dedicated and patient, they can safely accumulate resources. If, on the other hand, they become overconfident, don't accept advice from experts, or underestimate friends and opponents, they can lose money.

Profile of the Number 6

Personality Profile

Sixes are service-oriented with responsibility in the forefront. Their assertive traits are overinvolvement in the problems of others and a tendency to be self-righteous and worrisome. They can be veritable dictators at home, prone to arguing and easily upset. Their passive traits are a penchant toward martyrdom, resentment at being put in a servile position, and lack of concern for family and/or home. Sixes are constant complainers, always anxious, and carry the burdens of the world on their shoulders. When these traits are balanced, however, they have harmonious homes and serve humanity unselfishly. They are artistic in their work, conscientious, fair, and seek emotional balance.

Sixes' strong points include domesticity, responsibility, and service. More than any of the other numbers, their major concerns are emotional balance and security. They are usually born into disharmony and are often from a broken home; divorce or separation is common. This condition leaves an emotionally insecure child. Due to this background, sixes often experience difficulties adjusting to the responsibilities of home and family later in life. They often repeat the pattern established by their parents, and will have at least two marriages. However, if before becoming an adult, they can compensate, they may have long and happy marriages.

If not careful, sixes may become opinionated and stubborn, feel guilt without actually knowing why, and feel that people take advantage of them. Once they have matured and achieve emotional balance, they exhibit good taste and harmony in their surroundings.

Sixes can truly succeed in any endeavor they attempt sincerely. It is important for sixes to have positive attitudes and positive people around them in order to be personally creative. They are often "self-made," and others relate to them easily and help them along in life.

Love/Sex/Marriage Profiles

Number sixes experience life in the deepest senses, especially in sexual experiences. They are "on top of the mountain" or "in the valley," during their sexual lives. Love, for them, is tied directly to their sexual experiences. They use sex to express love, loyalty, and deeper feelings. They begin sexual activity in adolescent years and remain active until either bad health or death overtakes them. They learn early to use body language.

In their concept of marriage, sex is the most important link, and if sex is satisfying, they remain happy; even though other areas of the marriage may be off. They have an idealistic concept of married life, and as long as this idealistic partnership lasts, then the marriage is safe.

If they wait until their late twenties, sixes will probably marry only once. If they should marry earlier, several marriages will occur before they settle down. If sixes don't marry until their late thirties, they will again marry more than once, as their independence gets in the way of commitments. All sixes have active love lives.

On the surface, sixes are not openly affectionate; they hold affection to private moments.

Sixes are of slender build with dark eyes or eye areas. They have "bedroom eyes" and use them to convey their banked passion.

Sixes can have lots of patience with children, but Lord protect the child who is stubborn with a number six parent! They do not have a sense of humor with what they term sassy or impertinent children. They are strict disciplinarians concerning manners, behavior, and neatness.

Children are welcome in their home, but with restrictions. The children will have designated play spaces and are not permitted free access to other areas.

Home Profile

The profile of six homes is "sheer elegance." If they can afford the things they like, their home will reflect not only good quality, but will be picture perfect. They like color as a subtle accent, with dramatic flare brought in through furnishings, an unusual look in floors, and/or building design. They definitely are unusual. They require that their possessions have brand names; they believe in guarantees.

Sixes prefer to live in lowlands, around water or lakes, either natural or constructed. They like formal landscaping but prefer simple designs. They are picky housekeepers and like things neat and orderly both inside and outside homes. In art, their taste runs the gamut, from sculpture pieces to other art forms.

Number sixes like to entertain and cook, but only if they can restore order quickly. They like their food, table arrangements, and settings to look pretty. They like candles to help set the mood, and in most cases will have either a real or fake fireplace.

Health Profile

Sixes have unusual health problems and need to be aware that diet and exercise are very important, as they have weak recuperative powers. A good balanced mental state is essential to their overall health. They have a tendency to ingest too many liquids, and any beverage containing a stimulant should be avoided.

As sixes mature, clumsiness is likely to occur, along with colds with heavy mucus buildup, and bowel problems. The danger also exists for drug and/or alcohol problems. How they cope with stress depends on their mental attitude, and this can bring about more health problems. If depression and inability to express deep feelings are dealt with in the early developmental stages, most later health problems can be avoided. Chemical dependency does not usually become apparent until the late thirties, if it, in fact, becomes a problem.

Number sixes, due to their lack of interest in the physical side of life, must guard against becoming too sedate, or they increase the likelihood of health problems.

Money and Career Profile

Sixes have an intuitive flow concerning money and its use. They like to invest in diversified ways. Since they are geared toward service, they usually invest in areas that serve humanity.

Character traits that compromise financial success for sixes include being reliant on friendships rather than experts. Sixes like to sound out their business ideas with those they know and trust to give an honest appraisal. People will think they are easy touches and can be manipulated, though this is not usually the case.

Most sixes have strong social consciences and often try to compensate for wrongs because they realize that adequate finances can make up for hurt feelings or rectify social error.

Since sixes' byword is service to others, their occupations will bear this out. They make excellent counselors, ministers, doctors, nurses, teachers, or social workers. In business they are often assistants. Sixes often own their own business, especially if art-related; commercial design can lead to advertising and public relations. No matter what type of business they choose, they want quick profits. They often include, or give part of a business to, employees or friends, as they like to share.

In their stock market portfolio, sixes should invest a quarter of their cash in mutual funds, government bonds, or growth stock. Otherwise, they like short-term, high-risk speculations, as their intuitive quality assists them. Some of the major stocks that are the most oriented to sixes are: contraceptives, low-budget films, state bonds for civic developments, oceanography, antiques, and art galleries. Some sixes do well in the oil industry, pharmaceuticals, private churches and institutions, and any business connected with the arts, theatrical clothing, stage props, art supplies, and any devices used to explore (undersea or outerspace). Types of businesses or market investments that should be avoided are munitions, detergents, and the food industry.

Sixes should be careful of an urge to speculate on far-out schemes. They should check investment instruments for good credit and a reputation for honesty. They should also remember to keep some of the money earned as they tend to be overgenerous.

Sixes like to share their money with all family members and friends.

Profile of the Number 7

Personality Profile

Number sevens' byword is wisdom. Their assertive traits include being severely critical, overly analytical, intellectually conceited, vain, deceptive, aloof, eccentric, and faultfinding. Their passive traits include skepticism, inferiority complex, cynicism, supressiveness, coldness, introspection, craftiness, and a tendency toward emotional withdrawal. When balanced, they are excellent analysts, seek deeper truths, have good technical ability, and reach for faith and mystical or intuitive knowledge.

Number sevens are the searchers of the universe and need to understand themselves and the world around them. They are usually born into a family that is unable to provide higher education or training. If the resources are there, sevens seem out of step and unable to take advantage of them.

Sevens tend to be loners and need extra time and space to themselves. They are serious and should learn to be more light-hearted.

Sevens are dedicated to their goals and can attain much success. They use knowledge practically. They are aware of the spiritual needs of humanity, and if they follow the paths of enlightenment, they may find themselves serving humanity. Meditation will produce great understanding and peace for sevens. They can, however, intimidate others with subtle manipulation to gain control. They can also be cunning and deceptive. Usually pride and dignity are natural personality extensions, and they have a great sense of loyalty to family, spouse, work, or career activities. They have the makings of excellent parents, but they use reason and logic in parenting, which is often lost on their offspring.

Sex/Love/Marriage Profiles

Sevens are the most magnetic of the number wheel. They combine symbolic power and wisdom into their passionate natures and exhibit charismatic qualities without realizing their immense sexual attraction. This oozing of sexuality carries over into their business or social life.

Sevens learn about sex early, understand the ramifications of sexual activities, and learn early to be self-controlled. Rather than turn off the opposite sex, it seems to draw even more attention.

Number sevens are nice looking, and body builds are firm and lean. They dress either conservatively or very dramatically, depending upon their whim. Their dress only emphasizes the mysterious and enigmatic qualities they possess.

You'll find very few prudes among sevens. They like to experiment with lovemaking, and are considered the lovers of the number wheel, as they like to create a romantic atmosphere for love.

Number sevens usually have one or two rooms that young children are not allowed to use regularly. Kids are encouraged to bring friends home but are warned of the house rules.

Home Profile

Number sevens like nature and choose isolated homes or at least ones that give the illusion of isolation. They like gardens, low flowery shrubs, or low blooming ground cover. Some like what is now known as "natural yards." They usually cultivate vegetable gardens, grapevines, orchards, and the like. Sevens enjoy ponds, springs, lakes, or oceans.

Sevens are "pack rats," enjoy large rooms and built-in storage areas or furniture. They are generally good cooks and housekeepers, but don't like to deep clean; they are straighten-uppers. In addition, sevens love their home but also like to travel.

Sevens overall taste in decor is simple, with lots of different styles in accent pieces, and sedate or cool colors. In a five-bedroom home, they will have five differently styled bedrooms. Their homes will exhibit comfort, be functional, and have scattered accents. Bathrooms and kitchens are important, and sevens will spend a lot on gadgets.

Health Profile

The overall health of sevens is good. In the early years, health is a little precarious. Infant sevens are plagued by urinary tract infections, colic, and other related illnesses. The areas of health concerns for sevens are the bladder, urethra, kidneys, prostate glands, groin area, rectum, and/or colon. Usually problems are manifested as ruptures, fistulas, stones, and injuries.

Diet is important, and sevens are intuitively drawn toward appropriate diets. Most eat only when hungry and don't overeat. Exercise is normally high on their list, and they work out throughout their lives. Stress (self-imposed) will tend to deplete energy reserves quickly, as sevens tend to be intense in all activities. They need lots of rest and sleep.

As sevens reach the autumn of their years and their bodies change, they need to guard against weight gain and lack of adequate exercise, and to conserve energy.

Money and Career Profile

Sevens don't have boring or dull lives. They think creatively in terms of money, and know intuitively that they can reap the rewards. They give themselves totally to whatever they undertake. They can be secretive about personal plans and are tenacious in staying with planned strategy until it either proves successful or not. If their plan, after a reasonable time, doesn't pan out, they will alter their strategy.

Sevens exploit all opportunities to achieve goals. They increase money by making judicious investments; one success leads to another. They don't usually practice moderation in the stock market, so the broker will be their best ally. The bull market appeals to them, as does constant movement of their money.

The most likely careers for sevens are leadership roles requiring detail planning, managers of people, teachers, counselors, secretaries, accountants. They should invest in boating industries, food, oil and gas, and land development. They need to stay away from catering or hard sells in any industry.

Sevens must guard against allowing romantic and sexual interests to intrude into business areas and should not put all their eggs in one basket.

Profile of the Number 8

Personality Profile

The number eights of the world are unusual, as they represent the death of the lower mind and birth of the spiritual mind. Eights begin their serious work at about age thirty. Eights promote divine justice, trying to destroy the wickedness of ignorance in the soul of humanity. All number eights have to overcome physical obstacles placed in their paths so their minds can transcend to the spiritual planes.

This pattern for eights begins as they enter this world. They are usually born into families with one or both parents enforcing authority, rigidity of thought, religious doctrines, harsh ethical codes of behavior, or intellectual snobbery. Their childhood development centers on how they can flower within this structure and develop their abilities to balance parental requirements with personal goals. Their lessons on power and authority may be used as talent traits in working with either difficult people or business problems. They have uncanny insights into people and their characters.

All eights are filled with ideas and born with the knowledge of how things should work. They are simply drawing upon their own experience levels in childhood and reapplying this knowledge. They have to learn the proper ways money or resources should be handled, or they will repeat the same mistakes.

Number eights are the most likely to succeed, as their need for success is great. Their lives are a continual learning process. Some of their traits are dignity, caution, reverence, practicality, thoughtfulness, pickiness, diplomacy, profundity, positive attitude, magnetism, ambition, organization, concentration, and service to humanity. Eights have a downside, which, if not overcome, can cause them to become mentally dysfunctional or "broken in spirit." If they can correct it, they will not have to experience jealousy, selfishness, discontentment, capriciousness, suspicion, misuse of authority or power, gloomy outlook, avariciousness, impatience, or depression.

Eights must learn to become independent and stable, yet less fearful of receiving help. (They like helping others but are hesitant about seeking help.) They instinctively understand the cosmic law "You give back to the universe that which has been given to you." It is through this law that they can learn the proper use of authority and power and the leadership roles that authority and power attain.

Number eights can attract money easily, and if they use this talent correctly, it can and will serve not only them, but humanity also. They will, at some time or another, be placed in a position of leadership, authority, or power in some area(s) of their lives.

Sex/Love/Marriage Profiles

Traditionally, eights are portrayed as cold and calculating. This is far from the truth, for underneath eights' exterior are some of the most warm-hearted romantics in the world. While slaying with a glance, wounding with a word, stultifying by ignoring someone, they may be burning with desire in their secret heart; for eights have great big red, bleeding hearts.

Eights discover their sexual power early. They are lovers, desiring to please and fulfill, and are terribly tender. Their profound understanding of human nature and innate sense of how to arouse their partners make them desirable and sought after. They like to give gifts, letters, and even poems to those they love.

By the teenage years, most eights are experienced in sexual love, or at least understand how sexual love can bind them to another. They have certain ideals and retain the image of perfect "true" love in the romantic sense. They are ready for marriage but are picky. Poetic love stories fill their mind. They become great lovers, and retain, even enhance, the appeal as they grow older. Marriage is more common after thirty than before.

Eights can be jealous, demanding, and/or vengeful out of the bedroom. They are usually frustrated when they imagine they're rejected or unloved, as they are most likely insecure.

Eights dress well, speak eloquently, give the impression of born aristocrats and can be real merrymakers. They are usually slender and tall, but can look slightly plump.

Eight females are the symbols of motherhood, all-embracing restorers of self-confidence, givers of comfort and solace. All female eights are overprotective of loved ones.

Both female and male eights have tremendous patience with loved ones and inject their ambition and inspiration into their partnerships, either sexual or business.

Number eights are hard to know, as the discrepancies and contradictions in character and behavior are difficult to understand. Once past the exterior barriers, they are mates for life and love with great intensity and loyalty.

Eights enjoy children and are excellent preschool teachers. They like to help children accomplish little things and encourage them to reach out. They are not always consistent in their approach to discipline. They believe that once you've explained the why or why nots, the child should remember and do as instructed. As their offspring grow, the eight parents bind to them. They teach the child to fight, and respect their children enough to give them freedom to state their side. This freedom of expression helps the child verbalize her wants and needs.

Home Profile

You can bet that eights' homes will be very isolated. If in an arid setting, their home will sit well back from the main road, with a fence bordering property lines. If in a more tropical setting, look for a winding road to the highest ground. A more typical setting may include a forest or large stand of foliage camouflaging the entrance to their home. The style of homes is varied, but most will include a cellar or basement. Eights prefer open spaces with barns, animals, corrals, and so on.

The insides of their homes are built with stone, and unusual fireplaces are focal points. They may also have tiled floors, unusual lumber, and a combination of wood grains. Eights show a fondness for hinges, unusual door knockers, and gadgets for the kitchen and workshop. The actual home decor is on the practical side, using wood and metal.

In the kitchen, eights are very proficient and work hard to make meals a delight. They have a fondness for unusual foods.

Health Profile

Number eights have excellent recuperative abilities. In infancy they will be susceptible to colds, bronchitis, and/or other upper respiratory infections. During adolescence they will most likely have problems with their skin—eczema, impetigo, or bruises. As eights enter adulthood, they need to guard against skeletal dislocations and injuries, which in later life cause rheumatism and arthritis.

Eight children should follow stable programs of light exercise, as this promotes good muscle tone and keeps the skeleton stretched and supple. If they aren't careful, their knees and ankles will cause problems in adult years.

The diet for eights is important, but the types of foods are not as important as eating regularly. Eights have a tendency toward constipation and therefore need a diet including natural laxatives. They should avoid cold foods or drinks.

In early infancy, atmosphere plays an important part in eights' health. More than most, they need to be surrounded by happy, cheerful people, or they fall into despondency. This can be the biggest health pitfall for eights. They are prone to worry and exhibit nervousness, and should not let these tendencies take precedence over more positive health traits.

Number eights enjoy longevity and don't exhibit many physical signs of aging. Eights may look older in youth, but with age, appear younger.

Money and Career Profile

Eights' primary concern in the financial world is to be a provider for themselves and their family's future needs. They are also concerned about financial resources in old age.

Eights are always on the lookout to increase financial goals and will work diligently to overcome setbacks in their lives. They must learn to conserve economic resources and, until they do, aren't secure financially.

With determination and a goal in view, eights make it to the top of their profession. They accept starting at the bottom. Hard work doesn't worry them, as they consider it a prerequisite to success. It is determination to be independent and to rise above that helps eights climb to fortune and fame. They will persevere and proceed, always conscious of the need for personal and financial security.

In business, eights maintain their cautious attitude and seldom deal in speculative stock, preferring slow-moving but sound investments. Most don't like to play the stock market; therefore, a bull market is definitely best for them—including blue-chip stocks and bonds.

The types of investments that are best for eights are raw materials (especially iron), construction, iron stocks, computers, tool making, blue-chip stocks, bonds, oil, equipment, and household equipment such as stoves, refrigerators, washing machines, and dryers.

In general, eights' chances for financial success are excellent. They are not above using marriage as a stepping-stone to financial and social success.

Profile of the Number 9

Personality Profile

Number nines are perpetual dreamers and planners. They are idealistic, tolerant, and compassionate. They must not be stubborn in their pursuits of understanding, or they will lose their idealism and become cynical.

Nines are perfectionists and strive for perfection in marriage, social, and professional life. They like close friends or colleagues to achieve a high level of expertise or even perfection. Parents of nine children need to emphasize that although life is not always fair, the child should try to be fair in her dealings with life and people.

Number nines are usually born into families that are too reality-oriented. If nines are not careful, they will become caustic, sarcastic, and procrastinators. Nines are apt to lose their enthusiasm for life and will not complete or continue their previous goals. They will know of many things but be the master of none.

Nines can have trouble with money. They don't like to feel bought or "corrupted" by dollars, and feel strongly the unfairness of the inequality between the rich and the poor. They also tend to hang on to material possessions that may not be needed. Once they realize that money is not a corrupting agent, then wealth will flow toward them, as they have become more spiritual and released from the material things of this world.

Nines represent the leaders, justices, truth seekers, and scientists. They are cooperative, earnest, sociable, patient, and philosophical. These people can give much to our world. Their talents are great and many. They should guard against being radical, scattered, irrational, skeptical, anxious, or gullible, as they will then see the creative side of their personality begin to develop. Their lives are like adventures; unusual happenings and, of course, unusual people are drawn to them.

Sex/Love/Marriage Profiles

Number nines don't appear to have much sexual drive and frequently look more conventional or like weaklings. Female nines seem to be daydreamers or in a world of their own. Both sexes often hide their inner thoughts and harbor intense sexual/sensual feelings of love. They are excellent lovers and give mystical qualities to their lovemaking. The old saying "haste makes waste" doesn't apply to nines!

Their sexual activities begin when they decide the time is right. They are liberated and feel that people of each sex have the right to decide what, how, and when they choose to engage in sex. Female nines don't always feel they must marry if they become pregnant, nor should they be forced to give up their offspring for adoption. As a rule, nines continue their sexual loves until the end of their lives, with very few interruptions (for other than health reasons). They are not by nature promiscuous, but usually have more than one love affair during their lifetime.

Nines are known to be experimenters and usually don't recognize age differences as barriers. Most will marry rather early and have at least two marriages. They normally choose partners that are equal to themselves intellectually and who will enhance their social standing.

When nines become emotionally involved, the mate must realize that this is the most valuable gift nines can make to their marriage partner. If the partner is not aware or does not respond in kind, nines feel rejected and seek someone who will appreciate the gift.

Number nines are good parents and generally have no more than two offspring. They seem to draw children to them; they truly enjoy children and their great imaginations. They feel their children need broad-based education and should experience life so they can choose their own place in the sun.

Since number nines enjoy their offspring, they tend to be lax with discipline and lean heavily toward reasoning with their children, trying to help them learn mental control. They generally make good, understanding parents, and oftentimes treat their children as friends early on.

Home Profile

Number nines like to be near nature and prefer homes close to water. They usually choose hilly or uneven places where rivers or springs, or conduits run.

Homes are usually two stories and feature a steep roof, a location close to a main road, and a large garage area. Nines like large square rooms, but they don't require a great number of rooms.

Inside decor shows refined taste and has clean spartan lines. Number nines like bookshelves and a large desk. If not a typical desk, they will use a large, rectangular table so that they can spread things out. Nines are collectors of books, periodicals, antiques, maps, or anything rare and unusual.

Though nines like an orderly existence, they get sidetracked into intellectual pursuits and may not get back to basic home routines. They are good in the kitchen, especially in cooking good, plain foods. They like to putter and experiment with dishes of different cultures.

Health Profile

Number nines' health is wrapped up in their emotional personality. How they *think* they feel is how they *do* feel. As children, nines should be carefully monitored for diseases of the blood. Since a nine's parent can't see the onset of an illness, the child needs consistent health checkups.

Number nines tend to experience falls that involve the ankles, (either sprains or broken bones). And if not careful, they keep swollen ankles. They are prone to anemia and hay fever, and will also exhibit spasmodic or nervous diseases, along with cramps, and later in life, weakness of the heart.

As adults, they need to force themselves to get plenty of fresh air and lots of fresh vegetables and fruits in order to keep their health stable. They need to avoid fatty and greasy foods. Nines' nervous systems are sensitive, and proper diet and correct nutrients will keep infections and nervous problems to a minimum. The environment should be semiquiet but harmonious; nines need music to balance their nervous system. Most nines tend to be light-sensitive and will need glasses at some point.

In later years, nines will experience more stomach disorders, along with blood clots or heart defects. As a rule, their mind is good, along with their ability to conduct business as usual.

Money and Career Profile

Nines exhibit tremendous independence, and they are always the first to talk about being the master of their destiny and having free will. Their thirst for knowledge is remarkable. Money is never their guiding light, but more advanced nines realize that we live in a world where economics prevails.

Number nines appreciate that financial security leaves them free to do many other things. They aim for good living and protect their financial security. They are always prepared to consult an expert on subjects they aren't knowledgeable about.

Most nines are highly talented and can earn money using creative talents in almost any field. In business or the stock market, however, they tend to seek safe havens or respectable professions. They should not be associated with wars, weapons, or destructive chemicals, as they crave peaceful existences.

Most of nines' fortunes will be made with the judicious help of an adviser. If nines decide to invest in the stock market, the best bets are: research investments, computers, manufacturers of scientific instruments, corporate bonds, paintings, publishing, communication, and urban development. Stocks and bonds that they should avoid are those in the auto industry, synthetic foods, and food substitutes.

The major stumbling block to financial success is lack of attention to business, or having so many diverse interests that the nines become scattered. There is also a lack of ambition or drive necessary to be steady in the business world. But if nines go through the process of education, and center upon a goal, they will become financially successful.

Master Number Eleven

The number eleven is considered to be one of the three master numbers in numerology. The number eleven can also be reduced to the number two, so most of those characteristics will apply. Yet, as eleven is the first number of the "master" numbers, it has special qualities and abilities.

Elevens are total idealists and dreamers. This needs to be balanced, or they will not accomplish their role. All elevens have definite psychic/mystic abilities but are sometimes unaware of them. By the time elevens reach age twenty-five or thirty, they should be aware of their innate abilities. This can sometimes cause discomfort, especially if they don't have good spiritual bases or religious training. They are considered intuitive and strive for inspiration, not only for themselves but for others. Elevens should always follow their hunches, as this is the one way they can set themselves apart and understand their intuitive processes.

The very traits that set them apart also make elevens shy away from public attention, and this often produces intensely reserved personalities, who need to learn to make friends, mingle with people, experience life.

Number elevens are often born into families where spiritual training is not promoted, so elevens must seek it for themselves. They need to live humbly while in the public eye. They must guard their privacy, as their nervous systems are often strained by the inability to say the word *no*. They have generally good health, yet the health line is fragile and body structure delicate.

Number elevens are noted for a style that becomes their personality logo. They should wear smooth textures of fine woven fabric. They tend to choose the no-color or jewel tones.

Career possibilities for elevens are numerous. The best choices are diplomats, lecturers, critics, artists, television personalities, aviators, advertisers, directors, authors, or jobs in some way connected to the motion picture industry or any related field. There are numerous number elevens in the spiritual (preachers or missionaries) and metaphysical fields.

Number elevens need to learn self-discipline and to keep appointments, be on time, and forgive little slights, as their emotions are indeed sensitive. These people feel things deeply.

Master Number Twenty-Two

Number twenty-twos are the second level in the ascension to the masters, and their place is significant as it indicates that they have passed trials and been tempered with knowledge and understanding that is above average. It also implies that they will work with the masses to help promote universal love and understanding. Number twenty-twos have special insight into how practicality can work in promoting the universal concept of love. The influence of the twenty-twos can be far-reaching. They are able to bring system and order to this world; they are the organizers.

Twenty-twos have the ability to master anything if they so desire. Their concentration is intense, and they are able to hold fast to their goals or ideas. They possess the determination to bring to fruition what they have started.

They will start at the bottom of a chosen field, but are elevated shortly into a position of leadership. They command respect by their bearing without realizing it. Twenty-twos make good diplomats, CEOs of large corporations, ambassadors, analysts, financial advisers, or promoters.

Number twenty-twos always appear to be affluent even when they're not, and they don't usually remain in a sad financial state. Their mode of dress is an outward expression of their inward personality, and they should wear straight, tailored lines of good to excellent quality. They generally choose unadventurous colors, with texture producing a striking quality.

Twenty-twos are usually born into families that don't understand physical handicaps, and they may be handicapped—either physically or mentally. In early childhood, parental influence is critical. They must be encouraged to live up to their abilities and finish what they have started. They usually have latent artistic ability and don't normally use it for commercial gain. If twenty-twos are not advanced, they will work within a more restricted job situation such as foreman, clerk, and the like. Be sure you also read about the qualities of the number four. The number twenty-two, not developed, will resemble the four personality.

Master Number Thirty-Three

Number thirty-three is not commonly found in today's world, as this number represents the highest moral and spiritual universal master number. There are a few, but most are not developed enough to assume a personality without ego or other human frailties.

When you do find a number thirty-three, you are looking at one whose motives and actions are for the good of humanity, even if it involves personal sacrifice. These are the ones that have the strongest spiritual bonds. Their primary role in life is to bring an end to pain and suffering worldwide, and they will work tirelessly to this end.

Thirty-threes are the healers of the world, in both the spiritual and physical sense. They are the universal teachers and can transcend reality as most of us know it. They are the New Age pioneers, and as such they command our respect.

They are normally very calm people. They think before speaking, searching within to formulate responses that will serve humanity in the best way. They dress in conservative styles, in simple attire.

The underdeveloped thirty-three, if not careful, becomes self-righteous and can cause problems due to her limited viewpoint or understanding of how the universe should work.

Thirty-threes normally enjoy good health for the bulk of their lives but need help from other people (buffers) to preserve their energy. If not careful of diet, thirty-threes will subject themselves to fasts which can prove to have disastrous effects.

WHAT'S IN A NAME

Your name number is the second most important identity number assigned to you. Your name evokes certain feelings about you and determines how others will perceive you. Unfortunately, names are often handed down from generation to generation with little thought given to how the name will be received by the owner or by other people during their lives.

Just as our birth dates carry vibrations, our name and the numerical values assigned to the letters in our name also carry certain vibrations.

The name assigned at birth is divided into three sections—the beginning, middle, and end of the name. Each letter of the alphabet is assigned a numerical value, and those numbers added and reduced to a single digit represent the expression of the name personality. The number corresponding to the first letter of the name indicates the strongest attributes of the person. The number corresponding to the last letter of the name indicates the weakest attributes and/or the personality conflicts. The sum of the remaining letters of the name, when totaled and reduced to a single digit, indicate traits and talents assigned to that individual.

The total name number provides us with a summary of the person's qualities and helps produce a balanced personality profile. This is obtained by adding all the letters. Let's look at an example of how a name can influence a person. Using the following guide showing the alphabet and the numbers assigned to the letters, let us total the name John to see what is indicated:

1	2	3	4	5	6	7	8	9
A	B	C	D	E	F	G	H	I
J	K	L	M	N	O	P	Q	R
S	T	U	V	W	X	Y	Z	

$$\text{J} \quad \text{O} \quad \text{H} \quad \text{N}$$
$$1 + 6 + 8 + 5 = 20 = 2 + 0 = 2.$$

The name John has a total value number of 2. His strongest attributes are indicated by the number 1 (J being the first letter of the name), and his weakest attributes are indicated by the number 5 (N being the last letter of the name). His talents are indicated by the number 5 ($6 + 8 = 14$, $1 + 4 = 5$). To see what this indicates, look at the quick reference guide given below.

WHOLE NAME

Number	Definition
1	Ambition, creativity, changeable loner, egotist.
2	Support, cooperation, a follower, receptive.
3	Self-expressive, communicative, a party-goer.
4	Systematic, disciplinarian, self-disciplined.
5	Sensual, experimental, catalyst for change, speculative.
6	Responsible, instructional, loving, a server, parental, a showman.
7	Analytical, aristocratic by nature, scientific, spiritual, perfectionistic, authoritative.
8	Efficient, materialistic, executive, strongly disciplined, especially externally (never deviating).
9	Brotherly love, sophistication, dedication to perfecting skills and/or performance.
11	Extremely spiritual, high-strung, visionary, sensitive.
22	Intensely emotional, hyperactive, futuristic, uplifts the masses.
33	Spirituality, serving of the masses, great patience, extreme dedication.

FIRST LETTER (STRONGEST TRAIT)

Number	Definition
1	Independence, leadership, creative mental energy, pioneering in changes, restrictive.
2	Cooperative, receptive, naturally inclined to be emotionally supportive.
3	Creativity, self-expression, imagination, versatility in communication, optimism.
4	Self-disciplined, organized, practical in work, dutiful, conservative.

Number	Definition
5	Mental curiosity, nonconformity, unexpected changes, experimental.
6	Protective, responsible, adjustments for others, family/community harmony.
7	Introspective, analytical, aristocratic, spiritual curiosity, inclination to specialize, authoritative, seeks perfection.
8	Influences over others, material accumulation, disciplined, practical, problem solving, seeks affluence.
9	Compassion, empathy, philosophical judgment, communicates, expands culturally.
11, 22, 33	Don't apply.

LAST LETTER (WEAKEST TRAIT)

Number	Definition
1	Indecision, emotional judgments, lack of self-assertion, conflicts within.
2	Personalized sensitivity, preoccupation with petty problems, too concerned about peaceful surroundings, constantly nitpicking, conflicts within.
3	Erratic personality, scattered interests, superficial social concerns, reclusive.
4	Dislike of down-to-earth work, too much caution or a lack of self-protection, lack of practicality.
5	Inability to learn without experiencing everything, subconscious desire to be free of responsibility.
6	Jealous misgivings, stubborn sense of responsibility, imposes personal standards on others.
7	Aloofness, fault finding, lack of faith, inquisitiveness, gullibility in relationships.
8	Need for recognition, intolerance for inefficiency, lack of ambition.
9	Misplaced sympathy, impracticality, overly generous, egocentric.
11, 22, 33	Don't apply.

TALENT TRAITS

The following is a synopsis of the talent number, the number arrived at by adding up the number equivalents of all the letters between the first and last letter. This is also considered the lucky number in a person's life.

Number	Definition
1	You need to learn to incorporate initiative and directive independence along with originality into your career. You can expect to succeed through leadership, self-reliance, and by using proper methods. You will need to cultivate patience in order to have proper control over the success you want to achieve.
2	In your search for success and the proper use of your considerable talent, you will use cooperation and group efforts. Your best career opportunity is through others in partnerships using original ideas and concepts with detailed strategy. You will, over the years, develop a liking for the arts and need to cultivate a definite taste in them.
3	You will need to learn the correct form of self-expression either in written or spoken form through music, acting, or other arts. These areas will definitely bring money toward you.
4	Your best natural skill is your commonsense approach to managing anything, whether it be a large or small business, people, or objects. Use responsibility correctly and learn personal self-discipline along with practical problem solving. You can succeed.
5	Your best trait is the unconventional way in which you think and react in relation to new ideas. You are quick and inventive, as well as clever, and are able to do more than one thing at a time. You do, however, need to avoid tight scheduling whenever possible. Contact with the public or masses is your best bet for overall success.
6	Your home and community will be one of your major modes of self-expression. Your main

Number	Definition

abilities are to create beauty and harmony in either environment, as you are most likely destined to live a life that will suggest opulence, but only if you remember to give more than you receive. What you withdraw from the universe must be returned through helping others without selfish thoughts.

7 Your spiritual and technical ability is recognized by others and should be used with caution, as you will have much influence over others in these areas of your life. Money will come to you through investigation and by a broad base of knowledge. Avoid active partnerships, for they tend to restrict your natural ability to move from one field to the other or to incorporate many ideas and fields under one umbrella. Take time out for yourself. For example, take time for formal study, which you enjoy, and which is important to you.

8 Financial leadership and organization are your special keys to success. Keeping involved in community affairs, civic duties, and taking opportunities to mingle with prominent persons is where your special talents will surface. Your discipline and judgment of people will prove valuable to your overall success in achieving your goals. Develop a businesslike attitude and a straightforward approach to secure success in any of the many endeavors you may choose to pursue.

9 Your life's goals will indirectly involve the welfare of others. You will achieve them through any of the artistic abilities that you exhibit and your insistence on a quality (and you decide what "quality" is) in areas that you work or play in. Communication will play an important part in your overall life, as it seems to be your forte in life to reexplain what has transpired. Cultural growth, not material growth, should be your aim. You will attain money but won't keep it if money becomes your primary goal rather than a resource to

Number	Definition
	pave the way for others. Your talent is expressed through humanitarian concerns.
11	You have the unusual ability to weigh decisions and promote activities, with your innate ability to inspire. You can lead riots! These talents must be used wisely, or they can backfire and throw you into terrible situations or circumstances. Your spirituality is awesome and is the very core of your overall life activities. You will use your skill in communications to further spiritual growth in those around you. People will tend to listen and follow you, and your influence is immense. You need to be aware that you have a very sensitive nervous system and need to guard against overcommiting in your activities and against becoming too intense emotionally.
22	If you are a 22, then you have an incredible ability to solve problems, look for alternatives, create a better mousetrap, if you will. People will listen to and respect you for the directness and honesty that you exhibit. You represent the wisdom that we all wish we had in many areas of life. Your wisdom comes from within and seems to guide you through many of life's trials and tribulations, leaving you untouched, at least in the eyes of bystanders. This is not always so, but you do tend to be able to survive trials and tribulations better than most.
33	This is a very rare and uncommon talent number. The most that can be said about this number is that you are highly spiritual and totally unselfish. You will serve the public masses in a highly spiritual and unselfish manner.

SAMPLE READINGS
(WITH EMPHASIS ON MARITAL COMPATIBILITY)

These sample readings should help you understand how to bridge for various name traits; you might want to try your own reading for the names before you read mine. It's also interesting to see how two people's numerological readings can help them see potential strengths and weaknesses in their relationship. Numerological compatibility provides no guarantees that a marriage will succeed or fail, but it is an indicator of whether two people can complement and enhance each other and deal with problem areas effectively.

Husband: John Bell

Name Number

J   O   H   N   B   E   L   L
$1 + 6 + 8 + 5 = 20 = 2$ $2 + 5 + 3 + 3 = 13 = 4$
Whole name: $2 + 4 = 6$

Traits
  Strong: 1
  Weak: 5
  Talent: 5
  Whole First Name: 2

Birth Number

$8 + 2 + 5 + 1 + 9 + 6 + 4 = 35 = 8$

John's name indicates these characteristics:

Strong trait: 1	Independence, leadership, pioneering spirit, restrictive.
Weak trait: 5	Must learn by experience, has subconscious desire to be free of responsibilities.
Talent trait: 5	Unconventional in thought and reactions, experimental with ideas and concepts, quick, inventive, clever, can do more than one thing at a time. Needs to avoid overextension of his time. Best career involves contact with the public.
Whole first name: 2 (John)	Supportive, cooperative, follower, and receptive to ideas.
Whole name: 6 (John Bell)	Responsible, loving, good parent, showmanship.

Personality Profile: Filled with ideas; innate knowledge of how things should work; expert at reapplying knowledge from one area of life to another; excellent judge of character; can be diplomatic, profound, positive, organizer, and can have tremendous powers of concentration when working toward goals or projects. Must guard against impatience and gloomy outlook.

Sex/Love/Marriage: Romantic, overprotective of loved ones, has a way of injecting his ambitions and inspirations into partnerships (marriage or business).

Home: Isolated, on high ground, open spaces (inside), practical and functional furnishings, picky with home.

Children: Enjoys kids, isn't always consistent in discipline, teaches kids to fight for what they need and want, gives children freedom to achieve.

Health: Has excellent recuperative abilities; balanced diet is important; biggest pitfall is despondency. Therefore, needs harmony in environment. Ages slowly and looks youthful throughout life.

Money: Primary concern is to be a good provider. Accepts starting at the bottom and working up. Good investments: iron, construction, computers, blue-chip stock, oil, and publishing.

Wife: Dora Hall

Name Number

D O R A   H A L L
$4 + 6 + 9 + 1 = 20 = 2$ $8 + 1 + 3 + 3 = 15 = 6$
Whole name: $2 + 6 = 8$

Traits
  Strong: 4
  Weak: 1
  Talent: 6
  Whole First Name: 2

Birth Number

$3 + 3 + 0 + 1 + 9 + 6 + 6 = 28 = 1$

Dora's name indicates these characteristics:

Strong trait: 4	Self-disciplined, organized, practical in work, dutiful, and conservative.
Weak trait 1:	Indecisive, makes emotional judgments, lacks self-assertion, has internal conflicts.
Talent trait: 6	Home and community are major expressions in her life. She needs beauty and harmony in her home environment with the suggestion of an opulent lifestyle. Needs to give unselfishly of her time.
Whole first name: 2 (Dora)	Supportive, cooperative, follower, and receptive to ideas.
Whole name: 8 (Dora Hall)	Efficient, materialistic, strongly disciplined, good at implementation.
Whole name: 6 (Dora Bell)	(Most women take their husbands' last names, but even if they don't, they take on the qualities of the name.) Responsible, loving, good parent, showmanship.

Personality Profile: Leadership, needs harmony in environment, ambitious, original thinker, naturally enthusiastic, philosophical by nature, has strength of will to make marriage work (in unity). She is the ruler at home, is a strong parent, dutiful, and flexible. Best jobs include: management, self-employment, teacher, director.

Home: Prefers hills, barren landscapes, corner lots (facing east), fireplaces, lots of space, and traditional furniture. Is picky about her home, is oriented to neatness and cleanliness, is a specialty cook and likes a well-stocked pantry.

Children: Is gentle, likes to teach them, takes great pride in her children.

Health: Generally robust and vigorous, needs a definite routine for health maintenance. If not careful, she will tend to overdo it. Her health is tied to her emotional flows; if she gets unbalanced, this will cause health problems.

Money: Original sock saver of the universe—perceives money as a status symbol and is money-motivated to be successful. (Has a little hidden away that no one knows about.) Best investments: weapons, aerospace, defense, iron, steel.

The Couple

Compatibility Chart

When reading for compatability, you add the two people's trait numbers together for a composite number unless the numbers are the same. John and Dora share the number 2 in their whole name number. Number 2 represents supportive, cooperative, follower, and receptive.

John (1) + Dora (4) = 5   Strong trait
John (5) + Dora (1) = 6   Weak trait
John (5) + Dora (6) = 11   Talent trait
John (2) / Dora (2) = 2   Whole name

Strong trait: 5	Ambitious, sensual, catalysts for change, and speculative.
Weak trait: 6	Balance each other. Responsible, good parents, loving, showmanship.
Talent trait: 11	Spiritual, visionary, and sensitive.
Whole name trait: 2	Marriage would indicate a partnership that would be supportive and cooperative. They do not, however, lose their individuality (because their talent numbers are different).

Birth number: John (8) + Dora (1) = 9

Marriage: Nines like perfection in marriage, social, and professional life. They will complement each other. As parents they will emphasize that life isn't always fair, but children should be fair in their dealings in life. Spirituality is a fundamental part of their marital unity.

Sexual Area: Nines will use sexual activity with regularity and experimentation. If not careful, however, they can become too routine and passive as they take on life's responsibilities. They are slower to reach orgasm; the idea being that haste makes waste. They are excellent lovers, as they know how to use what they've got!

Home: They have refined tastes. They must have their own areas (spaces) at home. They collect books, lean toward the Spartan— clean settings with refined taste—they are not knickknack types.

Health of Marriage: Because they are so sensitive, they will be aware of how the other is feeling at all times. If not careful, one of the partners will ooververbalize what he or she feels problems are, which could blow problems out of proportion. The main requirements for a productive marriage are a semiquiet atmosphere and low activity levels. (Music will help provide calmness in a busy household.)

Joint Funds: They believe that charity begins at home. They appreciate anything high-tech, either as an investment vehicle or as a tool in their environment. They are usually self-employed. Both will have separate careers but will also be involved in a joint business venture on the side.

Good mutual investments for joint funds: research technology, computers, scientific instruments, publishing, and mining stocks (blue-chip).

Summary

All things considered, John and Dora, based on a numerological synopsis, have about a 60 percent chance of a happy marriage and a fairly affluent lifestyle together. Keep in mind that this synopsis does not include differences in cultural background, formal education, and other variables.

It's neat to note that neither will lose his or her individuality, and yet, in major areas of the marriage (such as parenthood), each has definite role responsibilities. One balances the other.

Since neither spouse has separate spiritual concepts, they will, therefore, form a staunch base of spirituality together.

Nicknames

If the person you are reading for uses a nickname, it is important to read for both the nickname and the given name. While the number relating to the name the client uses in day-to-day life tends to supply a more accurate picture of the client's present status than a birth name, you should point out the strengths and weaknesses of both names. For example, let's do a reading for Dora's brother who, like her husband, is named John. John Hall, however, often uses the nickname Johnny. There are some important differences between John and Johnny.

John's original (first name only) strength number is 1 (representing independence, creativity, energy, a pioneer of changes). His weak number is 5 (inability to learn something without personally experiencing it, subconscious desire to be free of what he considers to be responsibility). And his talent number is

5 (unconventional thinker, quick, inventive, clever, able to do more than one thing at a time, may tend to overreach).

The nickname Johnny retains the strength number 1, but his weakness is now a number 7 (representing aloofness, gullibility, faultfinding, and lack of faith). His talent number becomes 6 (someone who will express himself through home or community, cares about beauty, will most likely live a life of opulence, a giver). Thus Johnny will probably be less inventive and caring than John; he might tend to be shallower and more critical, as well.

$$J \quad O \quad H \quad N \quad N \quad Y$$
$$1 + 6 + 8 + 5 + 5 + 7 = 3 + 2 = 5$$

The nickname alters the personality number from 2 to 5, a number that enhances the weak traits of John. As a two, John is a cooperator, one who smooths things over, a receptive personality (the down side of John may be that he is too passive). As a five, however, Johnny is restless, speculative, the showman type—not a strong combination with his weakness and talent numbers. If the client calls himself Johnny as an adult, he may be too impulsive, and he may exhibit a latent tendency to be too one-sided.

$$J \quad O \quad H \quad N \quad N \quad Y \qquad\qquad H \quad A \quad L \quad L$$
$$1 + 6 + 8 + 5 + 5 + 7 = 5 \qquad 8 + 1 + 3 + 3 = 1 + 5 = 6$$
$$5 + 6 = 11$$

Since people are often identified by both first and last names, you might want to compare John Hall and Johnny Hall as regards the total personality number as well. Eleven represents extremes in spirituality; if he is not careful, Johnny might be high-strung, exhibiting nervous reactions and extreme sensitivity.

We now have a male who is drawn to experimentation, can be overly speculative, even "hyper." He is an individual of extremes, and may be quite difficult to deal with. This is a person who will probably have to overcome tremendous odds to make the best of his numerological leanings; I would probably advise this individual to use the name John rather than Johnny.

It is important to remember, however, that for certain career fields (sports, for example), Johnny might be the better choice, both aesthetically and numerologically. And of course, the inherent weaknesses and strengths of any name can be played up or overcome if the person is aware of these tendencies.

9
ESP—THE STRONGEST LINK IN THE LIFE-CHAIN

It has always amazed me that we slough off our first impressions of people, as this is the one time when our ESP kicks in automatically. These first impressions are ESP clues and are usually correct.

In Western culture, the accepted greeting is a handshake. Handshakes give substance to our initial reactions, as they involve both eye and physical contact, engage body sensors, and "turn on" the perceptual side of our minds. Thus, we are fed information that provides us with an instantaneous assessment of that person. Of course, our body language may appear accepting of an individual, but our feelings could be very different. You may smile while you're shaking that hand but inwardly be cringing. Body language, while a natural aggressive or passive response, is often manipulated socially. ESP cuts through this superficiality to provide true insight.

One of the purposes of this book is to help you shed this cloak of superficiality and recognize ESP signals as they occur. I have provided you with beginning points of reference (palms, cards, numerology) to help you become ESP-sensitive and to help you incorporate your sensitivity into your daily activities. It becomes a philosophy that changes your outlook, alters your thinking processes, and offers possibilities (instead of limitations) in day-to-day existence.

As you work through the processes of learning and developing your own ESP awareness, you will be drawn to "kindred spirits." You will easily recognize other ESP-sensitive people by their outward projections. The atmosphere around them draws you in and makes you feel genuinely welcome. ESP-sensitive people are courteous by nature, and are normally truly happy with themselves. They have strong and positive self-images and are naturally empathetic. They radiate these traits, and people involuntarily gravitate toward them. If you aren't aware of these people, sit up and take notice. They are easily recognizable once you begin to pay attention. Let me stress—these are normal, everyday people like you, who have problems and setbacks, too. They just deal with them in a positive way through ESP direction. They are always listening to their ESP, whether or not they are consciously aware of it.

If you are still skeptical, make the effort to "people watch" anyway. It doesn't cost a thing, and you have nothing to lose by noticing the people around you and how they interact. There *is* something going on. For the sake of argument, seek out people that fit the preceding description. Talk to them and learn something about their philosophies. You are bound to find that they follow an inner direction. Don't think of this as a test; instead, view it as an experiment in living. Once you begin to take notice of people, you will find it becomes second nature, and an assortment of information about these people will become available to you. Let me give you several examples of how this applies to daily living. This is your chance to tune in.

ESP AND WORK

There are hundreds of opportunities to use your ESP every day. For example, let's say you're at a job interview. When you first walk through the door, you will get a general feel for the office through the secretary or other office workers. (Is the atmosphere around them tense, friendly, indifferent, or what?) These are clues, given through psychometry, as to the characteristics of this particular environment.

Next, you meet the interviewer and shake hands. Don't let this golden opportunity to use your newly acquired ESP skills slip by. The handshake involves the sense of touch (psychometry) and also allows you to quickly scan the interviewer's palm (hand shape, skin texture, finger type, and—if you're quick—maybe even fingernails). While the potential employer has merely noticed whether or not your palms are sweaty and your grip is firm, you have gleaned an impressive amount of information about him (unless, of course, you are *both* testing your ESP skills). Because you actually touched the person during a handshake, your first impressions are going to be correct.

OK, you have made it through the office and the handshake. The interview is about to begin, and there are many clues you can pick up during this time. For example, voices can tell you a lot. Voices, like the eyes, are the mirrors of the inward person. Even if the interviewer smiles when he tells you to have a seat, you may sense *instinctively* that he doesn't want to be bothered. This is a clue. You are engaging in telepathy when your ESP tells you that one thing is actually going on when something else is implied— psychometry is also in gear. In addition, most people use their hands while they talk, and you'll get yet another chance to check their palms. More and more details are revealed.

In essence, *you* have become the interviewer and are making the decisions about the job. If you feel negative, don't take the job (unless, of course, you are desperate for the money; take the job and keep looking for another).

Once hired, you are usually lumped together with a large group of people. There is a lot of pressure to perform well. Your efficiency is being monitored, and you are more or less on display, with everyone watching to make sure you succeed. As a new employee, you need to tune in to your co-workers. ESP will help you discern the power structure of the office and lead you to the people you need for help and advice. ESP will also let you know who to avoid and who the troublemakers are. I call this an employee's "benefit package." You also have the option of "collecting" birthdays and doing numerological workups on people you want to understand better.

After you have been on the job for a while and acclimated to the work environment, you will need to decide where you want to fit within the work structure: this is the perfect opportunity for you to employ the practical skills for both goal setting and the realization of goals. As conditions begin to improve for you, as a result of visualization, co-workers absorb and reflect your positive attitudes and will respond in a friendly manner. As you interact positively with your co-workers, and attitudes are enhanced, this induces unity in your workplace. After all, ESP-sensitive people are always willing to go the extra mile, right? (And don't forget, the boss *will* remember your efforts when promotions and raises roll around.)

On a final note, you will know your ESP is in good working order when you can not only make small changes, but also perceive what needs to occur and actually have it on line before the need arises. Congratulations, you are on target—the proof is in the pudding!

Of course, employers can use ESP skills, too. In an interview, an employer is looking for a person with certain skill levels, someone who will "fit in" and become part of the team. While one applicant may have more obvious skills, an employer may end up hiring someone with less apparent skills whom he or she perceives has more potential to excel later on. Yet while the employer can utilize ESP techniques, he or she is in a different situation because an employer cannot hire someone based solely on intuition. He or she is restricted by conditions imposed by the company and has to follow their guidelines. There is a certain amount of leeway within these limitations, yet the employer must use caution.

Inner direction (ESP awareness) can be extremely helpful in general business flows. All businesses either promote or sell something. The ESP personality will have the advantage in business, as ESP-aware people can assimilate and use ESP information to help make a sale or acquire a customer. Through the handshake, you have gotten a feel for the person. A mini-palm reading helps to establish rapport quickly, by allowing recognition of specific personality traits. Telepathy may kick in. Dreams may provide ideas for new ways to approach the person. Meditation and visualization can help to set the scenario for empathetic, honest, and low-pressure sales. You are comfortable, and can relax and enjoy the process. Because you have been through it mentally, you are able to genuinely listen to your customer. The customer senses the interest and loves the attention; in short, the customer feels special. You used ESP to set a successful scenario; meditation, visualization, palm scans, psychometry, body sensors, and maybe more. Many benefits are gained by the ESP information-gathering processes. You may even gauge your success in the business world by the emergence of the following factors: a networking system with positive, friendly contacts, rewards and recognition within the organization (awards, merit raises, and promotions), and recognition in the business community.

By simply becoming a positive, optimistic, warm, and others-oriented person, you have gone full circle and drawn positive things back to you. The universal law stating, "What goes around comes around," is working *for* you. Using positive imaging, meditation, visualization, and ESP when it kicks in, you are becoming the person you wanted to be.

Take the case of my friend who had an idea that involved video lesson tapes and an educational television program. Although she had nine years of teaching and lecturing experience, she was totally out of her element with film projects. Initially, she tried to thoroughly research and develop her ideas to formulate a good game plan. This ran amok because she didn't have the resources or contacts needed. Finally, she simply put her ideas down on paper (defining goals) and yelled for help calling on the universe to help her achieve her goals. One by one, people and resources came into her life, thus enabling her to realize some of her primary goals. As they developed, she learned how to redefine goals and techniques in order to become successful. She employed visualization and meditation for the most part, sending telepathic messages that prompted responses.

A random polling of successful people showed that they daydream, or stargaze, not only to reduce stress, but also to assist themselves in unconscious decision making. What they are really doing is "clearing the slate" with meditation. This allows them to focus, zero in on, problem areas or decisions. Usually, they utilize meditation as a daily habit, and may meditate while commuting, while alone in the office, or in the tub or shower. Of course, there are no overnight success stories. Although some growth events may happen quickly, others take time. As positive events occur, either personal or financial, they can be equated with success.

SOCIAL ESP

The social aspects of ESP are slightly different and even more fun. Normally, you are using ESP because you enjoy it and want to see how well you do. And it is in practicing with friends—in in-depth concentration on ESP—that you'll probably make your greatest strides and receive some great early validation.

At a party, a friend might announce that you have been studying palmistry. You could end up reading every palm in the room, but don't complain; this is a wonderful experience for you, is entertaining for all concerned, and could reveal some tantalizing tidbits!

Telepathy can also be a lot of fun. Let's say that you and a friend are out on the town and spot interesting members of the opposite sex. You decide that it would be just a marvelous idea to use telepathy to get their attention. Bingo! It works. You and your friend are really excited when they ask if they can join you.

Another applicable form of telepathy, used in conjunction with visualization, is arranging for introductions with people you want to meet. You want to meet the CEO of a certain business, or a certain young man. By calling upon the powers of the universe to arrange the introduction, you have inadvertently begun visualization techniques, along with using telepathy as a conduit to attain his attention.

A card reading is probably the simplest ESP vehicle to use, and proficiency will be most beneficial to you, your family, and close friends. As card readings do reflect current events and trends, they are wonderful short-term helpmates, offering alternative solutions and insights. Card readings can provide advance notice concerning health matters, changes in finances, career opportunities, and romantic flows. They will help you recognize, or set, priorities. Cards can also reflect past events and trends that influence your current conditions. Its amazing how much you can learn about friends and spouses through cards. Oh, and did I mention how much fun they are?

Numerology is especially appropriate for learning about new friends, as you don't need their extensive participation to do a reading—just a name and a birthday.

Within the family framework, ESP can be very beneficial. Children, by following their parents' example, will begin at an early age to incorporate ESP into their lives. They may use visualization techniques to assist them in performing well in school, and regular mediation will notably reduce their daily stress levels.

Palmistry can greatly facilitate the rearing of children. By boosting your understanding of the child's personality aspects and indicating potential talents and interests, palmistry enables you to correctly motivate the child. Health information given in the palms will denote health tendencies. Remember, forewarned is forearmed.

Numerology is also an extremely helpful information-gathering process. Numerology, used in combination with palmistry, is doubly effective. The actual naming of a child can be deliberately planned to reflect certain connotations and traits. You could name your child with a certain image in mind, or choose a name that numerically matches or counters his or her birth number.

Your family can also benefit from regular card readings. The information gleaned will promote family harmony by allowing you to confront problem areas knowledgeably. Solutions, alternatives, and possibilities can be weighed and action taken with positive results.

THE PSYCHIC LIFE

I have purposely listed numerous applications of ESP. My goal is to enlighten and enable you to benefit in as many areas of your life as possible. This has not been an easy task, because most people have not been exposed to my method of thinking. The mental processes used in ESP are not logical in the normal sense. This is why some people find it difficult to incorporate this type of mental process into their lives. But if they let go of their preconceptions, ESP can become second nature. The vehicles in the previous chapters will activate this alternative way of thinking.

Until I wrote this book, I never attempted a formal breakdown of how and why ESP works and the mechanics of the vehicles. The processing cycles and thought patterns are so unconscious and automatic for me that I had never stopped to analyze them. By the same token, you can actually handicap yourself by limiting the boundaries of creative thoughts. Living in such a guarded state of thought will inhibit your originality.

I cannot stress enough that we all have psychic ability; a psychic monitor dwells within us, giving us amazing sensory faculties that enable us to "access" all sorts of information not available to us on this plane. Psychic energy is alive (albeit latent) in all of us and ready to be utilized as a supportive measure. Superstition, ignorance, or inexperience cannot negate ability. I cannot imagine having a resource or ability available and choosing to ignore it!

The use of ESP is tantamount to having a natural protective factor. ESP promotes well-being, always helps you, will never hurt you, and also saves you lots of grief. It is the most inexpensive counseling in the world, as it recognizes what you, and you alone, need—and it *is* accurate.

ESP opens communication lines and consequently helps with problem solving—not just for you, but for others as well. The self-esteem gained by all parties involved with ESP should never be understated.

The degree of psychic ability depends upon the refinement and sensitivity of the individual. Psychic nature is timeless and knows no limitation. When this pure psychic power is expressed by a highly developed soul, many things are manifested, and great intuitive insights are gleaned through one's psychic nature. Attaining this higher state of consciousness, or inner-core consciousness, increases your creative and prophetic abilities. To properly advance yourself in today's world, you *need* this psychic information.

Our world is very complex. New information to process and assimilate is never-ending. Attempting to keep up and advance oneself has resulted in a culture of people who are frantic, driven, unhappy, and "stressed out." You know some of these people and recognize many others. You may be one of them yourself. You may be doing all the "right" things for all the "right" reasons and still be frustrated. Something is missing in your life. You may feel that somehow, despite everything, you are missing the mark. Upon gaining an achievement or reaching a goal, have you ever felt depressed or let down?—"Is that all there is?"

ESP is the missing link, the Silver Thread, that enables you to become a whole person with inner-core (cosmic) connectedness. The practical and entertaining aspects of ESP are all well and good; however, you need to use ESP—in total—to achieve a perfect "rounding off."

In this book, I have given you the methodology that will lead you to this higher state of consciousness. I have carefully related a myriad of ESP usages. I have attempted to explain phenomena that exist simply because they exist. I have led you to the ESP well— whether you dip into the well or not is up to you. I can tell you, however, that if you do begin the process of incorporating ESP into your life, you will grasp its Silver Thread and be drawn into an unbroken circle of events.

Simply stated, the circle of events works in the following manner:

1. You begin to use ESP.
2. It works.
3. You now clearly are building faith in ESP.
4. ESP is a link to the mystery of life/the unknown.
5. The mystical is a key to the Supreme Being.
6. You are now communicating with the Supreme Being.
7. Now the circle is complete; you are one with the Supreme Being.

Notice that biblically, seven is the number of completion. For those of you into meditation, there are seven Chakras.

According to cosmic law, everything is connected. There is no past, present, or future; it is one and the same. Faith and the Silver Thread are the fibers that connect us to the Supreme Being. The Supreme Being is the life source, the beginning and the end, the alpha and omega—the infinity of cosmic law.

This spiritual base is crucial for consistent and beneficial use of ESP. First, you must be aware of a Supreme Being, and second, you must have faith and trust in order to accept that the Supreme Being has your best interests at heart.

The search for inner-core consciousness is what life is all about, and ESP can help you to a new understanding of what you are able to achieve by listening to your inner core. Previously I told you that ESP will never hurt you, lead you astray, or place you in jeopardy. It leads to fulfillment and great joy. Your spiritual foundation enables you to believe that you *are* loved and accepted, and you learn to run your life in this belief. Psychic communication becomes of paramount importance to you, giving you direction and balance.

Once these beliefs become your philosophy, you cannot avoid becoming closer to spiritual awareness. All three human dimensions—spiritual, mental, and physical—are joined by ESP inner-core consciousness. You have found the missing link, the spiritual core, and you are now whole and one with the universe. You are connected.

I call this connection "soul swelling" (it is an overwhelming upsurge of emotions that fills your entire being). Once begun, it never ceases. It's like the tide that ebbs and flows in constant motion. You now know that you are special and have a distinctive place within the universe. Yes, you can become confused, lose your place from time to time or even get off track. This merely alerts you to the fact that you are in need of spiritual replenishing. It is through this constant resurgence and listening that we retain our hope, optimism, and desire to continue the search.

I believe the Supreme Being gives you all of these abilities, and wants you to use them to your best advantage. OK, what about those who are skeptical or have suppressed this soul swelling? You may have a difficult time accepting the concepts or may have squelched the ESP flows with heavy defense mechanisms (much like children choosing to ignore parental advice). No problem, folks. If you don't have a good spiritual foundation initially, the Supreme Being will nudge or guide you in the right direction. He will begin by spoon-feeding you, a little at a time, until you are able to understand on your own.

Dreams are just one of the mechanisms that the Supreme Being chooses for communication with skeptics or ESP beginners. This is because even beginners will have an innate (although simplistic) understanding of what their dreams mean. If this particular method of communication doesn't work, and the message doesn't get through, He will be creative in communicating with you and find a way to communicate that you can understand and *cannot* ignore.

Skeptics and the inexperienced may find themselves in situations, or involved with certain people, that make them turn inward for direction. These persons, by being examples of how one should lead one's life become, in essence, missionaries. These people can be ministers, seers, tax accountants, friends. They have a radiant joy and zest for living. They are happy, contented, and problems don't seem to affect them adversely; although they may strive for more, they are satisfied with what they have. You may find yourself connected with one or more of these missionaries in some way. It will always be mutually beneficial, as everyone has a contribution to make in this world. They could be your cosmic teachers, and you the pupil. Sometimes books or classes can be your "teachers," too.

One of the roles of teachers is to get you over conceptual hurdles. One of the greatest anxieties expressed by the ESP novice is fear and learning how to deal with it. The novice does not want to lose control, feel out of control, or be controlled. But these are human concepts, not the Supreme Being's. Your teachers will help you learn to relax and let go of these inhibitions. You will learn that the universal laws give you "free will" and "freedom of choice."

These universal laws are wonderfully comforting. Everyone has a place in the universe. In the scheme of things, all people have a contribution to make, some talent (great or small) that makes them unique. You have a purpose for living that makes you special, and you need not necessarily recognize your niche in life to lead a happy, contented, fulfilling existence. Just being happy, in itself, may be the whole purpose of your life. He wants us to have peace of mind, trust, faith, and love: And the greatest of these is giving love in order to reach our full potential.

If you saw the movie *It's a Wonderful Life*, you know what I mean; in our lives we all touch many people. When the angel Clarence shows George what life in Bedford Falls would have been like without him, George is stunned. His brother never became a war hero, because George had not been there to save him from drowning as a young boy. His mother is a bitter old woman; his wife, a spinster. Even his first boss, the elderly pharmacist, suffered by not knowing George; without George to catch a pharmacological error, the poor man mistakenly poisons a young client and is shunned by the community. Even if you feel your life has been insignificant, the world would be immeasurably different without you.

The Supreme Being will subtly guide you toward the right path, at the right time, in order for you to gain complete understanding. When you are ready, the path will be revealed.

There are no accidents or victims. Everything has a cause and effect, and everything occurs for a reason. Have you ever had an occurrence that seemed very negative at the time but later turned out to be one of your greatest learning experiences? Or did you later feel that the event was the best thing that could have happened? This is what I'm talking about. If the Supreme Being can't get your attention one way, He will choose another. He will place you in a condition or situation, or with a person who *will* get your attention. Sometimes it comes in the form of a radical or amazing ESP phenomena. Sometimes it is exposure to a charismatic religious speaker. These are all *definite* attention-getters.

At some time in your life, something or someone will penetrate your barriers. This could happen early or late in life, but will happen nonetheless. It is like an eternal flame; it can dim and flicker, but it never dies. Your ESP inner-core consciousness is your eternal flame.

My personal spiritual concept is Christianity, therefore I am best able to express myself from a Christian point of view. Prophets are found within all religious sects and all have basically the same message: God (the Supreme Being) is love, and life through God is eternal. Each prophet was born at a certain time,

in a certain age, to satisfy a hunger for truth and knowledge and
to offer a spiritual assurance that we are all connected to a source
greater than either us or our physical world. I believe that Jesus
Christ is my Savior. I think He was born in the exact geographic
location that would best allow His message to be widespread. He
came as all prophets have, to teach us about universal love. He
taught what all prophets teach: God is love, love is all, all is at one
in the universe.

Christ spoke of self-will, free will, and perfect (God's) will. He
taught that God—the Father— is like a parent to all life in the
world. His message to us as His children is that everyone and
everything is perfected through His love. His creations have not
only order, but reason. By the grace of God, we are all born equal.
He gives us all abilities to attain spiritual growth and revelation.
All we need to do is listen and obey.

Without listening, we become confused. When we are confused,
we think God has moved away. Well, God hasn't moved—humanity has. We have become so scientific and logic-oriented that we
don't believe in anything we can't see, hear, or touch (and yet all
religious concepts include a Supreme Being that can't be seen,
heard, or touched). ESP follows the same concept. It is intangible,
but the results are not; initially, it is based on faith alone.

If you believe, as I do, that God would want to keep in touch
with us, His children, then believing in and using ESP will be no
problem for you. All parents want their children to keep in touch
with them. They don't care whether they write home, phone home,
or come home, as long as they do one of the three things.

Well, God wants us to keep in touch a little more often than we
have. He has sent many prophets to earth to remind us to do so.
But we haven't had a recognized prophet recently, so the New Age
movement is acting as our reminder—our prophet, if you will.
Our ESP inner-core consciousness is like a minor prophet. It is
our inner communication that keeps the link established between
the Supreme Being and us.

ESP is the ultimate form of communication. It is nonjudgmental
and does not seek to prove a point, but rather feeds out information. ESP is like the 1-800 line to God—you always get an answer,

it will always benefit you, and it will never harm you. All you have to do is ask, and He will answer. ESP merely clears the line so you can hear these answers. If you don't understand, or are so caught up in the mechanics of what is happening that you lose the message, another (ESP) message will come over and over until you get it right.

BIBLIOGRAPHY

Clarke, James Freeman. *Ten Great Religions*. Boston: Houghton Mifflin Co. with The University Press Cambridge, 1899, 1913.

Rhine, Louisa A. *PSI, What Is It?* New York: Harper and Row, 1975.

Time/Life Books. *The World's Great Religions*. New York: Golden Press, 1958.

The World Book Encyclopedia. Chicago: Field Enterprises Educational Corp., 1969.